growing
orchids

growing
orchids

The complete practical guide to
orchids and their cultivation

Brian & Wilma Rittershausen

Special Photography by Derek Cranch

HH
HERMES
HOUSE

This edition is published by Hermes House

Hermes House is an imprint of Anness Publishing Ltd
Hermes House, 88–89 Blackfriars Road,
London SE1 8HA
tel. 020 7401 2077; fax 020 7633 9499;
info@anness.com

Publisher Joanna Lorenz
Executive Editor Caroline Davison
Designed by Ruth Hope
Production Controller Ann Childers
Reader Kate Sillence
Photographers Derek Cranch and Helen Fickling
Stylist Gilly Love

Previously published as *The Practical Encyclopedia of Orchids*

10 9 8 7 6 5 4 3 2 1

Page 1 *Paphiopedilum insigne*
(left), *P.* Jersey Freckles (centre)
and *P.* Leeanum (right).
Page 2 *Odontocidium* La Moye.
Page 3 *Gongora maculata*.
Page 4 *Phalaenopsis* Silky Moon.

CONTENTS

Dactylorhiza fuchsii

THE WORLD OF ORCHIDS

Orchids are grown for the astonishing beauty and variety of their flowers. The most beautiful are the gorgeous South American cattleyas, with their often huge, sparkling, rosy-purple and mauve blooms; these are the aristocrats of the orchid world. Others have an altogether different appeal; these are the strangely weird, sometimes evil-smelling species, which are found among the bulbophyllums in particular. In between these two extremes are numerous delightful orchids of unlimited charm and desirability. It is from among this multitude of varieties that the vast number of collections is made up.

Part of the challenge of growing orchids lies in understanding their unique flower parts and exceptional plant structure. This book sets out to explore the world of orchids from their evolution in the natural world, the history of their early discovery and cultivation, and the many varieties that are available for growing today. Their cultivation is discussed in detail, giving the reader a clear insight into each plant's growing requirements.

Phalaenopsis Culiacan

WHY GROW ORCHIDS?

Orchids can charm and tantalize, fascinate and frustrate. They provide endless satisfaction, as you develop a special bond with a selection of plants that you will need to nurture and care for on a regular basis. Daily spraying, weekly watering and feeding, and constant attention to growing requirements, such as light, warmth and your orchid's general comfort, is a rewarding process. You will soon find that you wish to grow more orchids, and expand your collection to include some rarer orchids, as well as the more popular ones. With time, you will become an expert at growing and caring for your collection, and derive many hours of pleasure just admiring the results of your care and attention.

ABOVE *Many delightful hybrids, such as this* Phalaenopsis Sweet Sunrise, *have been bred using the Borneo species* Phalaenopsis violacea *as a starting point. The results are often flowers in extremely rich colours that appear on short flower spikes close to the plant, one bloom at a time.*

FIRST STEPS

Orchids are wonderfully accommodating plants that will succeed in almost any situation with comparative ease. This always astounds those who take their first tentative steps into the world of orchid growing. The reward of seeing the first signs of the developing flower spikes – those small, green shoots at the base of your first orchid – is an exciting event, surpassed only by the eventual opening of the glorious blooms. Often lasting for weeks at a time, these flowers will leave you in no doubt as to the pleasure that orchids can provide.

Orchids are lifelong plants: once acquired they will live for your lifetime and beyond, provided they are not killed accidentally or weakened by mismanagement. Always forgiving, orchids will continue to bloom under the most extreme of conditions, even sacrificing their own lives when a situation becomes intolerable and producing one final burst of colour in a last attempt to perpetuate themselves by seed production.

A century ago, when outrageously high prices were paid for the finest specimens, ensuring that orchids remained the preserve of the wealthy, orchids were considered difficult to grow, requiring specialist skills and the hot, humid atmosphere of a specially structured greenhouse.

Today, orchids are regularly on sale in garden centres, hardware stores and florists, as well as in specialist nurseries, where a wider variety is available. Orchids thrive on windowsills in apartments, offices and hotels, and in the small greenhouses of the serious hobby-growers.

Three Popular Orchids

The one orchid you will meet most often in homegrown situations is the delightful *Phalaenopsis*, softly hued, speckled or spotted, candy-striped or plain. In recent years these orchids have shot to fame and are now the most popular houseplant orchid. In white, pink and yellow colour combinations, phalaenopsis produce three to four attractive, dark to mid-green, broad, horizontally curving leaves, with thick, silvery white roots that have a strong tendency to meander outside their pot.

LEFT *The superb flowers of* Miltoniopsis *Faldouet have red-maroon petals and white lips, which are edged with mauve and streaked and spotted with maroon.*

Many other orchids will also thrive indoors with the minimum of care, but few can compare with the beautiful miltoniopsis, or pansy orchids as they are affectionately known. Their small plant size and large, decorative blooms create a summer show with a delicate fragrance. Look out for these orchids and similar adaptable kinds in your local outlet, and take one or two home. You will not be disappointed.

While it will not take you long to get to know and recognize these popular orchids, it will take a lifetime to learn about them generally, for there are far more of them than any other plant, and it is this endless search for further knowledge to understand the largest plant family in the world that makes orchid growing so totally absorbing.

Usually bought in flower, these will last for weeks at a time, and, before the first flower spike has finished, there is often another showing at the base with the promise of further blooms in the months to come. These plants are ideally suited to indoor culture, where they are unlikely to be exposed to the direct sun, caught in a cold draught or left to freeze on cold nights. The home is a place of warmth and comfort, which suits these tropical epiphytic orchids perfectly.

One further orchid that is frequently seen gracing large open areas is the *Cymbidium*. At home indoors or in the greenhouse, these robust orchids produce long, narrow, tropical-looking foliage that typically cascades below the blooms, which are carried on tall flower spikes with a dozen or more flowers. With almost unlimited colours available, there is no end to their variety; only blue has proved elusive

RIGHT *The lateral petals of* Cymbidium erythrostylum, *a delightful species from Vietnam, are thrust forward to hug the lip. The perfect, pristine-white blooms have produced some excellent hybrids.*

to the hybridizer. Cymbidiums mostly bloom in winter and spring, bursting into flower at a time when their vibrant shades and pastel colourings are a welcome contrast to the bare gardens outside. Their blooms will remain in perfect condition for months on end.

A GROWING COLLECTION

You may start with one or two orchids on your windowsill, but the interest seldom stops there. Orchids can become so compelling that you will never have enough – there will always be just one more plant that you absolutely must have. In no time at all, it seems, a small, contained collection swells into a larger one, and, when every windowsill and available space has been used up in the house, it is time to give this rapidly increasing collection a real home of its own in a conservatory or greenhouse designed especially for their comfort.

Committed growers cannot resist the temptation to acquire further additions at every opportunity, as can be seen by the flurry of purchasing that accompanies every orchid show. Do not forget that orchids grow: a plant that was purchased in a small pot can become a monster within a few years, taking up more than twice as much room.

If you have the patience to buy young plants to grow on, hobby flasks are an inexpensive alternative to

ABOVE LEFT Oncidium tigrinum *from Mexico is now rare in cultivation, but it has left its legacy in the number of fine hybrids, such as this* Odontocidium Tiger Brew, *that have inherited its yellow colouring with multiple patternings.*

LEFT *Stanhopeas, such as this* Stanhopea tigrina, *are extraordinary orchids which produce heavily textured, highly fragrant blooms from the base of the plant. The flowers are very short-lived, lasting just a few days before dying.*

buying flowering-size plants. These are sterile jars containing about a dozen plants, 2.5cm (1in) high, and they offer the great experience of growing the orchids on to flowering – a commitment that will take a few years. Twelve seedlings take up a lot less room than twelve flowering-size plants, and it is tempting to flower each one, before weeding them out and keeping just the best for yourself. The remainder make highly desirable presents to be distributed among friends, who will be delighted with their gift and may soon become orchid collectors themselves. Hobby flasks can contain seed-raised plants, which will all be different when they flower, or they may contain meri-stemmed plants, which will be identical. When you are considering buying a hobby flask, the seller will always be pleased to discuss these points with you.

A Specialist Collection

Having established your initial orchid collection with these easily grown types, you may later decide to specialize in whichever varieties appeal to you the most. Everyone has their own favourites, and you will become more discerning as you discover how many different orchids are available. Some growers prefer to concentrate on those small-sized plants with delightful, fascinating but minute blooms, as found among the pleuro-thallis and related orchids. Here you can find little gems that need the minimum of space. If bolder flowers fill you with awe, seek out the many variations in the paphiopedilums, those elegant slipper orchids, whose flowers exhibit the characteristic pouch, and where some of the most striking colours can be found. Winter-flowering and long-lasting, paphiopedilums need shady conditions and warm temperatures.

Whether your collection is housed indoors or in a greenhouse, there are different ways of growing orchids. Many of the epiphytes (those used to a tree-dwelling mode of life, such as coelogynes and encyclias) adapt extremely well to growing on slabs of bark, or on a large tree branch set up in a corner of the greenhouse as a permanent eye-catching display. On a smaller scale, an unused fish tank can make an ideal home for miniature orchids, where you can create a humid micro-climate to suit them.

As your interest in orchids expands, you may like to share your hobby with others. Information on your local orchid society should not be

ABOVE Paphiopedilum spicerianum, *a handsome species from India, is in the background of many of today's complex hybrids. The hooded dorsal sepal prevents water from getting into the pouch.*

hard to find, and from the regular meetings and lectures available you can increase your learning and enjoy the experience of seeing other members' orchids. You will also be able to exchange growing tips and advice. In addition, numerous workshops and open days are put on by the major orchid nurseries, while orchid shows provide further opportunities to learn and buy. By growing a few orchids, a whole new world opens up.

ORCHIDS IN THE WILD

Orchids represent the largest family of flowering plants in the world, and their diversity and distribution are virtually unchallenged in the plant kingdom. Every land habitat where it is possible for a plant to grow will contain orchids. They thrive on windswept mountain tops and in steaming tropical jungles. They cling to niches in the bitterly cold Arctic regions and in the hottest, driest deserts.

THE EVOLUTION OF ORCHIDS

A wide range of environments, from the seashore to the high alpine line, provide habitats for indigenous orchids. Within this global distribution, we find some 25,000 to 30,000 species. Since the beginning of modern plant classification, started by the Swedish naturalist Linnaeus in 1758, to the present day, taxonomists have continued to classify and reclassify existing species, as well as describing new ones. Every year, from some corner of the world, come new discoveries of orchid species. Some are so startlingly beautiful that it is hard to understand how they have remained undetected for so long, while others are so inconspicuous that it is clear why they have been overlooked. China, for example, is a huge country only recently opened up to Western exploration, and this has resulted in the discovery of some incredible *Paphiopedilum* species.

In addition to the vast number of species, there are some 100,000 man-made hybrids – a number that increases annually, as hybridizers the world over endeavour to meet an insatiable demand for more varieties. So great is the variation, it seems unbelievable that they can all belong to the same family of plants, which are classified according to the structure of their flowers and their resemblance to one another.

Orchid Distribution

It is their extremely small, dust-like seed that has enabled orchids to disperse and travel such great distances. Carried on the wind across continents and oceans, the seeds have helped orchids to colonize the world. Cypripediums, for example, are found circling the top of the globe in a line just below the Arctic Circle. Their far-reaching habitat has contributed to the emergence of many different species. Due to their often harsh habitats, some are extremely slow-growing, but once established in large populations they can exist for many years until they are disturbed.

ABOVE *New species of orchids are continually being discovered. In the latter part of the 20th century, some amazing, new paphiopedilums came to light in China, such as the golden yellow* Paphiopedilum armeniacum. *Nothing like it had been seen in the genus before.*

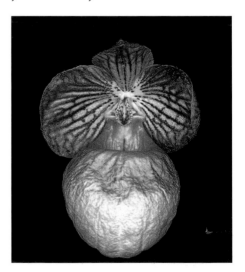

ABOVE *The beautifully striped and coloured species* Paphiopedilum micranthum *carries a huge, bulbous pouch which is quite untypical of the genus. Another recent discovery from China, it has produced a whole new range of hybrids.*

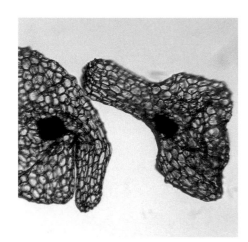

ABOVE *Orchid seeds are minute, no larger than very fine sawdust. Magnified hundreds of times, the fertile embryo of these* Liparis unata *seeds can be seen inside a protective covering. Seed capsules can contain anything up to half a million seeds.*

Ten thousand years ago, the last Ice Age covered much of the globe in a freezing grip. This huge shield of frozen water stretched from the North Pole, covering much of the Northern Hemisphere. This must have forced the orchids back from their original occupation of the land. Within the last few thousand years, as the ice shield receded, the orchids advanced again to regain the territories that they had occupied before the big freeze. In this way, the northern orchids have been moved backwards and forwards as a result of these dramatic climate changes. This has had a direct impact on their evolution. However, the tropical orchids in the forests close to the Equator remained largely unaffected by such climatic changes. The rainforests have hardly changed for millions of years. This has allowed the orchids to evolve without interruption, resulting in the greatest diversity to be found in these regions.

LEFT *Although the tiny, brightly coloured blooms of* Liparis unata *are just 1cm (¹/₂in) across, they are produced on flower spikes, which are 30cm (12in) tall. The sight of a large plant with several flower spikes is a sheer delight.*

LEFT Coelogyne mooreana *'Brockhurst'* FCC/RHS *is a superb species from Vietnam. It is unrivalled for its pristine white flowers which are enhanced by the deep golden lip. These plants grow well in cultivation and are all descended from a single clone which was imported into Britain around the turn of the 20th century.*

ABOVE *There are numerous orchids that are small enough to fit into a thimble.* Schoenorchis pachyrachis, *a species from Malaysia, produces its tiny flowers in profusion. Its small stature makes it ideal for growing on bark.*

Orchids and Other Organisms

In order to survive climate changes, orchids have evolved strange associations with other living organisms. Co-existing within the root structure of most orchids is a microscopic fungus (mycelium). This alliance forms a symbiotic relationship, whereby both the orchid and the fungus become completely dependent upon each other for their survival. The mycelium releases nutrients that are absorbed by the orchid, which in turn becomes the host for the fungus. Most orchids have their own specific micro-fungi, so there must exist as many different fungi as there are orchids. For a seed to germinate, it needs contact with the fungus from the beginning. For this reason, orchids are often found in large colonies, rather than growing as individual plants, because this close proximity to other orchids ensures that the necessary fungus is present.

Tropical epiphytes will also only grow on particular species of trees. In dense rainforest that has remained undisturbed for centuries, it is only certain trees that play host. The larger, more bulky orchids are confined to the main trunk or the first fork of a very large tree, while the smaller species will cling to the finer twigs and branches higher up on the outskirts of the canopy. As the leaf cover increases and becomes denser in evergreen forests, the orchids at the centre of such cover produce healthier and darker-foliaged specimens, but may not be as free-flowering as those growing on the edge. Here the plants will benefit from cooling prevailing winds and extra sunlight, flowering better as a result, although often with shrivelling pseudobulbs and yellowing foliage.

BELOW LEFT *A bluebottle is attracted to this* Bulbophyllum *species by the lurid red lip, which resembles an open animal wound. As it pushes deeper into the "wound", the hinged lip will catapult the fly's body against the pollinia.*

BELOW *This fly is attracted to a* Gongora *species by its appearance. Note the highly specialized pollinating mechanism which ensures the fly will be guided to the pollinia.*

RIGHT *This* Hexisea bidentata *from South America is being pollinated by a humming bird. This accounts for the flower being all red with no other decoration. Instead, it entices the bird with nectar.*

To achieve pollination, orchid flowers have also developed special relationships with insects, humming-birds and even small bats. In the case of insects, the relationship is formed with a group of insects or just one specific species. The insect is attracted to the bloom in its search for nectar, which is sometimes, but not always, given in return for facilitating pollination. The colour, shape and size of the flower are all significant forms of attraction. Many use mimicry to attract a certain bee or fly, and this is seen in the European species of *Ophrys*, where the lip of the flower resembles the female of the species; the male, believing it has found a mate, attempts copulation, but succeeds instead in pollinating the flower. In the bee orchid (*Ophrys apifera*), the orchid times the opening of its flowers to coincide with the emergence of the male bees, which appear on the wing about three weeks before the females. Once the females emerge, the male bee will lose interest in the flowers. The timing of this flowering is therefore critical for pollination.

There are some orchids, particularly among the *Bulbophyllum* species, that emit a strong odour of putrefaction. These have sepals or a lip in a dark reddish colour that resembles decaying meat, just the place where carrion flies and wasps would normally lay their eggs. In contrast, other orchids such as *Brassavola nodosa* carry a delicious night-time scent, relying on night-flying moths and other nocturnal insects for pollination. There are also the fabulous angraecums, which produce mainly white flowers that release their perfume only in the early part of the day to coincide with the time when their specific insect is active. Other species, such as *Oncidium flexuosum*, produce their flowers in a closely-clustered swarm at the end of a long, thin flower spike, which will attract little flying insects by the movement of the slightest breeze.

The unique partnership between orchids and their specific pollinators has evolved over an extremely long period of time, but it can be easily broken by man's unwarranted interference with the natural world through the indiscriminate misuse of insecticides, the felling of trees and the spread of agriculture.

LEFT *Burnet moths are attracted to the flowers of the terrestrial* Anacamptis pyramidalis. *The flowers are slightly fragrant, but carry no nectar.*

TYPES OF ORCHID

There are a number of different types of orchid which are classified according to the way they live and survive, whether they are supported by trees or rocks or grow in the ground. Some orchids have adapted to survive in different conditions.

Epiphytes

Those orchids that have evolved to live upon trees are called epiphytes. These are not the same as parasites, which owe their existence to nourishment taken out of the tree. Epiphytes take nothing from the tree upon which they grow, but merely take advantage of a loftier lifestyle and gain benefit from being closer to the air and light than the vegetation growing on the forest floor. This aerial way of life is not restricted to orchids, and they share this existence with bromeliads, ferns and mosses and other plants that creep along the branches, creating their own micro-climate high in the tree canopy. One further advantage of living in the tree canopy is the abundance of insect life, which is needed to pollinate the flowers. Orchids have found a variety of ingenious ways to attract specific insect pollinators to visit their flowers.

Epiphytes obtain their nutrients from the moisture in the air, and from any debris that has collected in the axils of the branches or beneath mosses where their roots will penetrate. Decomposing leaf litter and bird or animal droppings will make up the remainder of their meagre diet. Various epiphytic orchids have utilized every part of preferred trees. Some cling to the larger branches close to the main trunk, or hug the trunk itself, often growing to huge proportions that completely encircle the tree. Sometimes, the sheer weight of a two-ton mammoth orchid (*Grammatophyllum speciosum*) can make the tree crash to the ground. Other orchids, called twig epiphytes, cling precariously to the extremities of the branches, while some, such as *Psygmorchis pusilla*, even germinate and grow on the leaves of certain trees in Central America.

Being dependent upon the host tree, the orchids adapt a similar lifestyle. When the trees shed their leaves at the onset of the dry season to conserve moisture, many of the orchids do the same. Their aerial roots cease to grow and the growing tips become covered by the white velamen that protects them from damage and dehydration. Their growing season finished, the orchids remain in a dormant state until the onset of the first rains, which herald a new start when the plants become active once again. While the

LEFT *High up on the ridges that overlook these deep, lush valleys, epiphytic orchids cling to the exposed twigs. The weather conditions can be quite inhospitable, and the orchids must contend with the strong winds, rain and low temperatures of the Brazilian rainy season.*

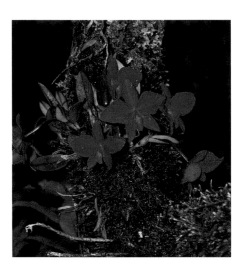

orchids are resting, they rely upon the stored moisture in their pseudobulbs to maintain them. After prolonged periods of drought, these pseudobulbs will begin to shrivel; this is a normal yearly process for many orchids.

With the start of the rainy season, new growth commences and new roots soon follow. The roots take up moisture to fill out the pseudobulbs once again. The newly developing growths rely upon the older, mature pseudobulbs for their source of energy until their own roots can nourish them. The ageing pseudobulbs will support the newer growths until they become exhausted and, in a dried and shrivelled state, eventually die. By this time, numerous new pseudobulbs will have taken their place, and in this way orchids can, in theory, live forever. In practice, they will thrive for hundreds of years, or for as long as their host tree remains standing.

For reasons not fully understood, many epiphytes select a specific tree on which to grow. This may be due to the texture of the bark in which they root, or it may reflect the nutrients available in the old bark. Likewise, some orchid species will only grow on one side of a tree, perhaps away from the prevailing wind.

ABOVE The scarlet flowers of the epiphytic Sophronitis coccinea *sparkle like bright gems on the trees of the high ridges of the Brazilian coastal forest where they can be shrouded in clouds for days at a time.*

ABOVE LEFT The tops of mountains in high-altitude areas, such as in the coastal Brazilian forest, can be covered in clouds for many days. This makes the area constantly moist from the dew that forms within the clouds.

BELOW The epiphytic species Scuticaria hadwenii *is a lovely orchid to see high up in a tree, with its long, terete leaves hanging down. It is fairly well camouflaged among the other forest plants.*

LEFT The beautiful epiphytic species Rodriguezia bractiata *from Brazil grows abundantly on fruit trees where the cascading white flowers look like snow in early spring.*

While epiphytes dwell upon living trees, a few orchids, such as the *Catasetum* species, are saprophytic, living upon decaying trees, where their roots penetrate the softer tissue beneath the bark. Their lifespan is more limited than that of the epiphytes, because dead trees in the tropics will remain for only a few years before fungi and termites take their toll. Therefore the saprophytes must be fast-growing and produce seed quickly so that the next generation can move on to other habitats.

Terrestrials

These orchids grow in the ground, and there is hardly any area where terrestrial orchids have not adapted to grow. They are found in places as diverse as the hot, dry Australian deserts, to the

shadier and gentler climates of temperate woodlands and grasslands. In North America, orchids such as the delightful *Cypripedium calceolus* grow in the cool forests, and other *Cypripedium* species are found in areas of Russia extending to the very edge of the Arctic Circle.

LEFT *The fragrant* Zygopetalum crinitum *enjoys a shady position away from the bright Brazilian sunshine. Many of these plants are found growing terrestrially under the trees.*

Terrestrial orchids may be found in solitary splendour or with just a few in a colony, while in other locations they appear in their thousands, tinting a grassy meadow purple or pink with their flower spikes (species of *Orchis* and *Dactylorhiza*). Among the terrestrial orchids there is as much variation as can be found among the tropical epiphytes. However, they have not excited the collector in the same way as the epiphytes, mainly because they are less easy to cultivate and less flamboyant in their plants as well as their flowers.

Typically, the terrestrial orchids grow a single leafy stem which rises from one or two underground tubers, or a mass of rhizomatous roots. These can grow either just below the surface of the natural grass-covering or deep in the soil, depending upon the conditions. The stem terminates in the flowering head, which may have from one to many blooms. While some species grow in sandy soils in arid places, others flourish in marshy swamps, where their tubers remain submerged in water for much of the year. During the winter, only the underground parts of the plant survive to reactivate new growth in the spring. Other terrestrials, such as *Phaius* and the evergreen calanthes, produce a creeping rhizome with pseudobulbs

LEFT *Growing near the base of a large tree, this* Gongora bufonia *will be a fantastic sight when its 11 flower spikes open and attract swarms of euglossan bees to pollinate it.*

RIGHT *This is a typical scene on a bromeliad-covered ridge in the Atlantic Forest of Brazil. Bromeliads are huge plants which grow on both the trees and the ground. Their centres are filled with water, which is a vital source of humidity. A* Scuticaria hadwenii *flowers in the centre.*

at ground level. The root system penetrates deep into the soil to find moisture and nutrients.

Not all terrestrial orchids with underground rhizomes live in cold areas. Many of the tropical species adopt this way of life, becoming completely deciduous and remaining dormant below ground level during the dry season. Their green parts emerge when conditions are suitable. These different habitats often merge, and epiphytes that fall from their host trees will, where conditions are suitable, be perfectly at home on the ground. Equally, terrestrial orchid seeds that have settled on mossy branches can find a suitable roothold and become established there. These orchids are great opportunists, and will grow well wherever conditions suit them. Stanhopeas and acinetas are epiphytes that produce pendent flower spikes. If they should end up on the ground, the plants will grow but are unable to bloom, because their flower spikes penetrate the soil and perish.

A few terrestrial orchids, such as *Bletia* species, produce pseudobulbs, and many of the species within the genus *Pleione* are also considered

RIGHT *Wet, boggy areas have formed on this rock which has a constant flow of water running across it. Held secure by tough grasses, and in bud, are large clumps of* Epidendrum aquaticum, *which loves having its roots in the water.*

terrestrial, although they too produce pseudobulbs; these remain above the surface of the ground, or become covered by the mosses and lichens among which they grow.

While the terrestrial species of Europe share many characteristics, in Australia some of the strangest types have evolved that have no comparison anywhere. The Australian terrestrials are worthy of study in their own right, but these plants are not generally found in cultivation, and knowledge of them outside Australia is gleaned mostly from other specialist publications.

Although the terrestrial orchids are not cultivated, they still have enthusiasts who would seek them out, returning each year to a favourable location to search for them in bogs, on hillsides and wherever else they may appear. These devotees are armed not with spades to dig them up but with cameras to photograph each individual and build up their own records

RIGHT *These seedlings of* Oncidium blanchetii *have been reintroduced into the wild in their native South-east Brazil to try to increase their diminishing numbers. These seedlings have all thrived and are now showing their flower spikes.*

of flowering data. For many orchid enthusiasts, the opportunity of searching and observing tropical orchids in the wild is an unattainable goal, but where there is the easier option of finding terrestrial orchids, the satisfaction generated is just as great.

One aspect that makes this so compelling year after year is the fluctuation in the number of flowering plants that may arise. In an area supporting hundreds of flowering plants in one season, you may be hard pressed to find a dozen the next. Terrestrial orchids are notorious for appearing sporadically over the seasons, and some species of *Orchis* can remain in a dormant state underground for many years before suddenly reappearing. In neglected gardens, unmown lawns can support many orchids where previously the lawnmower had decapitated the flowers. When prevented from flowering, orchids increase their vegetative growth below grass level, becoming more vigorous, so when the opportunity arises, they create an even better show of blooms. Where such plants are found in a lawn, do not treat the grass with selective weedkillers, or you will lose them.

Many of the terrestrial orchids use deception to attract insects to pollinate their flowers. In the genus *Ophrys*, commonly known as bee or spider orchids, the lip of the flower of certain species resembles either a bee or a spider closely enough to fool the male of the species into believing it is a female. While the bee or spider mounts the flower and endeavours to copulate, it receives or deposits pollen which is then delivered from one flower to another.

Terrestrial orchids are found worldwide, but many, like the epiphytes, are becoming increasingly rare in the wild, where habitats are being destroyed through urbanization, the spread of agriculture, mining or quarrying, or the application of fertilizer to improve grassland.

ABOVE *Some orchids, such as the terrestrial* Paphiopedilum gratrixianum *from Laos, have evolved specialized "pouches" in order to trap pollinating insects.*

ABOVE Cypripedium calceolus, *a lady's slipper orchid, is a hardy terrestrial which originates from Europe and North America.*

Lithophytes

Performing a balancing act somewhere between the epiphytes inhabiting the trees and the terrestrials in the soil are the lithophytes. These orchids make their homes on rocky cliff faces, sometimes on near vertical slopes where conditions are too extreme for much other plant life. Often these are limestone cliffs near to the seashore, or moss-covered rocks where there is some protection for the roots. The plants will find any small crevice where they can gain a hold, and cling on with their strong roots. The inaccessibility of some lithophytic habitats has allowed a few noteworthy orchids, such as *Phragmipedium besseae*, to remain undiscovered until recently, being detected only from the air.

Lithophytes obtain their nourishment in a similar way to epiphytes, relying upon regular mists and rain for moisture, but also having to withstand long periods of extreme dryness. Extra moisture and nutrients are obtained

ABOVE LEFT *The species* Cytopodium andersoniae *is managing to thrive by growing on this smooth, flat rock surface. It makes a striking sight with its long, tapering leaves.*

from roots that meander and penetrate into the crevices in the rocks, or underneath the mossy covering. Orchids that grow in this way include the pleiones and some species of *Paphiopedilum*. Often species that are epiphytic close to, or around, the base of trees become lithophytic when a suitable opportunity arises. Likewise, the terrestrial species of *Paphiopedilum* will also graduate onto surrounding rocks, where there is a sufficient covering of mosses or humus for their roots to remain covered.

In cultivation, lithophytes are treated in the same way as epiphytes. There are many examples among the hybrids, particularly with paphiopedilums and phragmipediums, of epiphytic species being crossed with lithophytic or terrestrial species within the same genus.

ABOVE Rodriguezia bractiata *is seen here unusually growing on a large boulder where it has landed after falling from the tree above. It has continued to grow successfully, surrounded by lichens.*

ABOVE Stenoglottis fimbriata *is a terrestrial orchid from South Africa.*

TROPICAL HABITATS

Tropical rainforests throughout the world are the natural home of the majority of epiphytic orchid species, which have evolved there for as long as the forests have existed. Thousands of different genera have adapted to an aerial way of life that gives each one an advantage over plants growing at ground level. They cling firmly to forest trees, often high in the canopy, where there is access to dappled sunlight filtering through the leaves in their growing season, and exposure to full light when the trees lose their leaves during the dry season. At this time the orchids often lose their leaves as well and enter a semi-dormant state, adjusting their season to that of the tree until rains activate new growth and leaves.

To cope with extreme conditions of wet and dry periods, orchids have evolved their own methods of survival; these include water-storing organs, known as pseudobulbs, and aerial roots through which they absorb the moisture that surrounds them. For most of the year, tropical downpours or frequent swirling mists sweeping in through the trees will give a steady supply of moisture sufficient for the orchids' needs.

Tropical rainforests extend around the world, stretching south of the Equator to Australia and New Zealand, where they become cooler, temperate forests and represent the southern-most limits of the epiphytic orchids. North of the Equator, epiphytes extend up through South America to Mexico and through Malaysia to the Philippines and South-east Asia,

creeping around the base of the Himalayas in Nepal. Conditions vary widely in these different areas, and orchids have adapted to each environment. Dry desert conditions or wet mangrove swamps are no barriers to these intrepid plants: there are orchids that have colonized every habitat offered by nature.

Forest and tree cover differ, depending upon the altitude, and so too do the growing conditions they provide. At sea level, forests are dense and lush, with little sunlight penetrating, while higher up trees begin to thin until the higher, dryer mountain slopes are reached, which offer very little protection from the elements.

RIGHT *This* Cymbidium aloifolium, *growing in the fork of a large tree in full sun in Thailand's Phu Kradung National Park, is a very resilient plant. It will tolerate a lot of tropical sun, and will grow quickly in order to produce large leaves during the monsoon season.*

ABOVE Seidenfadenia mitrata *is at home in the dry forest of Phu Kradung National Park in northern Thailand, where it grows on trees that are deciduous during the dry season. Just before the rains start the flowers are produced in great profusion, creating splashes of colour in the otherwise uninteresting jumble of branches.*

ABOVE AND LEFT Eria albidotomentosa *is a high-altitude species that grows on the ground or on rocky outcrops like a lithophyte. In their natural habitat, the mists that drift through the trees in the early morning supply these plants with heavy dew, which sustains them during the dry season. These orchids are great opportunists, creating a niche for themselves where other plants would not survive.*

ABOVE Coelogyne nitida *can grow epiphytically at the top of a very high tree or terrestrially on the ground. If the orchid falls from the host tree, it will survive as long as the competition from other terrestrial plants is not too great and the soil conditions are suitable. It will thrive and flower just as freely as it did as an epiphyte.*

The Effects of Altitude

Orchids are found at all altitudes, adapting to their surroundings and being completely at home. When in cultivation, it is the altitude at which a plant naturally grows that defines the temperature at which it is to be grown; knowing its natural altitude is more important than knowing its country of origin.

Generally, it is the shade-loving orchids such as the phalaenopsis that are found nearer to sea level; their wide, almost succulent leaves are designed to catch as much light as possible in areas of dense forest shade. Progressing to the higher altitudes and within reach of the snow line in the Andes of South America, cool-growing and shade-loving orchids such as odontoglossums and masde-vallias are encountered. Because of the rarity of the atmosphere at around 3,000m (9,850ft), the night-time frosts do them no harm, although in cultivation a temperature drop to around freezing would undoubtedly affect them. At an altitude of 1,250m

(4,100ft) in the Khasia Hills in India, the beautiful, sky-blue-flowered *Vanda coerulea* makes its home on stunted oak trees that are in full sun for part of the year and exposed to the fierce elements in a harsh, dry environment. At the other extreme, epiphytic lycastes often grow on the undersides of tree trunks leaning over water courses in heavily shaded areas.

Here, their leaves have become broad and softly textured in order to gain the maximum benefit from the meagre light available.

Dry, arid areas of the world experience extremely high temperatures, and in parts of Australia there exist some of the strangest of all terrestrial orchids, which cope with baking temperatures for part of the year.

RIGHT
Bulbophyllum blepharistes *is a small, insignificant species. Yet, it is interesting for its habit of growth, managing to grow successfully on bare, inhospitable rocks. Here, it is spreading across a lichen-covered rock. The pseudobulbs have long internodes.*

LEFT *When in flower, the species* Dendrobium trigonopus *creates striking splashes of yellow among the bare tree branches.*

RIGHT Vanda pumila *is a monopodial species with an extensive root system, which holds it to its host tree.*

Dendrobium
primulinum
*is one of the
prettiest of the
dendrobiums from
Thailand, found
in densely forested
land of the
Pai district. In
cultivation, this
orchid is sweetly
scented.*

The species
Dendrobium
pulchellum
*is shown
here growing
epiphytically in
the fork of a large
tree. This orchid
retains its leaves
on the newer
growth, but
flowers off the
previous season's
growth. It likes
dry, deciduous
woodland and
can be seen from
some distance
when in full
bloom.*

TEMPERATE HABITATS

Throughout the cooler, temperate regions of the world, orchids grow in the soil or in the leaf litter that covers the forest or woodland floor. Temperate forests cannot play host to epiphytes in the same way as in the tropics, because exposed aerial roots would soon succumb to the cold. In Europe, orchids colonize the hillsides, and are particularly numerous in Greece, Cyprus and Turkey, where agriculture has been less intensive than elsewhere, and the orchids thrive on the rocky mountainous slopes. Uncultivated marshy land is also a favourite habitat for many species in Europe.

It is known that native orchids, once established, dislike disturbance to land and cannot thrive in fertilized fields. For this reason, many have died out in meadows in which they had been growing in their thousands up to 100 years ago, but which have now been developed or cultivated. It is surprising, therefore, that when large road-building construction work has taken place, orchids are one of the first plants to colonize the disturbed earth.

In Britain, and elsewhere, orchids have gained a foothold at the edges of newly constructed roads, which, with their nutrient-poor soil, are unable to support many other flowering wild plants. These areas have become their haven, and as the latter part of the 20th century saw a vast programme of road building, so the sight of early

RIGHT *The greater butterfly orchid* (Platanthera chlorantha) *is a handsome, summer-flowering species with tall flower spikes. It is found growing on moorland and bracken-covered land.*

ABOVE *Land that has been built up with hard rubbish on an industrial site such as this reclaimed marshland can be quickly colonized. It is difficult to explain how some orchids – in this case the bee orchid* (Ophrys apifera), *shown right – arrive in such places or how, in a few years, large colonies can become established.*

purple orchids (*Orchis mascula*) flourishing in vast numbers alongside the verges of large roads has become a striking sight in early summer.

Both railway and road embankments are regularly maintained areas where large shrubs and trees – which would quickly outgrow the smaller-flowering plants – cannot establish themselves for very long. The regular

clearing of these verges means that they can remain as grassland where orchids can flourish. Such habitats soon become nature reserves in their own right, where many rare plants, previously unknown in certain areas of intensive agriculture or building land, thrive alongside urban development. Industrial wasteland, where factories

ABOVE *The early summer-flowering bee orchid* (Ophrys apifera) *is a well-known example of how orchids use mimicry to attract an insect pollinator. It needs a specific species of bee for pollination.*

have been removed and the area remains undeveloped, can support many wild flowers, including orchids, which are often the first plants to colonize such areas. Other man-made habitats that orchids are quick to colonize include disused quarries and clay pits, and the areas between sand dunes near the coast.

A better understanding of their soil requirements has enabled some orchids to become popular in gardens. *Dactylorhiza* and *Orchis* species readily propagate, and can be grown from seed by specialists. At one time it was considered almost impossible to raise native terrestrials from seed, but with modern techniques it is proving less of a

challenge. Even some of the cypripediums, which are notoriously slow to flower from seed, are being grown. As with the tropical epiphytes, the terrestrials have a specialized relationship with their pollinating insects (*Ophrys*, or bee orchids, are pollinated only by a certain species of bee), and a symbiotic relationship with a soil-dwelling fungus.

Temperate habitats colonized by orchids can be found almost anywhere in the world, including high altitudes in tropical countries, which means that orchids from totally different parts of the world can be grown together.

Orchids that grow in temperate regions are mostly terrestrial. These are often, but not always, smaller plants, which are less flamboyant in appearance than the tropical epiphytes. However, there are some gems among their number. The showiest of these, the lady's slipper orchid (*Cypripedium*) in particular, are often grown in alpine greenhouses, which are maintained during winter at temperatures just above freezing.

ABOVE *The lady's slipper orchid* (Cypripedium calceolus) *is a terrestrial orchid which grows in temperate regions. Although less flamboyant than the tropical epiphytes, it has a truly delicate beauty.*

LEFT AND RIGHT *This thriving orchid habitat was once a clay-spoil tip. Orchids are among the first plants to colonize such wasteland, working their way up from the surrounding soil. This common marsh orchid* (Dactylorhiza praetermissa) *is one of the tallest species found in Britain. If undisturbed, they will form large colonies, often competing with more robust plants such as gorse and willow. These plants eventually outgrow them, and, once deprived of light, the orchids will die out.*

THE HISTORY OF ORCHIDS

The early prehistory relating to orchids is sporadic and only partially recorded.It is known that in 500 BC the Chinese emperors coveted the indigenous species of Cymbidium, *such as* C. ensifolium *and* C. virescens, *for their sweet perfume. Confucius referred to all orchids as "Lan", and they held a high profile in the gardens of Chinese and Japanese cultivators. Other orchids, such as the fragrant* Dendrobium moniliforme, *were grown for their brightly coloured flowers. Of particular interest to the Japanese was the native species* Neofineta falcata. *Their fascination with this attractive, white-flowered species has endured through the centuries, and it remains as popular today. This species is greatly prized for the variegation of its foliage and those plants with the most prominent stripes are given preference. In Japan, as much importance is paid to the container as the plant, and elaborately designed pots are used to display orchids.*

RIGHT *The man orchid (Aceras anthropophorum) was once considered to be an aphrodisiac because the shape of the lip resembled the figure of a man.*

BELOW *The Aztecs used the ground seed capsules of vanilla as a perfume and food flavouring.*

EARLY HISTORY

In Europe, an interest in orchids can be traced back to Greek and Roman times. At that time, people knew only of the terrestrial orchids, which were vastly different from the tropical epiphytes. Like many ancient civilizations, the Greeks drew on the resources of the natural world, and the tubers and roots of most European terrestrial orchids were valued for various medicinal purposes. They studied the curious orchid flowers and believed that the different shapes revealed the beneficial effects of the plant. For example, the man orchid (*Aceras anthropophorum*) was thought to be an aphrodisiac because the shape of the lip resembled the figure of a man. The word orchid is, in fact, derived from the Greek "orchis", meaning testes, which refers to the tubers found in pairs in some species.

In the New World, orchids were used by the inhabitants long before the arrival of Europeans. Twenty years after Columbus landed on the mainland of South America in 1498, Hernando Cortes arrived in Mexico to overthrow the Aztec Empire and to claim Mexico for Spain. He found a species of *Vanilla* being cultivated for its perfume and, more importantly, for its culinary use. The Aztecs grew this vine-like orchid, which they called *Tlilxochitl*, for the seed capsules, which were ground and mixed with the brown seeds of the cacao plant to produce a bitter drink that is the basis of the chocolate we have today. Vanilla is still much in use today as a flavouring, but, while the seed capsules, called pods (beans), are in steady demand, artificial vanilla essence has lessened the need to cultivate plants. Today, the main vanilla crops come from Madagascar.

THE GOLDEN YEARS

By the late 18th century, the British Empire had spread across the globe. Merchant ships returned from the New World laden with previously unknown species of plants and animals. At the same time, the forerunner of the modern greenhouse was being developed to accommodate the newly arrived tropical plants, and especially orchids. These greenhouses were huge steel and glass structures with a system of heating by cast-iron piping and large, solid-fuel boilers. With steel in plentiful supply from the foundries, the construction of greenhouses developed into an industry supplying botanical gardens and large private country estates. Orchids became a status symbol for the rich and famous, and a lively trade ensued to satisfy this need.

Nurserymen and private collectors sponsored their own expeditions to send hunters to new regions in search of previously unknown orchids to add to their collections. There were many tales of daring exploits, hardship, disease and sometimes death in the world's remote tropical rainforests, but this did nothing to lessen the growing desire for orchids.

A few of the early stories have lingered and passed into orchid folklore.

The account most often retold is of the Madagascan species *Angraecum sesquipedale* and the prediction of Charles Darwin. The common name for this species is the comet orchid, which is a reference to the long spur at the back of the flower. Its specific name translates as "a foot and a half", and while this is a slight exaggeration, it describes the extraordinary appendage well. At first there seemed no logical explanation for the spur's length, but, after studying the flower, Darwin proclaimed that because nectar was held at the end of the spur, there must be a night-flying hawk moth with a tongue of the same length. It was not until some years after Darwin's death that such a moth was indeed discovered and named *Xanthopan morganii praedicta*. This example also emphasizes the fragile relationship that exists between one orchid and its pollinator. Should one become extinct, the other would die out in the wild; and yet there are many such insect-orchid associations that have existed virtually unchanged for thousands of years.

LEFT *At the end of the 18th century, merchant ships returned from the New World laden with newly discovered animals and plants, including orchids.*

ABOVE *The comet orchid (Angraecum sesquipedale) from Madagascar has an incredibly long spur at the back of the flower. This enables it to be pollinated by the night-flying hawk moth, which has a tongue of exactly the same length.*

LEFT *Phalaenopsis are strikingly beautiful, and have been popular among orchid collectors since the golden era of orchid hunting.* This orchid is Phalaenopsis *Flare Spots.*

The Orchid King

Probably the most distinguished nurseryman of the Victorian era was Frederick Sander, the man they called the Orchid King. His huge nursery was one of the largest in Britain, and he boasted of having orchid collectors in every corner of the world. When word reached him of a legendary red *Phalaenopsis*, he immediately dispatched a collector called Robbelin to find it. In 1881, Robbelin arrived at the small island of Davao in the Philippines, after searching the nearby island of Mindenoa without success. As his boat approached the shore of this previously unvisited island, the natives met them with hostility. Frightening warriors, with hair dyed bright golden yellow and bodies streaked with coloured paint,

threatened them as they approached. Robbelin considered turning back, but then he noticed that among the bright yellow heads were flowers of the sought-after *Phalaenopsis*. He made gestures of friendship and was allowed to land. He exchanged gifts in return for being shown where the red *Phalaenopsis* grew, and later left the island laden with a valuable cargo. The plants eventually arrived in England and were named *Phalaenopsis sanderiana*. The flowers, however, were never red, but a pale rosy-pink.

Another of Sander's collectors was making further discoveries in New Guinea. He encountered a village where the tribesmen laid the bones of their dead in graveyards and then decorated them with the finest orchids they could find. The plants

continued to grow, their roots firmly attached to the bones. This is how plants of *Dendrobium schroderianum* arrived at the salesrooms in London, attached to human skulls and accompanied by two native idols, said to have been sent to protect the souls of the ancestors on their journey. This was a condition insisted upon by the natives, who were persuaded to relinquish parts of their valued ancestors only after mirrors, beads and a roll of brass wire had been exchanged. The plants, still attached to the skulls, and the idols were sold as one lot and purchased by the Hon. Walter Rothschild, in whose collection they remained for many years. *D. schroderianum* was named after Baron Schroeder, who was a patron of Frederick Sander.

THE GREAT COLLECTORS

The vast majority of tropical orchids were brought into cultivation during the 19th century. For over 50 years, regular consignments containing tens of thousands of new species were shipped to Britain, leaving whole areas of rainforest stripped of their treasures. By the time they arrived in England, there were many losses. Orchids rotted in the holds of the ships or were eaten by the rats and cockroaches that infested the ships, until only a very few survived. Shipwrecks, not unusual occurrences in those days, also accounted for total losses of whole consignments.

The finest varieties of those plants that remained were sold at auction at hugely inflated prices, where competition among the wealthy collectors was fierce. In this way, the first of the prodigious collections of orchids were created; their equal has never been seen since. The lust for tropical orchids spread beyond Europe to the East Coast of the United States, and by the turn of the 20th century orchids were being grown on both sides of the Atlantic. In London, the Royal Horticultural Society appointed an Orchid Committee to set the standards for judging and awarding the best clones, and Britain maintained its lead in the introduction of new species.

ABOVE *This species,* Odontoglossum harryanum, *was discovered in Colombia and introduced into cultivation in 1886. It was named in honour of Sir Harry Veitch who acquired the first plants.*

LEFT *Sir Harry Veitch (1840–1924) was the second generation of the famous Veitch nursery in Devon, England. This nursery was founded by his father, James Veitch. Harry Veitch was the only orchid nurseryman to be knighted for his services to horticulture, in particular for staging the Great Horticultural Exhibition of 1812, which became the forerunner to the Chelsea Flower Show.*

Early Orchid Nurseries

The earliest nursery to specialize in tropical epiphytes and other exotic plants was that of Conrad Loddiges. He set up his nursery in the Hackney district of London. By 1812, he had established the largest collection of tropical plants known at that time. He published a journal, *The Cabinet*, in which he described many of the new plants. Other nurserymen followed, and the firm of B. S. Williams and Sons in Upper Norwood, London, and William Bull in the King's Road, Chelsea, London, were at the forefront of supplying orchids to owners of large estates.

By the 19th century, the Exeter nursery of James Veitch and Sons in Devon employed the greatest number of collectors to search for new trees, shrubs and other garden plants, as well as orchids. The firm of Sander's and Sons from St Albans came later, but rose to rival the most influential commercial establishments. Started by Frederick Sander, this company flourished through three generations of the same family before finally closing down in 1962. In its heyday, the nursery employed over 100 men, whose main activity was to unpack the stream of boxes that arrived almost daily and to sort out and pot up the new species. The nursery opened a branch in Bruges, Belgium, and later in New York.

A few orchid nurseries that had their beginnings in the 19th century are still flourishing today. These include McBeans Orchids of Cooksbridge, Sussex, which was started in 1879 by a Scotsman, Alexander McBean. Mansell and Hatcher's nursery in Leeds, Yorkshire, commenced in the 1890s, and in France, Vacherot and Lecoufle have been in existence since 1886, making theirs the oldest family-run nursery in the world.

In the 19th century, the orchid scene in Britain centred around four key people: the hunter, the botanist, the nurseryman, and the purchaser. Initially, it depended upon the orchid hunters who collected for the private growers and the nurserymen. The nurserymen established the trade

ABOVE Dendrobium loddigesii *from China was mentioned in George Loddiges'* Botanical Cabinet *in 1833. It was originally named* D. pulchellum. *George Loddiges (1784–1846) was the son of Conrad Loddiges.*

LEFT Cattleya skinneri *was named after George Ure-Skinner in 1838. It is the national flower of Costa Rica. For over 100 years, it has been used extensively in breeding to produce the multitude of hybrids that are around today.*

and acquired the knowledge needed to cultivate a wide range of orchids from different regions of the world. Most of the professional orchid growers started their apprenticeships at the nurseries and later found employment in the large collections. The botanical gardens employed botanists and taxonomists to classify and name the new discoveries. The upper classes of Britain and Europe were the patrons and they were willing to pay the huge sums often asked for the latest orchid sensation. In the size and number of their greenhouses, some of these private collections rivalled the nurseries who supplied them.

Early Private Collections

One of the most notable of the large private orchid collections was founded by Earl Spencer Cavendish, the sixth Duke of Devonshire. His name is immortalized in plants such as *Cymbidium devonianum* and *Oncidium cavendishianum*. The Duke pioneered the development of the large conservatory, such as can still be seen at the Royal Botanic Gardens at Kew, near London. A huge, cast-iron structure with small glass panes, the entrance was large enough to receive a horse and carriage. The Duke's gardener was Joseph Paxton, who became well known in his own right, and was later knighted for his services to horticulture and in particular for the construction of the famous Crystal Palace, which he designed for the Great Exhibition of 1852. Paxton's understanding of orchids and how they should be grown became the blueprint that others followed.

James Bateman amassed a huge collection of orchids at his home in Biddulph Grange, in Staffordshire. He published several notable works on orchids, including *Orchidaceae of Mexico and Guatemala* in 1843, and *Monograph of Odontoglossum* in 1867. He also sponsored collectors such as George Ure-Skinner, who explored throughout Honduras, Panama and Guatemala.

When Bateman sold his collection, the auction lasted for three days. Prices for the best specimens often exceeded the lifetime wages of the grower. Bateman is especially remembered for the genus *Batemannia*.

HYBRIDIZATION

Although each new species was greeted with enthusiasm, the first hybrids that appeared were met with both amazement and scepticism, for such an achievement was once thought impossible. The birthplace of orchid hybrids was the nursery of James Veitch and Sons in Exeter, Devon. A regular visitor to that nursery was John Harris, a local surgeon, whose interest led him to unravel the secrets of orchid pollination. He explained his theory to Veitch's grower, John Dominy. As a result of his experiments, the first orchid hybrid was flowered in 1856.

This was an evergreen *Calanthe*, which was named *C.* Dominyi after the raiser.

The new awareness of how orchid hybrids could be created led to many experiments with cross-breeding, giving botanists a clearer understanding of which orchids were related and would therefore interbreed. Orchids are extremely generous at providing abundant seed, but the masses of beautiful golden seed proved to be extremely reluctant to germinate or grow. Progress was slow until the botanists realized that orchids grew in conjunction with a microscopic fungus, without which the seed would not germinate. Following this discovery, in around 1903, the Frenchman Noel

Bernard isolated the fungus and placed it in sterile flasks on an agar base on which the seed was sown. The first results were amazing, and orchid seeds were germinated en masse. Where previously perhaps one per cent of seed sown would survive, now there was almost a 100 per cent success rate.

The first part of the 20th century saw an explosion of hybridizing and seed raising. In the 1920s, a further step was taken by L. Knudsen, an American scientist who bypassed the natural fungus and produced the nutrients artificially, using a technique that is still used, with a few modifications, today. Methods of raising orchids have improved so much that it is now possible

ABOVE *John Harris was a surgeon at the Devon and Exeter Royal Hospital in England. He had a great interest in orchids and was the first to suggest a way of pollinating the orchid flower. His observations led to the first hybrids being produced.*

LEFT Paphiopedilum *Harrisianum was the first* Paphiopedilum *hybrid to be bred. Registered in 1869, it was made by John Dominy at Veitch's nursery in Devon, England, following the suggestions of Dr John Harris.*

to bloom seedlings within three to four years from the flasks, whereas previously this had taken up to seven years.

The outbreak of the First World War interrupted the blossoming new science of hybridization because changes to the social order greatly affected the advancement of orchid cultivation. Many of the estates that had been holders of the large private collections had to be run down because their labour force was called to enlist, many never to return. The first great heyday of orchid cultivation in Europe had been brought to an abrupt end.

Following the war years, the coastal region of California from Los Angeles to San Francisco became an important orchid haven. In the warm climate, they could flourish out of doors with shade-cloth for protection from direct sun. This was a far cry from the long, cold winters in most of Europe. Cattleyas and phalaenopsis were found to do well in this climate and could be grown with no expensive heating bills. The same was true in New Zealand and parts of Australia, whose climate favoured cymbidiums, enabling them to be grown without artificial heating.

Europe joined in this new orchid bonanza, and commercial nurseries appeared in Germany, Holland, Belgium and Denmark. Most of these concentrated on producing new hybrids, untapping an enormous potential and taking advantage of the latest techniques, which offered unlimited opportunities. Increasingly, orchid

ABOVE *At the beginning of the 20th century Noel Bernard (1874–1911) successfully isolated the mycorrhizal fungi without which orchid seed cannot germinate. His work opened the way for seed raising of orchids en masse.*

ABOVE *Raising orchids from seed in jars is a modern method of propagation that owes its origins to the work carried out by Noel Bernard nearly 100 years ago.*

growers were coming from the middle classes, who lived in the spreading suburbs of the cities and grew their orchids in greenhouses no more than 10m (30ft) long. Interest had shifted from the declining estates, where few owners could now afford to maintain such large collections for pleasure, to the wider population.

Amateur societies dedicated to the advance of orchid cultivation started up, and in the United States the American Orchid Society was founded in 1921. This organization grew from small beginnings to a worldwide network, becoming the largest orchid society in the world.

Twenty years after the First World War, the orchid industry was again flourishing when the Second World War began, dashing all hopes of further progress. There was difficulty in obtaining fuel for amateur greenhouses, while commercial nurseries had to be used for the production of food crops.

CATTLEYA HYBRIDA PICTA.

FLORAL MAGAZINE NEW SERIES.

FAR LEFT *John Dominy (1816–1891) was orchid grower to the nursery of James Veitch in Devon, England. Assisted by John Harris, he became the first person to artificially raise orchid hybrids. He flowered his first hybrid,* Calanthe Dominyi *in 1856.*

LEFT Cattleya Hybrida *was one of the first* Cattleya *hybrids raised by John Dominy.*

BELOW LEFT Miltoniopsis roezlii *was discovered in 1873 by Benedict Roezl. Originating from Colombia, this lovely species was one of the most noted of his introductions. The species is grown today in collections, alongside the numerous hybrids that have been raised from it.*

The lack of skilled growers saw the demise of the last remaining large collections. At the onset of the Second World War, the best of the British stud plants, which were the finest of their kind in the world, were shipped to California, South Africa and Australia for safekeeping. *Cymbidium* hybrids, in particular, were to prove vital to the newly emerging orchid nurseries in these countries, giving them a much-needed boost to their own breeding lines. The most coveted were C. Alexanderi 'Westonbirt' FCC/RHS (white), the most famous *Cymbidium* of all time; C. Burgundian 'Chateau' FCC/RHS (bronze) and C. Rosanne 'Pinkie' FCC/RHS (pink).

The 1950s saw a reawakening of prosperity, which brought peace in Europe and a proliferation of hobby orchid growers. The hobbyists filled a niche by creating a new market for orchids that could be grown in the home or small greenhouse. Orchid societies sprang up, where amateurs assembled to discuss their hobby and show off their flowering plants. Today,

LEFT *Charles Vuylsteke (1844–1927) had a huge orchid nursery in Belgium. He raised new hybrids and produced the first bigeneric hybrid between* Odontoglossum *and* Cochlioda. *This was named* Odontioda Vuylstekea. *The genus* Vuylstekeara *is also named after him.*

is available on the Internet, where individual websites can be visited and ideas exchanged on a global basis.

Today, hybridizing has come a long way from the tentative steps taken by John Dominy in Veitch's nursery. The Royal Horticultural Society in London is the world authority for the registration of orchid hybrids, where over 100,000 have been entered. This astounding figure continues to rise by over 3,000 per year, testimony to an insatiable appetite for better plants. The majority of these new varieties are produced for the pot-plant trade, which

demands a supply of cheaply produced, easily grown orchids. Many more are brought into production and sold unnamed in the world's flower markets, there being little time or need for registration when a fast turnover exists. This mass increase in hybrid numbers is to be welcomed, because it takes the pressure off the wild species. These are no longer taken from their natural habitats to supply the home grower who, in turn, gets a much better quality plant from the many outlets now supplying orchids. Species in cultivation are kept in botanical gardens and specialist collections, which can care for them for posterity.

BELOW Vuylstekeara *Cambria 'Yellow' is a multigeneric genus which was named after Charles Vuylsteke in 1911. It contains the genera* Odontoglossum, Cochlioda *and* Miltonia.

orchid societies have become an influential force worldwide, catering for the ever-widening social aspect of growing orchids. They hold monthly meetings and table shows, and organize conference lectures, all with the aim of encouraging further interest in orchids and disseminating knowledge and awareness. Global events are now so numerous that there is one for every week of the year. With the relatively low cost of air travel, global events attract registrants from around the world. Interest is perhaps keenest in Japan, where orchid exhibitions are attended by hundreds of thousands of orchid fanciers and where prizes for the best plants start with a car. Every third year, the World Orchid Conference Committee stages an event that alternates its venue between the Northern and Southern Hemispheres.

This sustained interest in orchids has resulted in the publication of many volumes written for the beginner and specialized grower. The oldest journal in the world is the *Orchid Review*, started in 1893, which is published six times a year by the Royal Horticultural Society in London. Further information

THE BOTANY OF ORCHIDS

Orchids are primarily herbaceous or evergreen perennials. They range in size from Dendrophylax, *a plant that is reduced simply to roots, to the huge, bamboo-like* Arundina. *Orchids are distinguished from other plant families by their different habits of growth and by the distinctive structure of their flowers.*

ABOVE *When you cut a pseudobulb in half, you will see that it consists of a mass of fibrous material full of food to enable the plant to survive periods of drought.*

PSEUDOBULBS

Many orchids produce pseudobulbs or false bulbs, although this is not always the case. Those that do, develop a sympodial type of growth, where a new pseudobulb is added each season along a continually extending rhizome. In this way, the plant builds up a series of pseudobulbs that form a chain. The chain may divide when two or more growths develop from the last pseudobulb in one year. This is how large clumps can form over several years.

It is difficult to make comparisons with other structures and plants. A pseudobulb is unlike a daffodil or an onion bulb, which consists of a layer of sheafs, or false leaf bases, one on top of the other. It is also unlike a potato, which is a starchy, tuberous structure. Perhaps the closest is the creeping rhizome formed by members of the *Iris* family.

Inside, a pseudobulb consists of a fibrous material that can hold a great deal of water, conserving energy and storing moisture. In the wild, this ensures that the plant can survive periods of drought during the dry season. In cultivation, the dry season is represented by winter, when the plant goes into a semi-dormant state until the longer days of spring activate new growth. Pseudobulbs are the longest-living part of the plant and will exist in a dormant state long after the leaves have been shed. Leafless pseudobulbs are known as back bulbs. In evergreen types, such as cymbidiums, a healthy plant consists of more pseudobulbs in leaf than out of leaf. With the deciduous types, such as lycastes, a cluster of leafless pseudobulbs with only the leading one in leaf is normal.

Pseudobulbs have evolved into an unlimited range of shapes and sizes, from long, thin, pencil shapes to rounded or even flattened structures. They may be no larger than a pea, round and shiny, and delicious to look at when newly formed, as in the smaller coelogynes and bulbophyllums. By contrast, they may be the size of a tennis ball, as in the case of some cymbidiums. In cattleyas and allied genera, they become tall and club-shaped, swelling out from a narrow base adjoining the stout rhizome, while the one or two leaves are formed at the top.

Dendrobiums produce some of the longest pseudobulbs among cultivated orchids, and these become so elongated in some species that they are called "canes". In this genus, they

LEFT *A pseudobulb, such as this* Cymbidium *pseudobulb, grows above the surface of the ground or on a tree as an epiphyte.*

are mostly leafed along their entire length, as in *Dendrobium pierardii*. Many dendrobiums are deciduous and so remain in a leafless, dormant state for much of the year. Perhaps the longest pseudobulbs of all belong to the species *Grammatophyllum speciosum*. This giant orchid is known as the sugar cane orchid, a reference to its leafy canes that can reach a length of 5m (16ft), becoming pendent under their own weight. Between these extremes are numerous orchids that grow to a height of 1.2m (4ft), and as many again that are below 30cm (12in).

The strangest of all are the hollow pseudobulbs of *Schomburgkia tibicinis* and *Caularthon bicornutum*, two species with slits at the base of their hollow pseudobulbs. It is difficult to be sure why these have evolved, because they defeat the object of functioning as a

LEFT *This thriving* Odontoglossum *has a group of pseudobulbs, which support each other, and a new growth that will produce a further pseudo-bulb. In this way, orchids progress, developing new pseudobulbs each growing season.*

food store when they are completely empty. Usually occupied in the wild by a species of fierce ant, they can serve a dual purpose: providing a home for the insect, which, in turn, grooms the orchid and keeps it free from parasites and unwanted pests.

LEFT *The glow of light at the end of this hollow pseudobulb indicates the small hole at the bottom of the structure. In the wild, these orchids are infested with huge colonies of ants which live inside the hollow pseudobulb. The ant has a comfortable home, and the plant remains untroubled by parasites. This poses the question: "Which came first, the hollow pseudobulb or the ant?"*

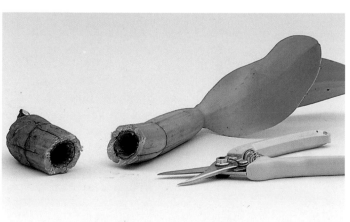

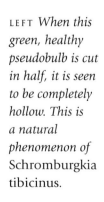

LEFT *When this green, healthy pseudobulb is cut in half, it is seen to be completely hollow. This is a natural phenomenon of* Schromburgkia tibicinus.

ABOVE *Some orchids, such as dendrobiums, have elongated pseudobulbs which bear little resemblance to the short pseudobulbs of other plants. These long stems or "canes" can reach lengths of anything up to 1–2m (3–6ft).*

LEAVES

The leaves of sympodial orchids are produced from the pseudobulb. There may be one or several. In cymbidiums, a number of long, narrow leaves come from the basal sheaths that cover the pseudobulb, and fall from the plant at a separation line that prevents any damage when the leaf is shed. Cattleyas produce just one or two broad, semi-rigid leaves from the apex of the pseudobulbs. Leaves vary considerably in colour from a light mid-green to dark grey-green. Some paphiopedilums and phalaenopsis are mottled with light and dark green shades. Not all sympodial orchids produce pseudobulbs. The paphiopedilums and phragmipediums, for example, form fans of leaves from a basal rhizome.

Monopodial orchids have a single vertical rhizome from which pairs of leaves grow at right angles. Vandas and phalaenopsis are the best examples of monopodial orchids in cultivation. While the vandas can become considerably tall, and at some stage in their life need to be reduced in height, the phalaenopsis are self-regulating, never attaining much

ABOVE LEFT *This* Paphiopedilum *has mottling on the surface of the leaf and dense, deep purple peppering on the underside.*

LEFT *The long stripes of* Oncidium incurvum *var.* variegatum *are not to be confused with a virus. This is a natural phenomenon which can occur in most orchids. Wherever variegation occurs, it is necessary for the health of the plant that there should be plenty of green pigment or chlorophyll to sustain the orchid. An all-white leaf will certainly die.*

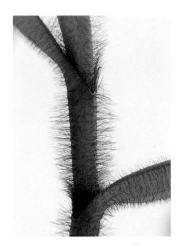

ABOVE *Some orchids, such as this* Trichotosia ferox, *produce plants covered with fine, brown hair, the purpose of which is not fully understood. It is thought that the hairs may provide a layer of protection in cold climates.*

ABOVE *The stems, new shoots and base of the flower buds of* Dendrobium infundibulum *are covered with thick, black hairs, creating a rough surface. As the new growth starts to age, the hairs become less apparent.*

ABOVE *Some orchids have a natural foliage variation. The new growth of this* Phaius maculatus *is a beautiful, pale green with yellow spotting.*

upward growth, because the older leaves are shed at the same rate as new ones appear.

The leaves of vandas and other monopodial orchids are semi-rigid, while those of phalaenopsis are broad and flat. In the wild, the latter plants are not subjected to extreme temperatures or bright sunlight, and their wide surface is designed to catch as much of the filtered light as possible. Some vandas, on the other hand, have rounded, or terete, foliage, which lessens the surface area on plants that can survive in areas of full sun. Leaves that remain for one or two seasons only are wide, soft and papery, such as with the lycastes, while leaves that are hard and leathery will live for much longer.

The leaves contain chlorophyll, which enables the plant to photosynthesize sunlight into energy. Some of the terrestrial orchids exist for long periods without leaves, producing foliage for only a short time during the growing season. A few orchids, such as *Rhizanthella* species, are subterranean, without any green parts, relying entirely on the microscopic fungus with which they form a symbiotic

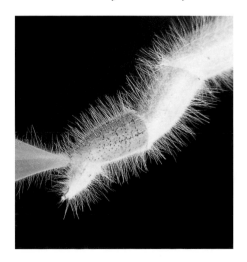

relationship. The nutrients that the orchid requires are provided by the fungus. Some leafless monopodial orchids exist, such as *Chilochista* species, that are no more than a cluster of roots, and it is the roots that contain the chlorophyll to enable the plants to photosynthesize. A few orchids have thick hairs on both sides of the foliage. The purpose of this is not fully understood, but it may be that they are a protection from insects or a means of preventing water lying on the foliage, which could be detrimental on cold nights. Other monopodials, including vandas, have leaf tips that are serrated; these enable the plant to dispose of any excess moisture taken up through the roots.

LEFT Dendrobium senile *has pseudobulbs and leaves covered with a layer of fine, white hair, which provides a layer of protection for the plant in its natural habitat.*

ROOTS

The roots of orchids are unique in the plant kingdom. They are thick and mostly white, but are not produced with the same abundance as in other plants. They consist of a thin inner core, with an absorbent outer covering made up of layers of dead cells. This layer, which soaks up water through its surface, is called the velamen, and it progresses behind the green growing tip. The tips of orchid roots are extremely vulnerable to damage and can be easily broken when they are outside the pot. Most orchid roots will remain in the container but, being naturally aerial, will often extend over the rim of the pot and continue to grow, suspended in air, or by attaching themselves to any surface they touch.

The roots are not permanent structures but are made annually, sprouting from the base some time after the start of the new growth. In the same way as the leaves are shed from the plant after one or a few years, so the roots die naturally to be replaced by those from the new growth.

In monopodial orchids such as vandas, the roots are made at intervals

ABOVE LEFT *The roots of epiphytic orchids such as* Encyclia radiata *are important. Not only do they supply the plant with nourishment, but they also attach the plant to its host tree.*

LEFT *Quite a number of epiphytic orchids produce masses of short, upright roots such as these* Stanhopea *roots. They grow like stalagmites, ending with a sharp point. The purpose of these upright roots may be to collect moisture or dead leaves and other forest detritus to form compost around the base of the plant.*

along the rhizome and seldom have need to go underground. Many orchids can photosynthesize through the roots, and in extreme examples there are a number of small epiphytic species that have become totally leafless, relying entirely upon a bundle of thick roots to hold the necessary chlorophyll.

The roots of some orchids are also extremely attractive; in phalaenopsis they are silvery white when outside the pot.

A few orchids, such as gongoras and *Ansellia* species, produce short side roots at an angle from the main ones. These are produced near the base of the plant and become hard and as sharp as needles as they mature. They form a dense, impenetrable barrier as a protection against pests that might otherwise attack their pseudobulbs.

Roots are extremely important to orchids. If they are killed through over-watering, they cannot be replaced until the plant makes new growth, which may mean the plant surviving for several months without roots and unable to take up moisture. If this happens, the pseudobulbs will shrivel and the foliage will become limp until new roots enable the lost water reserves to be made up. In the meantime, regular spraying will help to slow down dehydration.

ABOVE RIGHT *Ansellia africana* is a tropical epiphyte from Africa that produces masses of stiffly held aerial roots, branching in all directions. This does not always mean that the plant needs repotting.

RIGHT Phalaenopsis *roots are growing here in a transparent pot. This is to encourage the orchid to make pot, rather than aerial, roots, thus keeping it in contact with the compost (growing medium) and nourishment. It also allows the grower to observe progress.*

FLOWERS

While orchid plants themselves are
extremely varied, in their flowers
they know no bounds in terms of
variation in structure and colour.
The flowers are so diverse and often
incredibly beautiful, in stark contrast
to what some see as distinctly
unattractive plants. Many people are
amazed that such beautiful flowers
can come from what they consider to
be untidy or ugly plants, though to the
true enthusiast, most orchid plants
are handsome.

RIGHT *The striking* Paphiopedilum
Eustacenum *is a tall-stemmed, elegant
slipper orchid in which the more typical
lip or labellum has been further
modified to form a pouch. Above this
pouch, on either side of the staminode,
are two anthers.*

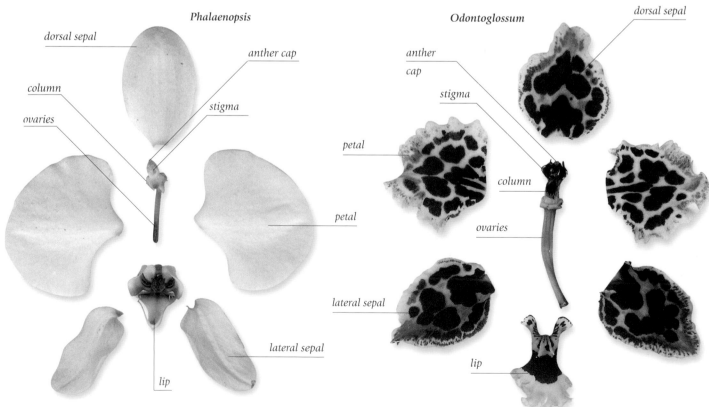

Phalaenopsis

dorsal sepal

anther cap

column

stigma

ovaries

petal

lateral sepal

lip

Odontoglossum

dorsal sepal

anther cap

stigma

petal

column

ovaries

lateral sepal

lip

Not all orchid blooms can be described as beautiful, however. While the most favoured and widely grown orchids are undeniably lovely, there are many whose flowers are curious, strange and even grotesque in appearance. The genus containing the greatest number of species is *Bulbophyllum*, but, among its thousand or so species, there are very few that could be described as pretty.

While all orchids conform to one basic design, this has been duplicated and modified a thousand times, each variation designed to suit one orchid's particular habitat or way of growing. One part of the flower has always

LEFT *Carrying its narrow-petalled flowers on tall spikes,* Zygopetalum intermedium *has a large, flared, prominent lip which is designed as a landing platform for a pollinating insect from where it is guided to the pollinia.*

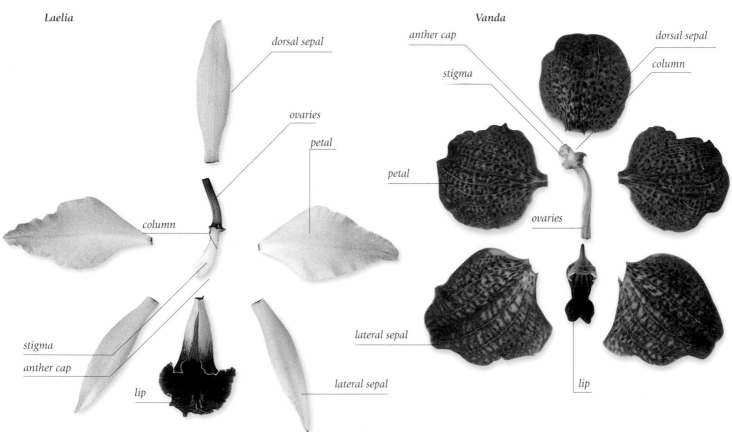

Laelia

dorsal sepal

ovaries

petal

column

stigma

anther cap

lip

lateral sepal

Vanda

anther cap

stigma

petal

ovaries

lateral sepal

lip

dorsal sepal

column

become much exaggerated, with petals or lip dominating the flower. All these modifications have evolved to attract a specific pollinator, and to do this some orchids have gone to extraordinary lengths.

Orchids are largely insect pollinated, and their flower structure reflects this. Each flower consists of six segments – three petals and three sepals – that are known collectively as the tepals. The outer three are sepals; the inner three petals. The third of the petals has developed into the labellum, or lip, which provides an ideal landing stage for the pollinating insect. Often the lip is lightly hinged, so that it can position the insect correctly for pollination, as well as ensuring that only the right-size insect enters the flower.

In many orchids, the lip is large and highly coloured and has a bright patterning quite distinct from the rest of the flower. At the centre are a number of ridges that guide the insect to the bloom. These are usually bright yellow and are called the honey guides. Above the lip is the column – a single, finger-like structure containing the reproductive parts of the flower. The pollen is found at the end of the column, usually in two, four or six masses. These pollen masses contain the pollen grains, or pollinia, which, unlike other flowers, are not in a powder form. They are held at the end of the column under a protective cap called the anther. The pollen masses are golden yellow and attached to a viscid disc by two thin threads. As an insect emerges from a flower, the sticky pad attached to the pollinia adheres to its head or thorax. The anther falls away as the insect flies off, carrying the pollinia to the next bloom.

On the underside of the column is a sticky patch. This is the stigmatic surface into which the pollinia are deposited. The pollen grains extend their growing tubes down through the centre of the column to reach the ovaries situated directly behind the flower, where they meet the thousands of unfertilized seeds. By the time fertilization is complete, the ovaries will have swollen into a large capsule containing up to a million minute, golden yellow, ripening seeds.

The largest of all orchid flowers is produced by the slipper orchid, *Phragmipedium grande*. In this species, the petals hang down to a length of 45cm (18in) when held out horizontally, and the flower measures a huge 1m (3ft) across. At the opposite extreme, there are minute species of *Stelis* whose flowers would be covered by a pin's head. In between are thousands of highly desirable flowers from one to several inches wide.

RIGHT Thunia marshalliana *is a lovely species that produces its flowers in close proximity to each other. The lip is densely haired and designed so that the pollinating insect can climb up to reach the pollinia.*

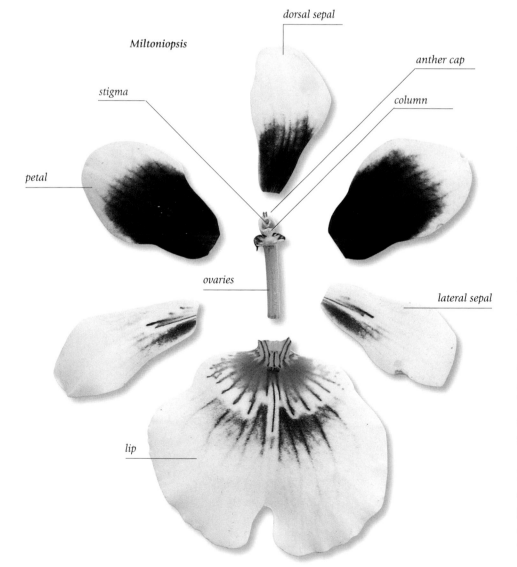

Miltoniopsis

dorsal sepal

anther cap

column

stigma

petal

ovaries

lateral sepal

lip

HYBRID ALLIANCES

There is no other plant family that will hybridize to the same extent as the orchid. They are highly evolved plants and many are still evolving. This, combined with their dependency upon insects for pollination, has influenced their ability to be hybridized, with f ew constrictions. In the wild, natural hybrids are a fairly common occurrence, and this is proved when a man-made cross produces flowers identical to the species. *Laelia gouldiana*, for example, is considered to be a natural hybrid between *L. anceps* and *L. autumnalis*.

In cultivation, hybridization has continued apace since the middle of the 19th century, when the unique structure of the orchid flower was understood. Many early experiments failed

RIGHT *Much influenced by the* Oncidium *in the make-up of this trigeneric hybrid, the flowers of* Wilsonara Bonne Nuit *are produced on tall flower spikes, the sepals and petals highly patterned.*

because the growers around at that time had little knowledge of compatibility or the relationships orchids had with each other. It was soon realized, however, that most species would breed readily with others of their own genus to produce interspecific crosses. It was also found that intergeneric crosses could be made between genera that were sufficiently related. It is this readiness to jump species and produce intergeneric hybrids that sets orchids apart.

There are some, such as the cymbidiums, that will only produce interspecific hybrids, and attempts to cross them with other, related orchids have largely failed. However,

LEFT
Odontoglossum *Violetta von Holm has tall, upright flower spikes of brightly coloured flowers in autumn. This elegant hybrid is raised from the species* O. bictoniense *and* O. rossii.

Cymbidium species from vastly different parts of the world, thousands of miles apart, will cross-breed, pointing to a close relationship between them that has endured despite a long separation from a common ancestor. *Cymbidium devonianum*, which originates from the Himalayas can be crossed with *C. madidum* from northern Australia; the resulting hybrid produces blooms that are midway between the species.

Among the slipper orchids, the paphiopedilums and phragmipediums appear similar. Hybridizing among the former has produced some fantastic results. However, there are no crosses with the South American phragmipediums. Although there appear to be similarities between the two genera, parallel evolutionary tracks have taken them down different avenues, segregating their genes, which, it appears, cannot be united. This is surprising, when we consider that a number of the multi-flowered, long-petalled *Paphiopedilum* species, such as *P. rothschildianum* and *P. parishii*, resemble phragmipediums such as *P. caudatum* and *P. pearcei* more closely than they do other paphiopedilums.

From among the immense number of hybrids raised, several alliances that contain numerous related genera have

RIGHT *Many generations of selective breeding with specific species has created* Brassolaeliocattleya *Nuance 'Elegie' which has lovely, lime-green flowers with a deep yellow lip. This modern hybrid blooms during the autumn.*

FAR RIGHT Laeliocattleya *Elizabeth Fulton 'Histoire' is a unifoliate hybrid that produces a single leaf per pseudobulb and colourful flowers in a striking combination of yellow sepals and petals with a deep magenta lip.*

RIGHT *Hybrids such as* Dendrobium *Emma White and Trakool Red are raised in South-east Asia for the pot-plant and cut-flower trade. From there they are shipped to countries around the world. The flowers are exceptionally long-lived.*

FAR RIGHT Phalaenopsis *Brother Wild Thing is one of a new range of fabulous hybrids that provide multi-coloured flowers with an attractive design on the sepals and petals. They are exceptionally free-flowering and will bloom several times during the year.*

emerged. Among these the most favoured are the *Cattleya* alliance, the *Odontoglossum* alliance and the *Vanda* alliance. Within these three natural genera, alliances can be found consisting of anything from two natural genera (*Laelia* × *Cattleya* = *Laeliocattleya*) to six (*Cattleya* × *Brassavola* × *Broughtonia* × *Laelia* × *Schomburgkia* × *Sophronitis* = *Mooreara*), and, in a few instances, nine (*Cattleya* × *Brassavola* × *Broughtonia* × *Cattleyopsis* × *Diacrium* × *Epidendrum* × *Laelia* × *Schomburgkia* × *Sophronitis* = *Sallyyeeara*). Here, there appears to be no limit on the multiples, which have led to some astonishing results.

The spectacular vandas from South-east Asia appear, at first glance, to be compatible with the vast number of angraecoid orchids from Africa and Madagascar. The foliage of *Angraecum sesquipedale*, for example, resembles that of the vandas more closely than those other monopodials, the phalaenopsis. However, the vandas are closer in evolutionary terms to the phalaenopsis, and these two will hybridize, along with many others that make up this alliance but that look totally different.

At present, we are denied a union between the angraecums and phalaenopsis, and can only speculate on what the results might be. A few hybrids from the crossing of angraecums and vandas have been achieved, but with little result.

ABOVE Laeliocattleya *Chinco is a superbly coloured hybrid that produces rich purple flowers with a deeper lip that is not over-large for the flower. The plant blooms during the autumn.*

WHERE TO GROW ORCHIDS

More people are growing orchids today because they are so easily available, and the hybrids being raised, mainly in Europe and Asia, are designed specifically as pot plants. Phalaenopsis and miltoniopsis take the lead because they are the most adaptable and easy to grow and flower, with many other types adding interest and variety. These orchids are mass-produced in huge quantities to satisfy a burgeoning demand for houseplants with a difference. Orchids bred for this purpose have opened up a new indoor growing experience with individual sprays of blooms lasting for eight weeks or more at a time; compared to other pot plants this represents extremely good value. For the more serious orchid grower, a well-maintained greenhouse offers a much wider choice of plants, and for the specialist preferring to concentrate on a particular genus or group, a greenhouse becomes a necessity. In between the windowsill and the greenhouse are sun lounges and conservatories, both of which can accommodate a few orchids. However small or large the space you can devote to growing them, orchids will give you lasting pleasure for years to come.

Dactylorhiza fuchsii

GROWING ORCHIDS INDOORS

There are several advantages to growing orchids in the home. You do not have to go to any great expense to provide warmth, provided there is central heating already installed in all rooms. Very little equipment will be needed when you start with just a few plants, and that can be added to as the collection grows, as it surely will.

ABOVE *Cymbidiums are large orchids and this* Cymbidium Jocelyn *makes a striking centrepiece in a living room.*

POSITIONING ORCHIDS

Orchids growing in your home benefit from the regular attention you can give them. Like the much-loved cat that sits in her favourite chair and receives a stroke every time you pass, your orchids will be admired every time you pass them by. In this way, you will notice immediately when a new growth or flower spike appears or when the surface compost (growing medium) has dried out, quickly learning to judge their requirements as you gain experience. The more time you spend around your orchids, the more attention you are going to give them. In summer, keep a hand-held spray bottle nearby and regularly mist the leaves lightly when you pass by. Should the orchids be receiving too much light so that their foliage changes colour, you will notice this and can remove them to another, more suitable place, long before any harm is done. In this way, your orchids become

your constant companions, and it is surprising how attached you can become to them, doting upon their every need and enthusing about new leaves or roots as they appear.

Take a look around your home to decide which would be the most favoured position for your first orchids. The ideal aspect for summer growing is a window that receives either the morning or evening sun, but not direct sun during the hottest part of the day. Most indoor kinds will be happy with this situation. Those orchids that like the shadiest places, such as phalaenopsis and paphiopedilums, will do equally well in a window that does not receive too much sun in summer. Cattleyas and dendrobiums are examples of orchids that like a considerable amount of light, and these would be well suited to a window that receives a great deal of sun, provided there was some shading between the plants and the glass. Blinds or net curtains would be sufficient to prevent burning from direct sun, while giving the plants the extra light they

need for optimum growth and ripening of the pseudobulbs. In the winter, most orchids will be comfortable in a well-lit window, because the sun will not reach high enough in the sky to cause any problems with burning. The high-risk time here is in the early spring, when the sun begins to climb higher each day, gradually gaining strength. Certain plants will quickly need to be moved to a less sunny aspect.

Whichever room the orchids are growing in, they need to be close to the window and the light. Indoors, this light is usually available from only one direction, so remember to take full advantage of it. Always place the orchids so that the back of the plant is facing the window, with the new growths facing into the room. In this way, tender new leaves cannot become accidentally burnt, and the older pseudobulbs can be well ripened to assist flowering. In winter, the plants can be turned around so that it is the new growths that receive the most light. Most orchids will grow better close to the window than in the centre of a room, unless it is particularly well lit with a high ceiling and white walls. An area like this would suit phalaenopsis very well. While orchids are in flower, they can be brought into the room for display for as long as the flowers last, then returned to their growing area.

Orchids should not be stood so close to the window that their leaves touch the glass. Ideally, double-glazed windows are best, so that in winter the cold does not impinge on the plants. Blinds or curtaining prevent the plants from being too close to the window, which is ideal. On winter nights, ensure that heavy curtains are drawn behind the orchids, leaving them inside the room. In summer, windows can be left open to give the orchids a flow of fresh air whenever the weather is warm enough, but this should not cause a cold draught.

Be aware of those places that could be harmful to orchids. Do not stand the plants directly in front of, or above, an open fire, where they will quickly succumb to overheating and dehydration. Remember that appliances such as the fridge in the kitchen and the television in the living room both give out warmth when working, which is harmful to orchids placed nearby. Also, avoid any area where the plants will be in a draught (draft) from an open doorway or other source of cold air. Finally, wherever you place your orchids, take care to prevent them being knocked over or damaged by pets or children.

RIGHT Paphiopedilum insigne *can be displayed to good effect on a windowsill. Be sure to protect the plant from direct sun, with blinds or thin curtains.*

ORCHIDS THROUGHOUT THE HOME

In the kitchen, a wide windowsill will accommodate several orchids, but make sure that they will not be exposed to too much hot steam from the washing-up bowl or, worse, a steaming kettle. There may be more than one suitable aspect in the living or dining room, provided these are kept at a comfortable temperature. Bedrooms, which are often colder at night, will be suitable for the cooler growing orchids, which need a night-time drop in order to grow and flower well. Spare bedrooms are perhaps less suitable because such rooms are often left unheated and unvisited on a regular basis, and plants remaining here may be forgotten for days, and, with little rise in the daytime temperature, can become very cold indeed. These sterile rooms will not provide the stimulating conditions in which orchids grow. The bathroom is often considered an ideal place because of the steam created when the bath or shower is running. However, this creates rapid changes in temperature and humidity, which plants can find hard to tolerate. In addition, the bathroom is most often the worst-lit room in the house. Usually any light comes from a small, frosted window, which is insufficient for most orchids. Bathroom-grown orchids are often distinguishable by the light coating of talcum powder covering their leaves. This, in itself, is dangerous to orchids, clogging up the leaf pores and preventing them from ventilating in the normal way. In a house, an ideal position can often be found in a window halfway up the stairwell. Wherever there is sufficient light and warmth, orchids will grow, provided a suitable growing area is set aside for them.

Cellar culture is practised in countries such as Canada, where excessively cold winters prevent the use of greenhouses. The cellar, which is usually heated, is adapted to grow orchids by the installation of electric lighting and benching with humidity trays, and a system of catching the surplus water to be recycled or drained away. This system works well in these colder countries, where the orchids are brought out for the summer and grown in the conventional way. In other situations, however, this system is not worth the cost and effort involved in converting an area, and the plants grown in this manner rely more upon their summer growth to keep them surviving through the winter.

Growing Orchids in a Conservatory

Many houses today have a built-on sun lounge or conservatory, which offers a very satisfactory home for orchids. Often these areas contain garden furniture, and the main idea is to provide a place to relax that catches the sun's warmth on those days when it is too cold to sit outside. An area for orchids can be created in the same way that space is provided to grow them indoors, except that here there is more room, and particularly more headroom, which means that larger orchids such as cymbidiums can be grown. If the construction has glass to the ground, the orchids can be grown at floor level, and may need some shade from blinds pulled down at the side,

LEFT *This beautiful arrangement of orchids includes* Dendrochilum glumaceum *(left),* Encyclia cochleata *var. 'Yellow Burnham' (centre), and* Coelogyne Intermedia *(right).*

ORCHIDS SUITABLE FOR GROWING INDOORS

Brassia verrucosa
Coelogyne cristata
Cymbidiums (small-growing)
Dendrobium infundibulum
Encyclia radiata
Laelia anceps
Lycaste aromatica
Lycaste skinneri
Miltoniopsis (all)
Odontoglossum (intergeneric)
Oncidium ornithorhynchum
Paphiopedilums (all)
Phalaenopsis (all)
Pleiones (all)

ORCHIDS SUITABLE FOR GROWING IN A CONSERVATORY

Anguloa clowesii
Angulocaste hybrids
Brassia verrucosa
Cattleyas (all) plus allied genera
Coelogyne cristata
Cymbidiums (small-growing and larger-growing)
Dendrobium infundibulum
Encyclia radiata
Laelia anceps
Lycaste aromatica
Lycaste skinneri
Miltoniopsis (all)
Odontoglossums (intergeneric)
Oncidium ornithorhynchum
Paphiopedilums (all)
Phalaenopsis (all)
Phragmipediums (all)
Pleiones (all)

LEFT *A bedroom is the perfect setting for a specimen orchid such as this* Phalaenopsis *Little Skipper 'Zuma Nova', with its delicate, pink flowers.*

with the roof area painted with shading material. This would only be necessary to prevent the sun shining directly upon the leaves. Orchids placed on the floor would need to stand on concrete or tiles, which can be wetted without harming any installations, and some means of channelling away surplus water would need to be set up. Alternatively, where the floor area is carpeted, the plants would be better housed on the sort of staging used in greenhouses. Here the same humidity tray system can be put into place to give the orchids the all-important microclimate, with some moisture rising around them. It should also be possible to spray the foliage without worrying about surplus water.

The temperature will need to be controlled to prevent the area from over-heating during the day or else becoming too cold at night in winter. If there is no form of heating in the conservatory or sun lounge, it may only be necessary to run an extra radiator from the central heating in the house to the area, at very little extra cost to the heating bill. However, this must be kept on all night in winter to maintain a steady warmth for the plants. Otherwise, it may be necessary to install an electric fan heater to heat the place in winter. This can double as a cooling fan in summer. As with green-houses, the smaller the area, the greater the fluctuation of temperature in the shortest time, and in summer it will probably be desirable to leave the door open if that is the only source of fresh air. Conservatories that are shaded by large trees nearby are the most suitable, and the danger of overheating in summer is greatly lessened.

METHODS OF DISPLAY

Growing areas can accommodate from just one to many orchids. However, an orchid plant placed in isolation, with nothing around it to stimulate growth, will not succeed. A barren windowsill can be likened to a desert, until a few adaptations are made to make the area habitable. A narrow windowsill may have to be widened by attaching a wooden shelf to give more space and increase the growing area.

Humidity Trays

This area can be used for humidity trays. These are available from garden centres and other outlets in many shapes and sizes with differing designs. The humidity tray is a shallow tray without holes, because it needs to hold water. Place a quantity of expanded clay pellets in the tray to about 2.5cm (1in), or just below the rim, and partially fill with water. Now you have created a base for your

orchids to stand on where they will receive a small amount of moisture from the evaporating water rising around them; at the same time, the plants will be standing above the water, so their roots will be kept wet but not immersed.

LEFT Encyclia cochleata var. 'Yellow Burnham' is an extremely popular orchid, which grows well indoors. It can reach over 30cm (12in) in height.

You can have as many humidity trays as you have room for, standing a few orchids on each and allowing sufficient room between them for air to circulate. Place a few smaller pots of ferns or other green plants in between the orchids; these can be kept wetter than the orchids by plunging them directly into the pellets. The green plants, which may be colourful busy Lizzies (*Impatiens*) or any of the small-growing creeping plants that will not become so large as to overgrow the orchids, will do much to create a good growing environment, increasing the humidity around the orchids and generally brightening up the setting. *Tradescantia* can be trained around the edge of a humidity tray to good effect, but its speed of growth will necessitate regular pruning. It will be necessary to top up the water in the trays from time

LEFT A group of orchids should be placed on a humidity tray covered with a 2.5cm (1in) layer of clay pellets and partially filled with water. As the water evaporates, the orchids receive a small amount of moisture.

to time, always making sure that the orchids are standing above the water and not with the base of their pots in the water. (This would cause the roots to drown and the loss of its roots can be serious for an orchid.) Orchids growing in humidity trays will need to be removed for watering. The best place to water the plants is on the kitchen draining board or in the sink. Because of the nature of orchid compost (growing medium), a lot of water has to be used at one time, and unless a system of catching the water and channelling it into a container is installed, which is almost impossible indoors, the plants are better taken to a watering place.

Where a single plant is being used as a specimen to enhance one small window, for example, it is even more important that there is some moisture surrounding it, and a small humidity tray or saucer becomes necessary. Add other plants to the tray for effect, or arrange large pebbles or sea shells to create a pleasing attraction with the orchid as centrepiece.

Growing Carts

An alternative idea to growing on the windowsill is the growing cart on wheels. Growing carts are available from most garden centres and are designed for indoor plants. They have the advantage in that the plants can be

ABOVE *Small pots of green plants can be placed among the orchids. They help to create a good growing environment for the orchids by increasing the humidity. Here, a collection of paphiopedilums includes* Paphiopedilum *Leeanum (inset top),* P. *Jersey Freckles (inset centre), and* P. insigne *(inset bottom).*

wheeled to a light position close to the window during the day and moved back at night. It also makes the chore of taking plants out for watering much easier. Some orchid plants can become top heavy, particularly when they have outgrown their pots and are in need of repotting, and these are best handled singly rather than risk their falling over

LEFT *Orchids can be displayed in unusual containers, as this twiggy, wall-mounted pot shows. This* Vuylstekeara Cambria *'Lensings Favorit' has red and pink flowers, with mottling on the petals and sepals.*

while being moved in the cart. A free-standing coffee-type table situated in front of a window can be used in the same way, without the need for installing a wider shelf.

Growing Miniature Orchids

Some growers delight in the very tiny miniature orchids, which can be grown in pots as small as 3cm (1¼in) in diameter. These little gems of the orchid world have a great following, and can be every bit as enjoyable to grow as the larger, showier kinds. However, their small size can create problems of keeping them wet enough and preventing rapid drying out, particularly in the summer. One successful method of growing miniature orchids is to enclose them in a growing case. An old aquarium used for tropical fish is ideal, and these can often be picked up very cheaply if they are no longer watertight.

First establish whether or not there are any leaks around the base; if there are, fit a humidity tray into the base. Place pebbles or expanded clay pellets in the base to create your own individual tank effect. You now have a miniature orchid garden to house those tiny plants that would otherwise dry out too rapidly. Place this in a bright spot, but not too close to a window where it

LEFT *For growing miniature varieties indoors where less headroom is needed, a disused fish tank can be suitable. Place some pebbles in the base and keep them wet in order to provide a humid environment for the orchids. Add a few ferns or other green plants.*

ORCHIDS SUITABLE FOR
GROWING IN A SMALL
GROWING CASE OR
GLASS TANK

Coelogyne corymbosa
Cirrhopetalum guttulatum
Dendrobium cuthbertsonii
Encyclia polybulbon
Ludisia discolor
Masdevallia tovarensis
Masdevallia Whiskers
Mexicoa ghiesbrechtiana
Neofineta falcata
Oncidium cheirophorum

RIGHT *An excellent way to grow a few orchids indoors is to set up an orchid growing case just large enough to accommodate a few plants in flower. The door can be opened to provide fresh air and control the temperature.*

may overheat. It is a good idea to place a minimum/maximum thermometer inside the aquarium to assess the temperature range you have created. During the summer, the aquarium can be left open at the top; close it down only when warmth needs to be conserved. By setting up a horticultural fluorescent light tube above the plants, it is possible to place the aquarium in an unlit corner that would otherwise be unsuitable for growing orchids. This idea can be adapted to a smaller or larger degree. For just one or two very small plants, use a large glass such as a brandy glass laid on its side, and create a miniature landscape inside for one or two little plants. Alternatively, you can build your own indoor growing case as large as conveniently possible and with the inclusion of electric lighting. This will provide a permanent

home for those plants that do not need bright light. These include the phalaenopsis and paphiopedilums. The lighting can be controlled so that the plants receive up to twelve hours of "daylight" daily throughout the year. This can greatly assist the flowering of orchids during dull periods.

An indoor case can be a simple design fitted into an existing window-

sill, or it can be quite an elaborate affair, with built-in ventilation from fans, and some lighting to stimulate the plants in winter. This can be placed almost anywhere in the home to provide an eye-catching display, with something of interest always flowering in the case. The larger the case, the greater the number and the size of plants that can be grown.

COLOUR AND SCENT

If you are growing your orchids indoors you may want to be more selective about the range of colours from your orchid blooms. With such a vast choice of hues and shades, it is possible to arrange your colour schemes to suit any room or personal choice.

The following charts will give you some at-a-glance ideas for this. Everyone has their own ideas and favourite colours, and their own preferred places in which to show off their treasured blooms. While in flower, and most orchids will last for several weeks, you can display your plants wherever they can be seen at their best. This may not be the best place for growing them in, but while in bloom a plant standing on its own with an attractive pot cover

can be most dramatic. If you also choose your orchids to bloom at different times of the year, you can have a plant in flower for most months of the year, ensuring that your favourite position is always filled with at least one plant in bloom.

To make the most of your blooms, stand a plant where it will create the greatest impact, but remember that you will need to water the plant in the usual way. If you do not stand the plant on a damp base, you will need to remove it for watering and replace it after the pot has drained.

The flowers of some orchids can also be highly scented, which adds immeasurably to their overall appeal. The richly coloured flowers of *Zygopetalum maxillare*, for example, are strongly scented. *Brassavola cuculata*, which is sometimes called the ghost orchid, has drooping flowers of a ghostly appearance. It blooms during the autumn and is highly fragrant at night.

LEFT *Well-chosen colour combinations can create beautiful effects, as is shown by this display of pale pink* Phalaenopsis schilleriana *(left) and the deep pink* P. Mad Milva *(right).*

ABOVE A Phalaenopsis *Mad Milva will do well as the centrepiece of an orchid display, provided it is kept out of direct sunlight. The flowers are delightful with cerise pink petals and sepals, with a darker pink lip.*

RIGHT *Orchids can be displayed in most rooms in the house. This pale lemon* Phalaenopsis Barbara Moler × Spitzberg *looks perfect in a blue bathroom.*

ORCHIDS FOR SCENT

Anguloa clowesii
Brassia verrucosa
Cattleyas and allied genera
Coelogyne ochracea
Dendrochilum cobbianum
Encyclia radiata
Gongora galeata
Lycaste aromatica
Maxillaria ochroleuca
Maxillaria picta
Miltoniopsis
Odontoglossum laeve
Oncidium ornithorhynchum

ORCHIDS WITH BRIGHTLY COLOURED FLOWERS

Phalaenopsis Mad Milva

Reds and oranges
Cattleyas
Cymbidiums
Encyclia vitellina
Epidendrum radicans
Lycastes
Masdevallia Copper Wing
Miltoniopsis
Oncidium Sharry Baby
'Sweet Fragrance'
Phragmipedium besseae
Sophrolaeliocattleya Jewel Box
'Dark Waters'
Sophronitis coccinea
Vuylstekeara Cambria
'Lensings Favorit'

Oncidium
Sharry Baby
'Sweet Fragrance'

Masdevallia
Copper Wing

Vuylstekeara
Cambria 'Lensings
Favorit'

Dark pinks
Angulocaste
Cattleyas and allied genera
Cymbidiums
Dendrobium nobile hybrids
Laelia anceps 'Guerrero'
Laelia purpurata
Lycastes
Miltoniopsis
Odontoglossums
Phalaenopsis Mad Milva
Phalaenopsis Purple Valley
Pleiones

Dark purples
Ascocendas
Cattleyas and allied genera
Odontoglossums

Bright yellows
Anguloa clowesii
Cattleyas and allied genera
Oncidium Boissiense
Oncidium sphacelatum
Phalaenopsis

Phalaenopsis
Purple Valley

Cymbidium Mini Ice 'Antarctic'

Greens
Brassia verrucosa
Coelogyne Green Dragon
'Chelsea' AM/RHS
Cymbidium Mini Ice 'Antarctic'
Epidendrum Orchid Glade
Paphiopedilums
Paphiopedilum Clare de Lune
Phragmipedium pearcei
Trudelia cristata

Epidendrum
Orchid Glade

ORCHIDS WITH PALE-COLOURED FLOWERS

Phalaenopsis Little Skipper 'Zuma Nova'

Pale pink
Cattleyas and allied genera
Cuitlauzina pendula
Cymbidiums
Dendrobium nobile hybrids
Laelia anceps
Lycastes and angulocastes
Lycaste skinneri
Miltoniopsis
Odontoglossums and allied genera
Phalaenopsis Brother Stripe ×
Phalaenopsis amboinensis
Phalaenopsis Little Skipper
'Zuma Nova'
Pleiones

White and cream
Aerangis luteo alba var. *rhodostricta*
Angraecum sesquipedale
Anguloa eburnea
Cattleyas and allied genera
Coelogynes
Cymbidiums
Dendrochilum glumaceum
Dendrobium nobile hybrids
Lycastes and angulocastes
Masdevallia tovarensis
Maxillaria ochroleuca
Miltoniopsis
Odontoglossums and allied genera
Phalaenopsis

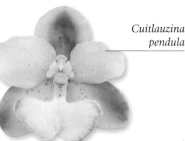

Cuitlauzina pendula

Masdevallia tovarensis

Lilac and lavender
Cattleyas and allied genera
Miltoniopsis
Phalaenopsis

Pale lemon
Cattleyas and allied genera
Cymbidiums
Dendrobium nobile hybrids
Lycastes and angulocastes
Miltoniopsis
Odontoglossums and allied genera
Phalaenopsis

Phalaenopsis Brother Stripe × *Phalaenopsis amboinensis*

Gongora maculata

Lemboglossum (Odontoglossum) bictoniense

Bi-coloured orchids
Calanthes
Cattleyas and allied genera
Cymbidums
Epidendrum pseudepudendrum
Gongora maculata
Lycastes
Miltoniopsis
Phalaenopsis
Rossioglossum Rawdon Jester
Thunia Gattonense

Multi-coloured orchids
Dendrobium nobile hybrids
Odontoglossums and allied genera

GROWING ORCHIDS OUTDOORS

Taking care of orchids growing outside differs little from the care that is needed to grow orchids indoors. However, you need to be more aware of the day-to-day conditions, which can change dramatically, and treat your orchids accordingly.

TEMPERATE REGIONS IN SUMMER

In temperate regions of the world, orchids that are normally grown indoors or under glass can be placed outside for the summer growing season. A carefully chosen position will provide your plants with conditions that are nearer to those of their natural habitat.

Orchids that benefit most are light-loving, cool-growing types such as cymbidiums, odontoglossums, coelogynes, encyclias and dendrobiums, all of which have fairly robust foliage that may become a little spotted or marked throughout the course of several months but will not come to any harm.

Those orchids with softer, wide-leafed foliage, such as lycastes, anguloas and the deciduous calanthes, would very soon become notably spoiled by blemishes as a result of the effects of the weather. The exceptions are the cool-growing varieties among the pleiones. These plants always do better in a cooler environment for the summer, and any spotting of their foliage usually comes late, at the season's end, just before the leaves turn brown and are shed.

Masdevallias and other small-growing related genera are shade-dwellers that would be particularly unhappy placed in the open. In no time a rapid loss of their almost succulent leaves would result. Their culture is more specialized, and difficult enough to achieve in the greenhouse.

Among the intermediate genera, those members of the vast *Cattleya* alliance do well in tropical gardens, but in temperate regions the foliage is prone to heavy marking by the excesses of wind and weather. Cattleyas retain their leaves for a number of years, and if they are spoilt at an early age, you have to live with a

disfigured plant for a long time. Although they like the warmth, cattleyas can easily be burnt by direct sun, and for this reason are better protected from the vagaries of a temperate summer. In tropical regions, however, these orchids will excel under shade cloth, which gives them a constant supply of fresh air without exposure to direct sun.

The hard-leafed encyclias and a number of *Oncidium* species, which include the tough, mule-eared species such as *Oncidium splendidum*, will take more light than most. The response of their foliage to any extra sunlight is a reddening of the leaves.

LEFT *Like many cymbidiums,* Cymbidium *Bethlehem 'Ridgeway' can be grown outdoors in summer in temperate regions.*

Those orchids termed warm-growing include the shade-loving phalaenopsis and a number of the paphiopedilums. Generally, none of these is suitable for outdoor growing, except in the tropics. The temperatures at night are too cold for much of the summer, and the lush foliage of phalaenopsis will suffer from the elements, causing premature leaf-loss and the death of the plant in extreme cases. The paphiopedilums are altogether too soft-leafed to cope with outdoor conditions, and it becomes impossible to keep the centre of their growths from filling with water when it rains. In a short time this can result in rot to the centre of the growth. These orchids are not suited to a temperate climate, even in summer. In a mixed collection of various orchids, it can be trial and error that decides those plants that will benefit from summering outdoors.

Do not attempt to take outside very young plants, or those growing in particularly small pots. Exposed to the elements, small pots are extremely difficult to keep wet, and at best will be wet one day and dry the next. It becomes impossible to retain an even level of moisture at the roots, which is conducive to all good orchid growing. Small pots are also in danger of being blown over by the wind or even trampled by pets. Orchids that have outgrown their pots are also at risk of being top-heavy and are easily knocked over and damaged. These same orchids are also extremely difficult to keep watered, and once they have become dry it is almost impossible to get water down to the roots without a long soak in a bucket of water.

Other orchids better left where they are include those that are producing their flowers during the summer period. Developing buds and flowers are the first to suffer from dampness, rain and wind. It also becomes difficult to keep

ABOVE In many temperate areas of the world, Dendrobium nobile, *a Himalayan species, can be grown successfully in gardens, hanging from trees in large baskets. The night temperature has to drop quite low, however, to enable them to flower well.*

the buds free of aphids and attacks from slugs. Newly repotted orchids should not be taken outside until they have started to make their new root systems.

A sick plant may improve under outside conditions. Cymbidiums, for example, growing indoors under poor light will produce a soft, lush foliage with over-long leaves that are limp and dark green, weakened by the lack of light. In a greenhouse or conservatory, soaring summer temperatures may produce a similar reaction, resulting in a weakened plant that is under stress and fails to bloom. You may also notice these symptoms in other light-loving orchids, and these will also benefit from being placed out-of-doors. At first, their response may be dramatic, and a sudden leaf-loss may result. Once the plants settle in and new growth starts, however, you will notice a complete change in the thickness and length of the leaves, and, together with a much sturdier appearance, the plant adapts and develops a much hardier growth. By the end of the growing season, a plant will look noticeably different, with pseudobulbs varying in their shape from the previous ones. This is the proof that your orchids have thrived and appreciate the more natural surroundings you have provided for them. By the time the cymbidiums are ready to be returned to their winter quarters, they will be bristling with flower spikes.

The *Odontoglossum* types, in particular, will reflect their change of surroundings and the extra light by the reddening of their leaves. Provided the amount of light they receive is not overdone, and they are not exposed to bright sunlight, this reddening will do no harm; it can be likened to a suntan and is not sunburn. During the following winter, these leaves will regain their mid-green colouring.

If you do not have a garden, your orchids can still enjoy the advantages of being outside for the summer. They are equally at home on a patio or even a balcony, provided they are shaded from direct sun during most of the day. Ideally, select a spot that is reached by either the early morning, the late afternoon or the evening sun only. This will ensure that the plants are in the shade during the hottest part of the day. Standing them against a white-washed wall will give them the added benefit of light reflected from behind. A roof garden may have just this situation.

In a garden, there are a number of places that will provide a good summer home for your orchids. It may be alongside a fence, a wall or a hedge, which will provide the necessary protection from the sun. Trees may also offer a shady place, but fruit trees should be avoided if there is any danger of ripe fruit crashing on the plants. They also harbour aphids and other pests that will get on the orchids. Do not place the orchids where they will be in the way of regular hedge trimming or lawn cutting, because you will tire of repeatedly having to move the plants.

Having chosen the ideal position, erect a bench for the plants to stand upon that is at a convenient

height for you to water and attend to them. Ideally, stand the orchids on grit or expanded clay pellets in water-filled humidity trays. This will ensure some moisture around the plants at all times. There should be no problem with water overflow, which will normally run away into the surrounding ground. Any orchids growing on a balcony outside your window may have to be brought inside for watering if surplus water may cause a problem.

Avoid standing the orchids directly on the ground, where the pots will be subjected to infestation by all types of ground-dwelling pests. To prevent the orchids from being blown off their bench during very windy weather, it is a good idea to place a small railing around the edge. If you cannot find a sufficiently shady place for the orchids erect a shade-cloth roof above the plants on the bench, leaving open ends or sides to allow a free movement of air.

Orchids that are mounted on bark can be hung in trees, but they will require constant daily watering to ensure that they get enough moisture. Vandas, stanhopeas and other orchids in hanging baskets can be treated likewise. Aerial roots should remain active all through the summer and they will grow steadily if they are kept well sprayed.

When to Put Orchids Outside

In countries with a temperate climate, it is safe to place those orchids that will benefit from the air outside in their pots by the end of late spring or the beginning of early summer. By this time the danger of

THIS PAGE Encyclia brassavolae (*top*), E. alata (*left*), E. cochleata (*centre*), *and* E. radiata (*right*).

THIS PAGE Cymbidium *Cotil Point (left)*, C. *Sleeping Lamb (centre)*, C. *Candy King (right), and* C. *Baltic Starlight (bottom)*.

frosts should be well past, and the temperature change from inside to outside not so great as to cause undue stress. Choose a day when the weather is settled and heavy rain or wind not expected. Keep a close eye on the orchids and note any changes that occur. Any plant that immediately loses a lot of leaves may not be well suited to outdoor culture and would be better off coming back inside. Otherwise, expect some leaf-loss as the plants adjust to their new environment.

By the end of the summer, usually approaching the end of early autumn, the nights become colder as the weather deteriorates, and it is time to bring your plants back inside. Do this before the first frost appears, unless the orchids are well protected by tree foliage above them, in which case they may stay out a little longer, especially if the flower spikes are not yet showing.

Before bringing the plants back inside, check for pests. Out-of-doors they can harbour insects, such as earwigs and woodlice, which will be out of sight beneath the leaf-bracts and will need to be searched out. Check the compost (growing medium) for ants' nests and vine weevils or their grubs. Destroy these by

soaking the plant in a bucket of water for up to an hour. Check for the more easily seen pests such as slugs and snails, and also for the smaller, more troublesome red spider mites and aphids. Tidy up your orchids at the same time, removing all old bracts on the cymbidiums, and cutting off any broken or brown leaves. Pull out any weeds that have grown in the compost, including mosses and ferns; these may look nice growing with the orchids, but they will clog up the compost, making watering more difficult. Once the plants have been overhauled, they can be safely returned to their warmer winter quarters, having enjoyed their stay outdoors. The plants will be better prepared for flowering, and you will be wonderfully surprised at the improved quality of the blooms that will undoubtedly follow.

Growing Orchids in the Ground

In temperate parts of the world, notably Europe and North America, there is a growing awareness that it is possible to grow certain terrestrial types of orchid in the garden all year round. Orchids that were once plentiful before becoming extremely rare through overcollecting and destruction of their natural habitats, are now grown artificially in order to supply a need for garden cultivation. Such a plant is the lovely *Cypripedium reginae*, the pink and white lady's slipper orchid. Similarly, *C. calceolus*, which was once common in both Europe and North America, is being successfully grown commercially as a pot plant and garden plant, while at the same time, efforts are being made to reinstate its beautiful yellow and brown flowers back into the wild in Britain, where it has virtually become extinct.

Other European orchids available from commercial nurseries include *Dactylorhiza* hybrids, with tall, vibrantly coloured spikes of mauve flowers. These orchids can be established in specially prepared ground beds and left to mature into good-size colonies over many years.

ORCHIDS OUTDOORS IN TEMPERATE REGIONS

Orchids that can be moved outdoors:
Coelogynes
Cymbidiums
Dendrobiums
Encyclias

Terrestrial orchids that can be grown outdoors:
Cypripedium calceolus
Cypripedium reginae
(lady's slipper orchid)
Dactylorhiza

TROPICAL REGIONS ALL YEAR ROUND

In tropical climates, which include parts of the United States, Central and South America, parts of Australia, South Africa and South-east Asia, orchids can be grown permanently out-of-doors. The shade-loving genera can be accommodated beneath shade-cloth houses, which are open at the sides to allow air to flow through. This is the method used by commercial nurseries. Alternatively, the plants can be naturalized on trees in the garden. Here, once in position, they can grow into magnificent specimens with the minimum of care. Orchids growing naturally in this way need to be comfortable with the changing temperatures throughout the seasons. Cool-growing orchids will not do well in a tropical garden, which may be too hot for even the warmer-growing orchids. Some need a lower temperature at night if they are to bloom, and may need to be brought indoors at night, where air conditioning maintains a lower temperature.

Cattleyas are especially suited to naturalizing upon trees, and in their native Central America many are grown in this way in gardens, where they are a common sight flowering on the trunks and branches of trees. Where conditions are right for them,

RIGHT *This beautiful yellow* Promenaea xanthina *has been reintroduced on to this tree in its native Brazil where it naturally grows on the lower trunk of trees at high altitude in cloud-filled, humid rainforests.*

their aerial roots will be strong and active and provide most of the nourishment needed.

Conditions are not always ideal in the tropics, however, and the plants can suffer from weather extremes greater than in a temperate garden. When a hurricane hits, the plants can be damaged and dislodged from their host and perhaps blown away and lost forever. If a tree falls, it becomes an urgent task to rescue all the orchids growing there.

ORCHIDS FOR TROPICAL
REGIONS ALL YEAR
ROUND

Cattleyas and allied genera
Phalaenopsis
Vandas and allied genera

LEFT *This stunning red* Masdevallia
infracta *is the only species of this genus
to be found in the Brazilian Atlantic
Forest, enjoying the high humidity and
shady conditions to be found there.*

ABOVE *The miniature species* Oncidium
longipes *grows and flowers easily
when established on trees in this
Brazilian garden. It is a charming species
which is frequently cultivated because it
is relatively easy to grow.*

RIGHT *Here we can see three different
types of tropical orchids growing together
on a tree stump in a Brazilian garden. A
native* Encyclia oncidioides *is in flower
with a* Bulbophyllum *above and a tall
terete* Vanda *on the left.*

CARING FOR ORCHIDS OUTDOORS

One of the key points to bear in mind if you are growing orchids outdoors is that the conditions outside can change much more than they would indoors, especially in western Europe.

Outdoor Care in Temperate Gardens

During periods of hot, dry weather, the plants will need regular overhead spraying. In the home, this would involve a light misting of the foliage, but outdoors it should become a drenching. Cymbidiums, for example, can be liberally hosed down with no ill effects. This saturation will also assist in keeping pests at bay, particularly red spider mite,

TIPS ON CARING FOR ORCHIDS OUTDOORS

Establish plants in trees in gardens or grow in pots on patios

Water and feed regularly

Protect from bright sun

Watch out for local pests

Orchids growing on trees should be kept well sprayed during the dry season

which is prevalent in most gardens during the summer. Hosing down will naturally wet every part of the plant, but in view of the faster rate of drying out, water inside the new growths will evaporate before it can cause any harm. In the same way, plants may receive hours of steady rain without coming to harm.

ABOVE Bulbophyllum frostii *is sometimes called the clog orchid because the flowers resemble the well-known footwear. The lower sepals are fused, forming a pouch-like slipper, while the petals and lip are almost hidden inside the flower.*

However, during spells of very wet weather and low temperatures, new growths may rot, and you will need to make some provision to protect the orchids from excessive amounts of rain. If you have only a few plants, it may be easier to move them to shelter. Alternatively, a polythene (plastic) "tent" can easily be erected over the plants. The only danger here is that when the sun comes out again after the rain, the plants inside the "tent" may experience a sudden rise in temperature if the polythene is not removed quickly.

Spraying the foliage is no substitute for watering the pots, and the aim should be to keep the orchids evenly moist at the roots to ensure a steady rate of growth. During the hottest months of the year, watering can be more beneficial if it is done towards evening, when the sun has left the plants and the temperature is cooling down. In this way, the compost (growing medium) will remain moist for longer and keep the roots cool. Check daily to see if watering is needed, and give plenty each time to ensure a thorough wetting.

LEFT
Laeliocattleya *Quo Vadis 'Floralia' is a lovely variety that shows all the best qualities of the modern* Cattleya *hybrid. The large, showy flowers will last for three weeks or more and are produced in the spring and autumn.*

Orchids that are suspended in the branches of shady trees will do well, provided they receive sufficient moisture. There is a danger of forgetting those that may be some way from the main growing area, or it may become an effort to remove the plants repeatedly for dunking. Ensure that all your orchids are in a convenient situation where their daily requirements do not become a chore or they are at risk of being left unattended.

In outdoor conditions, pseudobulbs will quickly shrivel if water is withheld for any length of time, and in this situation it may be some weeks before they plump up again. Shrivelling during the growing season will reduce the plant's capacity for developing good-size pseudobulbs, which in turn will affect its flowering ability.

Artificial feeding can be increased in relation to the extra light the orchids are receiving. The occasional foliar feed (spraying the foliage with liquid feed) will ensure that the leaves remain a good mid-green. This is especially useful for any orchids that turn slightly yellow after being placed outside. Otherwise, continue with the feeding regime, alternating between plain water and feed-water. Orchids with good aerial root systems, such as the vandas, can have their roots as well as their leaves regularly sprayed with feed-water.

Outdoor Care in Tropical Gardens

In tropical gardens where the orchids have become permanently attached to trees or other structures, the plants will look after themselves once they have become established. Some form of artificial feeding will be beneficial where this is practical; if not, the plants will grow naturally. Phalaenopsis, which in the Northern Hemisphere are grown

indoors all year, can do extremely well outdoors in tropical areas. The plants should always be established so that their fleshy leaves hang down, as those of the species do in their natural habitats. This ensures that water does not lodge in the centre of the plant but becomes self-draining. This is less easy to do with some of the modern hybrids, whose leaves have lost the elongated shape of the species and have become rounder and more rigidly upright. Look for plants of the right shape for this purpose.

In parts of the world where year-round sunshine is guaranteed, the vandaceous orchids come into their own. The brilliant colours of the

ABOVE Phalaenopsis *Yalta is a rare example of a peloric flower that has mutated to produce three petals, all of which are lips instead of the normal lateral petals. Such novelties in orchid flowers are not unattractive.*

modern hybrids are the envy of those of us residing in cooler climes. In the tropics, they grow with total ease, continuing to produce their superb blooms throughout the year. These lovely plants, with their tall, monopodial foliage and vigorous aerial roots, are grown in vast quantities in large ground beds made up with suitable compost. Today, these are grown for the cut-flower trade as well as the export market.

GROWING ORCHIDS UNDER GLASS

Many growers start with a few orchids indoors before graduating to a greenhouse and greatly widening the choice that can be grown. Greenhouse culture is more demanding than growing orchids indoors, but the rewards are many and a different approach to orchid growing is possible.

UNDER-GLASS CULTURE

In addition to having plants in pots, growing orchids under glass enables you to grow them mounted on bark or attached to tree branches. The latter can make attractive and unusual additions in the greenhouse, and can be set up at one end to create a pleasing, eye-catching and permanent display. Some orchids can be grown in open slatted baskets, and by using these different methods every available space can be utilized.

It is surprising how many orchids you can fit comfortably into a small greenhouse. However, if you are considering purchasing a new greenhouse for your orchids, it is always best to obtain one that is larger than you think you will need. Your collection will grow, as will the individual plants, all of them requiring more room as time goes by. Also, the smaller the greenhouse, the more difficult it becomes to control, and temperatures can fluctuate extremely quickly in a small space, thus threatening the well-being of your orchids.

Ideally, the greenhouse should be sited so that it runs from north to south. This means that the plants inside will receive the maximum amount of light, although much depends upon the space you have available for your greenhouse. In years gone by, the greenhouse was usually built at the bottom of the garden, often some way from the house. This means a long walk on cold winter nights to ensure that all is well with the heating and plants. The closer your greenhouse is situated to the house the better. You are likely to visit the greenhouse far more often if it means just stepping outside the back door, rather than having to negotiate a slippery path on a wet winter's night.

The greenhouse should not be placed too close to large trees. The trees will restrict the available light, and the glass roof will be covered by debris from the trees, which will encourage the growth of algae. An open site will also prevent insects from the trees being blown in through the

LEFT *This is an ideal greenhouse, built on a brick base with a bottom ventilating system and ridge ventilators. An extractor is situated at the end of the roof. The rolls of lath blinds are brought into use on hot, sunny days.*

LEFT *This large-scale, tropical indoor garden contains a a mixture of foliage plants and orchids in bloom. Grown together in this way, they provide their own environment.*

open ventilators, which is how many pests enter the greenhouse in summer.

There are many differing designs of greenhouses available from various manufacturers. When choosing the right type for orchids, look for one with the most ventilation. Ideally, there should be bottom or side ventilators as well as top ones, but this is not always possible. For orchids, the ideal greenhouse has a brick base. You may prefer to build this yourself, adding the sides and a glass roof with a timber or aluminium frame. The brick surround should be built to staging level, which will help to keep the greenhouse warmer in winter. If your greenhouse has glass right down to the ground, use bricks or polystyrene (plastic foam) panels to insulate the

lower half. Install slatted wooden stagings that have been treated to prevent rotting; they should be raised to a higher level at the back to help with watering and caring for your orchids.

To make the most use of the space available, two narrow paths running down each side, with a central staging below the apex of the roof, is most beneficial. This will enable you to make full use of the central ridge board in the roof of the greenhouse for hanging up plants in baskets. The floor of the greenhouse, apart from the paths, which can be concreted, can be left as bare earth. This will enable you to plant out a number of green plants, such as ferns, which require fairly wet, shady conditions, and greatly assist in maintaining

a good growing atmosphere. In a small greenhouse it is not a good idea, however, to grow climbing plants that will eventually occupy the roof area. Climbers, such as stephanotis or hoya, tend to drop blooms on to the orchids below, causing rots if they are not picked up quickly, as well as dripping their sugary nectar, which causes moulds, on to your orchids below. As the climbers grow, they will restrict more and more light from the orchids and will outpace every other plant in the greenhouse, in addition to harbouring pests such as scale insects.

Leave room for an inside water butt (deep sink) in which to dunk plants, and install a mains water tap and hose to make watering and damping down easier.

CREATING THE RIGHT CONDITIONS

Having set up your greenhouse with the correct equipment and prepared it for orchids, use the central staging for the largest plants that need the most headroom. Above these, along the ridge board and elsewhere, suspend orchids, such as vandas and stanhopeas, that like to grow in hanging baskets. These can be attached by the clips that are supplied with aluminium greenhouses, or you can hang them from hooks in timber rafters. Bear in mind that these plants will have to be taken down for watering to prevent too much surplus water from splashing on to the plants below.

The side benches can accommodate orchids in pots; place those that need the most light on the brightest side, with shade-loving plants being shielded by the others. Behind these, on either side of the greenhouse, attach wires or wooden trellis to the inside of the glass on which to hang orchids that grow on slabs of bark. The end of the greenhouse can be used to grow further orchids permanently on a small tree or branch.

Creating the right conditions for the orchids is a combination of providing humidity, warmth and fresh air. These three important factors must always balance each other, so that the atmosphere always feels right when you enter the greenhouse. Orchids like to be warm and comfortable, and only when there is an imbalance of these conditions, resulting in either a cold and damp atmosphere, or a hot and dry one, at the other extreme, will problems arise.

You will need to visit your greenhouse two or three times a day, if possible, to check that the temperature

and humidity are right. A visit first thing in the morning is a joy. This is the time when those fragrant orchids in bloom give off the strongest perfume; the scent of their flowers in the moist morning air

ABOVE *Galvanized mesh benching on a wooden frame is an ideal surface on which to grow your orchids.*

LEFT *A novel way of growing orchids in a greenhouse is to mount them on a branch to form a miniature tree. The tree will require constant spraying to prevent the plants drying out completely.*

RIGHT *These orchids show the variation to be found within the vast* Cattleya *alliance. They are all intermediate-growing plants which will produce flowers throughout the year. They are, from left to right,* Laeliocattleya Beaumesnil 'Parme', Potinara *Rebecca Merkel,* Epicattleya *Elphin Jade and* Laeliocattleya *Persepolis × Shellie Compton.*

is one of the delights of orchid growing. A midday visit will be needed to adjust ventilators or increase humidity in summer, and a final visit last thing at night is advisable to check that all is well.

HEATING

The heating system should be large enough to maintain the greenhouse at the required minimum temperature. It is better to have a larger heater working at half its maximum output than to have a smaller one working at full capacity, which is likely to burn out within a comparatively short time.

Types of Heater

Thermostatically-controlled electric fan heaters are clean and easy to use, providing warm, moving air in the greenhouse, which makes them ideal. Because they dry the air, you will need to stand a water-filled tray directly in front of the heater so that the air carries some moisture with it as it passes over the water. Ensure that there are no orchids standing directly in front of the air flow, because this will cause dehydration. In summer, the same heater can be used as a cooling fan to circulate cool air and reduce the temperature.

Other forms of heater, such as paraffin- and gas-burning heaters, which are available for greenhouses, are only suitable for orchids if used with care. They emit ethylene fumes which can cause bud-drop and other problems.

Insulating the Greenhouse

In winter, save as much heat as possible by insulating the inside of the greenhouse with double-glazing, using polythene (plastic) sheeting or panels on the sides and roof. This should be installed a few inches from the glass, in order to create a layer of still air in

LEFT *A three kilowatt fan heater with a built-in thermostat is a good way of heating a small greenhouse.*

between, and should form a complete seal. To put up the insulation, you will have to remove those plants growing on the sides of the greenhouse and replace them when the polythene is in position. Remove the polythene in the summer, and replace it each year. You will need to allow fresh air in, so cut the polythene to fit around the ventilators, in the same way as the door, and insulate the door panel separately. One disadvantage of this method of insulation is that the condensation that forms on the polythene will drip onto the orchids that are growing beneath.

Alternatively, where it proves difficult to insulate the inside of the greenhouse because of moving any orchids in the way, try using a heavy-duty polythene on the outside of your greenhouse, completely sealing it and fastening it down. Done with care, this should withstand even the strongest winds. One further advantage is that any condensation will simply run down the glass and not drip onto the orchids.

RIGHT *Soil-warming cables under the ground or in sand benches are ideal for propagating orchids or raising young plants.*

ABOVE *This piece of greenhouse equipment is a sophisticated thermostat, which draws in air through a built-in fan. It can be used to control temperature or ventilation, as required.*

Heating a Conservatory

To heat a conservatory or sun lounge, install an extra loop off the domestic heating system. A strategically placed radiator or two, with their own thermostat controlling a small pump, will provide heat whenever required. As the domestic system will already be producing heat from a central boiler, be it mains gas, electricity or oil, the added cost of heating the conservatory is not as great as having a separate heating system. Use two thermostats, one to control the night temperature – set just above the minimum required – and the other to control the day temperature, along with a time clock to differentiate between the two. It is essential to install a maximum/ minimum thermometer next to the thermostat as they are notoriously inaccurate. By double checking the thermostat with the thermometer, you will be able to provide a more accurately controlled temperature.

Checking the Temperature

Heating in winter is the most essential part of orchid growing. While the plants can survive being dry for short

ABOVE *Polythene (plastic) bubble insulation keeps down heating costs and prevents any violent fluctuations in the temperature.*

LEFT *A blue-flame paraffin heater can be used where no other source of heating can be installed. Ensure there is always a flow of air around the plants and that fumes can escape. Always fill a heater outside the greenhouse.*

periods, they will suffer if they get too cold. One bitterly cold night without heat can seriously harm the orchids. Monitor the heating continually, by making it part of a daily inspection. Check that the daily temperature is correct by consulting a maximum/ minimum thermometer, and keep a record so that you build up a pattern showing the average and also noting any severe drops. You can then adjust the thermostat accordingly.

VENTILATION

Fresh air is important at all times to prevent the air inside the greenhouse from becoming stagnant. Ventilation also controls the temperature and helps to prevent overheating.

In early spring, there will be days when the increasing power of the sun heats up the greenhouse with amazing speed, and it will be necessary to open the ventilators to prevent a sudden rise in temperature (although, even with ventilators, this will be difficult to reduce until the sun goes off the greenhouse). Early in the year, this may mean that several daily visits are needed to check the temperature and adjust the ventilation accordingly.

As spring advances into summer, ventilation control becomes easier, and once the summer shading is in position, this will prevent sudden rises in temperature. Also, you can be more sure that the temperature will not drop drastically, and the ventilators can be left open all day, gradually extending the period until, by midsummer, it becomes safe to leave them open permanently both day and night. This is a lovely time for the orchids, which benefit from the cool, fresh air at night, and in the morning the greenhouse is slower to heat up to the maximum day temperature. During this time, if additional ventilation is needed, you can safely open the door to create an even greater flow of air. However, if you do this, you may want to install a gauze-lined inner door to prevent cats from wandering into the greenhouse. It is also a good idea to install an alarm system for when the door is open and the greenhouse left unlocked.

Once the nights begin to get colder, you will need to close the ventilators earlier in the evenings to conserve as much natural warmth as possible until the heater is in operation. On cold, wet evenings, this becomes more urgent to prevent a drop in temperature that would leave the orchids cold all night. Likewise, in the mornings, it may not be possible to open the ventilators until the greenhouse has warmed up

BELOW *Opening the windows at the right time is not always possible, but automatic window-openers will do the job for you.*

LEFT *Extractor fans are excellent for reducing the temperature quickly in an over-heated greenhouse, and will assist with the ventilation.*

LEFT *In a small greenhouse, extra air movement can be created by opening the door. Be sure to cover the opening with gauze netting to stop insects or pets from entering.*

sufficiently. The aim should be to maintain a steady temperature that rises and falls according to the time of day or night, without causing sudden changes from one extreme to another.

During the winter months, on sunny days or even dull days when there is little wind, it is possible to open the ventilators for short periods to freshen up the air inside the greenhouse and to help to reduce any condensation. Opening the ventilators just a crack is often sufficient to achieve this, and is an important part of winter care. When insufficient ventilation is given, the air can become stagnant, encouraging the growth of moulds and rots. This can be prevented by opening one ventilator for a short period during the middle of the day.

Some greenhouses are equipped with a ventilator on both sides of the roof. This creates more opportunities for opening the ventilators, and on windy days you can open the ventilator on the leeward side to the wind. Bottom ventilators, sited on both sides of the greenhouse, just above ground level, are ideal for creating a natural current of air from the bottom to the top. This current of air creates a natural cooling breeze through the orchids.

This is important for odontoglossums, although not really necessary in a tropical house with phalaenopsis.

Ventilators can be installed to work automatically, opening and closing with the rise and fall of the temperature at a predetermined setting. Alternatively, some growers prefer to use an extractor fan. The type that is installed for domestic use in a bathroom or kitchen is adequate. The fan will pull the hot air out of the greenhouse but it will also reduce the humidity and moisture, so it becomes necessary to install a misting system fitted below bench level to keep the floor permanently moist. Fresh air entering the bottom ventilators will collect moisture, which is carried through the orchids before being expelled at ridge level by the extractor fan.

RIGHT *A circulating fan in a small greenhouse will keep the air moving and fresh when ventilation is not possible.*

An alternative is to install a small electric circulating fan. This is different from the extractor fan, and only moves air around the greenhouse, freshening it up and keeping it buoyant, to prevent spotting on flowers, which can occur when the air is still and the humidity builds up. These fans can be a nuisance when you enter the greenhouse because you feel as if you are standing in a draught (draft). A pull switch by the door solves this problem, allowing you to turn the fan on and off when entering and leaving the greenhouse.

SHADING

The greenhouse will need to be shaded for about half the year. Shading is important to prevent the orchids from being burnt by the sun; it also assists in keeping the temperature down. It will become necessary to shade the greenhouse as soon as the sun begins to gain power, in early spring. If you cannot get any form of shading into position soon enough, it can be a good idea to provide your orchids with temporary protection by placing single sheets of newspaper over their leaves by day. This will ensure that they do not suffer until you can get the summer shading into position. However, it will not help to reduce the temperature, and the covering up of the leaves should only be used as a temporary measure.

There are several types of shading available, but the most popular today is greenhouse netting, which can be purchased on the roll and is placed on the outside of the glass. For a small greenhouse, you can make up panels of netting that can be placed in position on hooks screwed into the glazing bars. In this way, the shading is easily and quickly put up and taken down again. This means that on dull, cloudy

days the panels can be removed altogether, and replaced when the sun comes out. This type of shading should be placed about 15cm (6in) from the glass in order to allow a flow of cooler air in between. The panels will shade the glass and cool it down before the sun heats it up. For orchids, it may be necessary to use a double layer of the netting to provide sufficient shade.

Another very simple form of shading is to use paint shading on the outside of the glass. This can be made up to manufacturers' instructions and painted on in the spring. As the year progresses, the shading weathers,

ABOVE *Shade the greenhouse during the summer to prevent scorching and to control the temperature. Fix net shading to the inside of the glass using plastic plugs if the greenhouse is made from aluminium.*

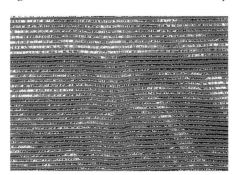

ABOVE *Aluminium greenhouse shading, which is easily fixed to the outside of the roof, will shade the orchids on the inside and reflect the heat.*

ABOVE *Be sure to cover the ventilator opening, while allowing the vent to be fully operational. Otherwise bees, which will pollinate the orchid flowers, will gain entrance.*

ABOVE It is important to protect orchids from the scorching effects of the sun. This gauze netting will also help to keep down the temperature inside the greenhouse.

ABOVE Paint shading helps to cool the greenhouse in summer. Applied at the correct dilution, it will be slowly washed off by rain and may need replacing before the autumn.

becoming slowly washed off by the rain, until by the autumn it gradually allows more light to filter through to the orchids. By the time the orchids are ready for full light once again, whatever paint shading remains can be cleaned off. It is often a good idea to use paint shading and netting in conjunction with each other. This has the advantage in that you can remove the netting at the end of the summer, leaving the reduced paint shading in position for a bit longer, which gives the orchids time to adjust to the extra light in two stages.

The ultimate luxury in shading is blinds that automatically roll up and down in response to a light-sensitive cell. They will not be in use on dull, cloudy summer days, but as soon as the sun appears, they will roll down over the greenhouse. Alternatively, you can have louvre-blinds that adjust according to the amount of light. This equipment is expensive to install and it must be maintained in perfect working order.

It is possible to have a fully automated greenhouse, where heating, spraying and ventilation are carried out automatically. Modern labour-saving devices make the pleasures of orchid growing much easier than they used to be, when hand-stoked boilers had to be made up late at night and roller blinds were constantly needing manual adjustment, according to the immediate weather conditions. These automated

greenhouses take all the strain out of orchid growing, but they are still only as good as the person in charge.

Labour-saving devices should be an asset, not a liability, so use them to the best advantage, always making sure that spare parts are readily available, especially with fan heaters. Do not wait until anything breaks down before finding a replacement. Two fans used alternately can be a good idea.

LEFT Early spring sunshine can catch growers unawares. A quick way to protect the orchids from sunburn is to lay newspaper sheets lightly over the foliage for a few hours until long-term shading can be put into place.

DAMPING DOWN

Damping down is a daily routine carried out throughout the year. It is best done by using a garden hose connected to the mains water supply. With a spray nozzle attached, soak the floor area beneath the staging, wetting the plants that grow there, and wet the staging between the orchids. The overhead spraying of leaves is part of damping down in the summer and whenever conditions permit.

In the spring and summer, damp down the greenhouse in the morning as soon as the temperature starts to rise, and lightly spray over the foliage. This raises the humidity immediately, and you will smell the moist atmosphere that is indispensable to good orchid culture. On sunny days this humidity will have evaporated by midday, when another damping becomes necessary. At the height of summer, you can repeat this again towards late afternoon. As evening falls, all surplus water will have dried up, but as the temperature drops, the humidity will rise naturally and remain at a good level for most of the night. During the summer, this will be good for your orchids, but as winter approaches, together with lower temperatures, you will not want to add further humidity by damping down after midday. In winter, it is

ABOVE RIGHT Humidity is important for the welfare of the orchids. In a greenhouse, regular, daily damping down of the floor area can be done with a rosed water lance from the mains water supply.

RIGHT Under-bench misting with sprinkler rails soaks the floor. The water will evaporate and produce humidity.

LEFT Orchids growing on bark will require constant spraying with water over the leaves. Once a week, add a feed to the hand-held spray bottle, according to the manufacturer's instructions.

necessary to damp down the floor and between the orchids only once a day, in the morning. Overhead spraying of the leaves should be discontinued at this time of year, because the leaves will take too long to dry up, and this may result in rots and blemishes. Also, as many of the orchids will be resting at this time, their foliage should be left dry.

During spells of wet winter weather, damping down can be dispensed with altogether: there will be sufficient moisture to balance the low temperature and light levels, as well as spilled water from the watering of those orchids that need it.

For the busy person who is away all day, it can be a great advantage to install an automatic damping system.

This consists of one spray rail underneath the stagings and one above, both of which can be used independently so that you can wet either underneath the plants or the foliage as necessary. The spray rails can be thermostatically controlled to cut in every few hours in the summer, thus preventing the complete drying out of the greenhouse while you are away.

In the same way, the ventilators can be controlled to open automatically as the temperature rises. These adaptations can be a real bonus if you cannot be there to look after the greenhouse at all times, and they also mean that you can go on holiday, knowing that your orchids will not be neglected.

ABOVE *The fine nozzles on the spray lines emit a fog, producing humidity for the plants. These spray lines are mostly suitable for larger greenhouses.*

ABOVE *Humidifiers will produce microscopic droplets of cool moisture. The fog created provides an ideal level of humidity for a small greenhouse.*

CARE AND CULTIVATION

Anyone can grow orchids, all you need is an affinity with plants. You do not necessarily require a garden or a greenhouse. There are orchids which you can grow quite easily in the home, provided a few of the conditions required by orchids are understood and carefully followed. If you live in a tropical region, you can obviously grow the vast number of tropical orchids outdoors, but if you live in a temperate part of the world, you can grow a limited number of hardy orchids in the garden or in patio planters. These are, in fact, becoming more popular as specific nurseries are offering them for sale. If you are fortunate enough to own a greenhouse, or have plans to acquire one, then the whole unrestricted world of orchids opens up, giving you limitless opportunities to grow, and become acquainted with, the numerous orchids which are available. This section describes in detail how to grow various orchids in whatever situation is available to you.

An automatic overhead spraying system

TOOLS AND EQUIPMENT

The tools and equipment that you will need in order to care for your orchids depends on the scale on which you plan to grow them. If you only want to grow a few orchids in pots indoors, then you will need very few tools. However, if you wish to develop a large orchid collection in a greenhouse, then you will need much more specialist equipment.

plant labels

watering can

LEFT *Depending on the type of orchid, orchids can be grown in a variety of ways, including in pots of varying sizes and in open slatted baskets, as well as on bark, pieces of tree fern and on special orchid rafts.*

BASIC TOOLS

Few tools are required in the management of orchids, and very little equipment is essential. When starting out with a small collection, it is not necessary to install expensive pieces of equipment, but, as time goes by and your interest in orchids develops, you will find out which accessories can be added to improve the growing conditions.

A pruning knife that is always ready to hand will probably be the most useful tool in your orchid tool kit. Keep the blade sharp and regularly sterilized every time it is used to cut into any part of the plant. At repotting time it will be useful for cutting away dead parts or for dividing up individual orchids. Some growers prefer to use scissors or secateurs (pruners) for this; it depends on which you are most comfortable with. Keep a jar of denatured alcohol handy into which your tools can be dipped. This will prevent the spread of viruses or other diseases which may be present in one plant.

The basic equipment that you will need before you start growing orchids in a greenhouse are a heater and a maximum/minimum thermometer. It will be important to keep an eye on the temperature both day and night. Other accessories, such as the ones illustrated here, can be added if required. If you are starting your orchids indoors, you will only require the maximum/minimum thermometer. But here you will also need a humidity tray and pebbles as a basic kit to ensure that some humidity is created around your plants.

scissors

multipull-headed misting nozzle

thermometer

pruning knife

hand-held spray

secateurs (pruners)

ABOVE *A large pump spray such as this will hold much more water than a hand-held one. It is ideal for damping down a small greenhouse.*

saw

GROWING MEDIUMS

Many orchids can be grown on bark as well as in a variety of compost mixes (growing mediums), but whatever compost is used, the main criteria are good aeration and swift drainage. Most orchids cope with their roots being cramped in a container, provided that the compost is open and allows some air to circulate through and around the roots.

COMPOSTS

The tropical epiphytes have evolved by growing upon the branches and trunks of trees, where their roots either hang, suspended in air, or travel along the bark, seeking out crevices and gaining access to the humus or decaying leaves in the axils of branches. In this way there is always plenty of air around the roots, hence the importance of a light, well-drained compost (growing medium).

Terrestrial orchids vary in their soil requirements. Some prefer grassy meadows with a well-drained subsoil, others like peaty bogs that are permanently wet, while in the tropics many live on the open savanna plains where, during the dry season, they become completely dehydrated because of the shortage of moisture in the soil. Their rhizomes may be either just below the surface or very deep, depending on the species. Their root system may only penetrate the mossy soil covering or push deep into the subsoil in the search for permanent moisture.

Early Organic Composts

After some disastrous experiments and false starts in the very early days of orchid culture, one of the first composts (growing mediums) used was composed of hard, firm chunks of sedge peat mixed with a heavy loam or leaf mould. The mix was too dense and, since the roots could not penetrate very far through it, good root systems were not always developed.

It was not until the early part of the 20th century that a better compost (growing medium) was found, and this consisted of *Osmunda* fibre and sphagnum moss. The roots of the royal fern (*Osmunda regalis*), were used at that time as ballast in ships returning to Europe and Britain from the United States. It had no other use until orchid growers discovered it. Once it became popular, it was imported in huge quantities to satisfy the demand, along with other species of *Osmunda* from around Europe and Japan. It arrived in large chunks, which had to be cleaned, stripped out into single fibres and chopped. The prepared fibre was then mixed with fresh, living sphagnum moss, locally gathered from bog areas. It took great skill to work with the compost to ensure that the springy material and the orchid were sufficiently firm in the pot, but not so firm that water could not penetrate easily. In those days, the manner in which a plant was potted had a great bearing on how well it grew. Although expensive and time-consuming to prepare, this formed an ideal compost for over 50 years. One of the reasons that orchids rooted so

LEFT *A range of suitable plastic and clay pots and composts. The composts include (anti-clockwise from bottom left): Rockwool, hortag, fine bark, sphagnum peat and coarse bark.*

ABOVE *Polystyrene (plastic foam) chips are an ideal material to use for drainage.*

well in it was thought to be the living moss, which formed a green growing mat on the surface. However, once the feeding of orchids became fashionable, this killed the moss, causing the compost to deteriorate and decompose to a soggy state. The search was on for something better.

Bark Compost

All the necessary requirements for a new compost (growing medium) were found in the bark of the American redwood cedar, although in Britain, where plantations of Corsican and Scots pine were being felled, the bark from these trees proved a good substitute. The bark compost was much cheaper to produce and easier to handle than the old moss and fibre mixture, and today it is sold all over the world specifically for orchids. It is produced from locally felled trees and supplied through specialist nurseries and larger garden centres. It comes in graded pieces, suitable for seedlings or mature plants. It should not be confused with the bark sold by garden centres for mulching flowerbeds.

Orchid bark is slow to decompose and will not break down when fertilizer is added. It will remain in a good state for several years, slowly releasing its nutrients. It retains just the right amount of moisture for the roots, but without remaining too wet after watering. It can be used on its own or other materials can be mixed with it as required.

If you find that your orchids are suffering from dryness, and you have difficulty in keeping the bark compost (growing medium) sufficiently moist, add about a third of sphagnum moss or other fibrous peat to the mix. A peat substitute will do as well, although it may need sieving to remove the finer particles. This will provide a slightly wetter mix, which can be an advantage if you cannot attend to your orchids as often as you would like. To this basic mix you can add a small percentage of charcoal, which will ensure that the compost stays "sweet" and does not become soured. Use only granulated horticultural charcoal as supplied by specialist nurseries or garden centres. This is not the same as barbecue charcoal, which has been treated to burn slowly and is unsuitable for orchids.

LEFT *Sphagnum moss can be purchased as compressed slabs. When these are wetted, they will swell to their original size and can be used in orchid compost or for lining orchid baskets.*

Coarsely shredded bark

Bark and coconut fibre

A coarse compost mix containing bark and fibrous peat

Inorganic Composts

In addition to the organic composts (growing mediums), there are a number of man-made materials that provide synthetic alternatives. These are cheap and easy to use, and have the advantage in that they will not decompose and therefore cause the roots to rot.

These materials include Rockwool, which is produced for the horticultural industry from spun volcanic pumice. Rockwool looks like discoloured cotton wool, and the surface is sometimes stained green with an algae that grows in response to the nutrients. It provides a hydroponic base for vegetable crops such as aubergines (egg plants), cucumbers and tomatoes, as well as cut-flower carnations. Rockwool is long lasting and enables plants to be grown under a complete and accurate feeding programme. It is available in two forms: absorbent and non-absorbent. The first retains much more water around the roots, which suits some orchids, while a drier

compost is provided by the non-absorbent type. Many growers like to mix the two together to provide an ideal medium that holds sufficient water over an extended period, but has the capacity to support pockets of air. Rockwool is poured lightly into the pot and needs no firming down. When using Rockwool, use gloves and a mask because the glass fibres can irritate the skin.

Another widely used material, which performs in much the same way as Rockwool, is horticultural foam. This can be used with either Rockwool or organic bark and peat mixes.

Perlag and perlite are both porous horticultural products made from ground volcanic rock. They can be used on their own for certain orchids, such as cattleyas, or used as an aggregate to open up either Rockwool or bark and peat mixes. In Hawaii, volcanic pumice is available locally and widely used for orchids in that part of the world.

The advantages of these inorganic materials are that they are very light, easy to use, and, when the plants are repotted, the old mix can be left, causing less root disturbance. However, it becomes necessary to supply the orchids with sufficient nutrients by artificial feeding, since there is no food value in the man-made materials.

You can easily transfer an orchid growing in an organic compost (growing medium) to an inorganic mix, or vice versa, but do not be tempted to mix the two compounds in one pot because they both require different watering techniques.

Some orchid growers like to mix up their own special brand of orchid compost (growing medium) from locally available materials. These materials may include dried oak leaves and beech masts, mixed with live sphagnum moss. While these may be successful when made up by an experienced grower, beginners should seek advice from their local orchid nursery.

INORGANIC GROWING MEDIUMS

Rockwool is a potting medium favoured by some experienced growers

This fine but open mix, made from bark, perlite and peat, is ideal for terrestrials

Horticultural foam holds moisture and is used in compost instead of peat

Perlite is a fine, granular material, which is ideal for keeping compost open. Add to horticultural foam, peat or peat substitute

Perlag is larger and coarser than perlite, and can be used for drainage in the base of pots

Hortag consists of pellets of baked clay that can be used for drainage or as a bench covering to hold moisture

REPLACING COMPOST

In time, bark- and peat-based composts (growing mediums) will break down, which is why regular repotting is important. A plant that suddenly loses much of its foliage, or shrivels, may have lost its roots, and this will become apparent when you knock the plant out of its pot and examine its condition.

Compost (growing medium) that is in good condition should have a pleasant, moist smell. If it smells sour, it has probably broken down to the extent that the plant can no longer gain any benefit from it. Compost that has deteriorated will have dissolved into small particles; these will wash through to the bottom of the pot, clog up the drainage and cause water to stagnate, thus speeding up the whole process of decomposition.

Insect pests, such as woodlice, will also break down compost (growing medium) and can cause rapid deterioration. Once the compost has broken down in this way, the roots cannot thrive and will quickly die. Speedy repotting is essential. First cut away all the dead roots and remove all the old compost, then replace it with fresh material throughout.

Roots that can be seen to circle the rim of the pot without penetrating to the bottom indicate that the compost (growing medium) is unsuitable. The cause may be that the compost is too dense for the roots to penetrate, and once again repotting may be needed. Phalaenopsis are particularly reluctant to immerse their roots in a compost that they do not like, and will prefer to extend their roots over the rim of the pot into the air, where they will adhere to any surface with which they come into contact. These orchids particularly like a loose, open compost where their roots can breathe.

Most composts (growing mediums) are supplied in a dried state to lessen their weight, but they need to be moistened before they are used. Remove just enough compost from the bag to serve your purposes, and water well, leaving it overnight to drain. The next day it will feel just right to work with. Do not return any unused damp compost to the bag, but leave it to dry out first. If it is returned to the bag while it is still wet, it will produce a mould, which will spread to the rest of the contents of the bag. Always store orchid compost dry, but use it moist.

BELOW This Cymbidium *Mini Ice 'Antarctic' looks striking in a square galvanized container. Where space is limited, this smaller-growing hybrid is ideal and will provide plenty of flowers during the early spring months. Keep the plant watered all year, and apply feed during most of the year.*

POTTING AND MOUNTING ORCHIDS

Orchids can be grown in a number of different ways, depending on how they grow in the wild. They are suitable for potting into a variety of containers, as well as for growing in orchid baskets and mounting on bark.

ORCHIDS IN CONTAINERS

Orchids will grow in almost any type of container, but for practical purposes they are usually cultivated in plastic pots, which are light and easy to use. They also stay clean in a humid environment and can be washed and reused. Terracotta pots are also suitable – and were once considered preferable to plastic pots because they kept the roots cooler in high temperatures – but they are costly and the larger sizes can be considerably heavy. Also, being porous, they dry out much more quickly, and it is easier to maintain a constantly moist compost (growing medium) with plastic pots.

Orchids need to be grown in as small a pot as possible. They can easily be overpotted, and, where there is a great mass of compost (growing medium) around the roots, there is a danger that they will not be able to extract the water around them fast enough, which means that they will rot. Overpotting leads directly to overwatering, with disastrous results. On average, orchids need repotting about once every two years. Older established plants may be left for longer, especially when they do not outgrow their pots, while young plants need to be moved on every six months or so in order to maintain a steady rate of growth.

Repotting Orchids

Once a plant has filled its pot, and there is no more room for the formation of new pseudobulbs, it is time to repot it into a larger container. Some orchids, particularly cymbidiums, which have an extremely thick and vigorous rooting system, will often push themselves up by their roots before filling the surface area with pseudobulbs. These need to be repotted as soon as possible because it is extremely difficult to water them when they are above the rim of the pot. Orchids will also need repotting when the compost (growing medium) has deteriorated to such a degree that you can easily push your finger through it.

LEFT *Orchids can be displayed in a variety of different containers. This collection includes, from left to right:* Ludisia discolor *in the pale green pot,* Miltonidium Pupukea Sunset *in the small, square pot, and* Miltonia confusa *in the large, square pot.*

Dropping On an Orchid

As soon as an orchid has filled its pot, and there is no room for the development of new pseudobulbs, repot it into a larger pot.

❶ This cymbidium has outgrown its pot and has started to push itself free with its roots.

❷ Slide the orchid from the pot and check over the root system. The roots here are healthy and do not need trimming.

❸ Select a pot the next size up from the original one, and line the base with polystyrene (plastic foam) chips.

❹ Place the plant in the pot so that the oldest part is in contact with one side. This leaves plenty of room for the new growth to take place on the opposite side of the plant. Leave a gap of 2.5cm (1in) at the top of the pot for watering.

❺ Feed in a fresh compost (growing medium) of the appropriate grade, and firm it down with your fingers. (If the orchid is fine-rooted, you may need to use a thin cane for this.)

❻ Flood the pot with water in order to settle the plant. Make sure that the water drains away rapidly, so that the roots are not standing in water.

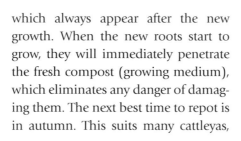

The best time for repotting is in the spring, but not if a plant is in flower. Most orchids commence their new growth at this time, and the ideal moment to repot is when the new growth is a few inches high. This is just before the formation of the new roots, which always appear after the new growth. When the new roots start to grow, they will immediately penetrate the fresh compost (growing medium), which eliminates any danger of damaging them. The next best time to repot is in autumn. This suits many cattleyas, which can often produce new roots at this time, as well as young seedlings, which need to be kept growing forward throughout the winter. Plants in the *Odontoglossum* alliance, and any others that continue to grow throughout the winter, can also be repotted now. Do not repot orchids, such as coelogynes or encyclias, that are about to commence their winter's rest.

To repot your orchids, you will need a potting bench or worktop with sufficient room on which to operate. Have ready a supply of previously dampened compost (growing medium), variously sized pots and some crocking material for the base of each pot. This may be broken polystyrene (plastic foam) chips or chips of the type used as packing material. You will also need a pair of secateurs or scissors and a sharp pruning knife, as well as a sterilizing agent and a few sheets of newspaper.

There are two basic methods of potting. The first, "dropping on", is done when young plants do not need any root pruning and when the compost (growing medium) is in good condition, and can be left intact. Because this causes no disturbance, dropping on can be done at almost any time of the year, but avoid the hottest and coldest months when the plants may be stressed or growing slowly.

The second method of potting is to completely repot the orchid, stripping out the old compost, discarding any dead roots and removing surplus leafless or dead pseudobulbs. This method can be used for splitting up large plants and reducing their size where necessary, so that they can often be returned to the same size pot.

Dropping On

To drop on a plant, remove its pot by up-turning and tapping the pot on the edge of the bench. It should slide out easily, and you should see a ball of white roots holding the compost in place. Select a new pot that is about 5cm (2in) larger to give sufficient room for another one to two years' growth. If it is a young, immature plant that will need dropping on again in a few months' time, you need only use a pot about 2.5cm (1in) larger. Place a layer of the crocking material at the base of the pot, and a small amount of compost (growing medium) on top. Stand the plant on this, ensuring that the base of the new

growth is level with the rim of the pot. If it stands higher, remove a little of the old compost from around the base until you can sit the plant deeper in the pot. Position it so that the older pseudobulbs are against one side of the pot, allowing space for the plant to grow towards the other edge. If you are potting a phalaenopsis or similar monopodial type, place the plant at the centre of the pot, bearing in mind that it will grow upwards rather than outwards.

Hold the plant, and pour in the compost (growing medium) all round, firming it down until the pot is full. Use the same compost that the plant has been growing in, and do not attempt to mix bark or peat with Rockwool or a similar synthetic material because both types require slightly different watering treatments. If you are using Rockwool, pour this into the cavity in the same way, but do not firm down as you would with bark or peat. Keep the Rockwool loose and open, making sure that the plant remains steady and firm.

Repotting and Dividing

Older plants that have, over the years, produced a large number of pseudobulbs, will have several that are leafless. These may not be dead, and if they are still plump and green they will have some life left in them. At present they are supporting the newer, leafed pseudobulbs, passing on their stored food supply to the younger part of the plant. However, if there are more pseudobulbs out of leaf than in leaf, they will become a drain on the main plant and need to be removed. Where there is more than one new growth, it may be possible to separate the plant into two or more divisions, provided each has at least one new growth. To maintain flowering, a division should have at

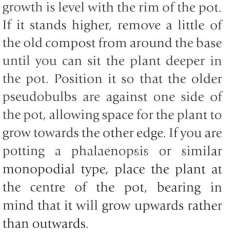

LEFT Gongora maculata *can be grown in a pot or hanging basket in a fine bark compost (growing medium). It will need to be watered and fed during the summer.*

Repotting and Dividing

This method involves completely repotting the orchid, stripping out the old compost (growing medium), discarding any dead roots and removing surplus leafless or dead pseudobulbs. It can be used for splitting up large plants, so that they can often be returned to the same size of pot. You can separate the plant into two or more divisions, provided each has at least one new growth. Separate the orchid into as many divisions as you wish, but bear in mind that to maintain flowering, a division will need to have at least three pseudobulbs in leaf with one new growth.

❶ This *Cymbidium* has been in its pot for some years. It has lifted itself up by its roots and is ready for dividing. Have ready fresh compost and crocking material for drainage.

❷ Remove the plant from its pot and, using a sharp pruning knife, cut between the adjoining rhizomes and through the rootball.

❸ The two halves, consisting of an equal number of pseudobulbs and new growths, are ready for preparation.

❹ Prune off all the dead roots and remove the old compost (growing medium), retaining a reasonably sized rootball.

❺ Choose a suitably sized pot and place a layer of crocking material in the bottom. This is usually polystyrene (plastic foam) chips.

least three pseudobulbs in leaf with one new growth. With this in mind, you can separate your plant into as many divisions as it is safe to do so. Any leftover pieces of less than three good pseudobulbs will not flower for another two to three years.

Because such plants may have been in their present pot for more than two years, they will be extremely pot-bound and difficult to remove. You can try tapping out, and running the pruning knife around the inside rim to loosen the roots, but if it is still firmly attached you may have to cut away the pot. This is often necessary with cattleyas,

❻ Place the plant in the pot so that the base of the pseudobulb is below the rim. Hold it firmly in the desired position with one hand and pour in the compost with the other hand.

❼ After potting, label each piece with the date of potting and the name of the plant. The divisions will not need to be disturbed again for two or three years. Water after a few days.

LEFT Cymbidium *Embers 'Yowie Bay', a miniature orchid, can be grown indoors in good light or placed out of doors for the summer growing season.*

BELOW
Phalaenopsis *Mad Milva will flower for several weeks. It should be grown in a warm situation, but not in direct sun.*

whose roots will adhere to the inside of the pot. Before you start, lie some newspaper on the bench and keep the plant on this. All the old material that you remove can then be easily discarded, and the old and new compost (growing mediums) will not get mixed.

Having removed the plant from its pot, examine the roots, which should be white and fleshy. Any blackened roots are dead and need to be cut away. This can be difficult where there is a solid ball of roots, and in this case it is better to cut down through the entire rootball at a point where you want to divide your plant. Sever between the pseudobulbs, and the plant will then pull apart. At the centre of the rootball will be the oldest decomposed compost (growing medium) and dead roots. Tease out all the old compost and roots, and cut the dead ones back to the base. Dead roots will be hollow, and the outer covering may peel away, leaving just the inner, wiry core. Some of the live roots can be considerably long, and these need to be trimmed back to a length of about 15cm (6in). Leave just the right number of pseudobulbs on each piece, making sure that there are more in leaf than out of leaf. Usually, you need to leave only one or two dormant back bulbs for support. Remove the remainder by cutting through the rhizome – taking care not to slice through the base of the pseudobulbs – and place these on one side. If you wish to add to your stock of plants by propagating, these back bulbs can be potted up on their own. They will often produce a new growth, which can be grown on to flower within a few years.

Where before you had one untidy-looking plant, you will now have two or more smaller, neater plants. Repot these in pots of a similar size to the one the old orchid came from; this should leave sufficient room in each pot for the plant to grow on for another two years. Place the plant to one side of the pot, with the oldest pseudobulbs at the back and the new growths facing forward. Crock the base of the new pot and place sufficient compost (growing medium) on top so that when you insert the plant, the base of the new growth will be level with, or just below, the rim of the pot. Fill in with compost – tucking some under and around the roots to ensure that there are no open spaces – until the plant is firmly in position and the compost finishes below the pot rim. This will ensure that when you water the plant the compost will not be washed over the rim.

Not all large plants need to be divided into smaller pieces, unless you want to increase your stock. Smaller-growing species that will not become unmanageable can be left as one specimen plant, provided that most or all of the pseudobulbs are leafed. Where there is a cluster of leafless pseudobulbs at the centre of a plant, these need to be removed or reduced in number before they weaken the plant. The exception here is with the deciduous lycastes and angulocastes, where only the leading pseudobulbs are in leaf at any one time.

When you have divided your plant, remember to write out new labels for each piece of the plant. Return the plants to their growing area and give them a light overhead spray to prevent any dehydration through their leaves after the root pruning. Water the plants after a few days, having allowed time for damaged roots and cut ends to heal partially before being wetted. Careful watering will be required for a while until you can be sure that new roots have started to grow from the new growth. When this happens, normal watering and feeding can resume. After repotting, expect your plants to shrivel slightly or shed some foliage until the new roots grow. This is the reason

ABOVE Dendrochilum glumaceum *will give up to three weeks of strong fragrance while it is in bloom during the early spring.*

why it is best to repot in the spring, just prior to the formation of the new roots. Repotting a plant at the wrong time can cause stress until the new roots take over from those severed during repotting.

After about six weeks, tap out one plant, and check the new roots. You will be surprised at the progress of new white roots extending through the compost (growing medium). If this is not the case, and the plant continues to shrivel, it may be late in growing and will benefit from being placed in a propagator, where a little extra warmth will start it growing.

ABOVE Miltonia confusa *is a fragrant species from Costa Rica which produces its flamboyant, red-and-green flowers mainly during winter and spring.*

ORCHIDS IN HANGING BASKETS

An alternative method to growing your orchids in plastic pots is to use hanging baskets. This is ideal for those orchids that prefer more light, or that have drooping flower spikes. The stanhopeas produce their flower spikes from the base of the plant, and these burrow through the compost (growing medium) to produce their flowers underneath, or at the side of, the basket. If these are placed in conventional pots, they will not be seen to flower.

There are a number of suitable containers for suspending stanhopeas and others, from slatted wooden baskets, which can easily be made of 1cm (½in) timber, to aquatic plant baskets, available in green or black plastic, which provide plenty of spaces for orchid roots and flower spikes to protrude. Smaller plants grown in baskets can be left for several years until they completely obscure the container. From time to time they need a little extra compost (growing medium) pushed around them where this has washed out.

ABOVE **Cymbidium** *Sarah Jean 'Icicle' is a pretty hybrid which will enhance any situation. Keep the plant well watered throughout the year, but avoid getting too wet in winter. Place in a cool room away from any source of heat or draughts.*

ORCHIDS FOR HANGING BASKETS

Acineta superba
Bulbophyllums (all)
Cirrhopetalums (all)
Coelogyne cristata
Cymbidiums (some)
Dendrochilum cobbianum
Encyclia radiata
Gongora maculata
Miltonia flavescens
Stanhopeas (all)

Making and Planting an Orchid Hanging Basket

Slatted wooden baskets can be made easily from 1cm (½in) timber. Hardwoods, such as oak or teak, will last a long time without rotting. You may prefer to use softwoods which are cheaper. The slats provide space for the roots and flower spikes to protrude. The potting method is the same as for any other container, but if the basket is shallow you will need to remove part of the rootball so that it fits the space. Smaller orchids will eventually obsure the hanging basket completely if left undisturbed for several years.

❶ An orchid basket can be made out of hard or soft timber. When the orchid has outgrown the basket, in about three or four years' time, it can be thrown away and a new one made.

❷ You will need 18 lengths of timber to make the basket. Decide on the width and depth of the basket, and then cut the timber to length. Nail the lengths of timber together in alternate layers.

❸ To plant up the orchid, you will need a lining material such as sphagnum moss, bark compost (growing medium), a pair of secateurs (pruners) and plant labels.

❹ This *Stanhopea* has been in its basket for many years and is ready for dividing. The old basket easily falls away so that the plant can be cut up using the secateurs.

❺ Take each new division and trim back some of the dead roots. Remove any unwanted backbulbs.

❻ Line the basket with the moss, coconut fibre or some similar material.

❼ Hold the *Stanhopea* in the basket and fill in with compost. The plant will stay in this basket for three or four years.

❽ Within a year the *Stanhopea* will be flowering. The long spikes penetrate through the compost to form a chandelier of blooms.

ORCHIDS ON BARK

A number of the smaller-growing epiphytic species make ideal subjects for growing on bark. This is an acceptable and delightful way of growing many orchids. The advantages are that you can save valuable staging space in a greenhouse, using the side walls to good advantage.

Ideal plants for bark culture are those in which the pseudobulbs are grown on an upward-growing rhizome, such as

Oncidium flexuosum, Maxillaria tenuifolia and a number of bulbophyllums.

Your plant may already be growing more out of its pot than in, and there may be a number of aerial roots that have not entered the compost (growing medium). Remove the plant from its pot and take away all the old compost and any surplus backbulbs. The plant is now ready to be mounted onto the bark.

Have ready a supply of material to place around the plant for moisture retention. This can be a mixture of sphagnum moss and coconut fibre, both

of which are available from specialist nurseries. Select a piece of cork bark, or similar wood, of a size to accommodate the plant, allowing room for growth. Insert a length of wire to make a hook in the top of the bark. You will also require a length of thin, plastic-coated wire and a pair of small pliers.

Place a wad of the supporting moss and fibre around the base of the plant, without covering the pseudobulbs, and place another wad directly on the bark. On top of this, place your plant with the new growths at the top, facing towards the bark. If the plant has a downward-growing habit, such as *Brassavola nodosa*, reverse it. Once the plant is in position, hold it firmly and place a band of thin, plastic-coated wire around the base to secure it in position. Take care to pass the wire around the medium and rhizome, without cutting into a pseudobulb. Pull the wire tight and twist it using the pliers, then cut off the ends. Place another tie farther up, if necessary. When finished, the plant must be secure on its bark. If it is loose, it will not root into the bark or progress well. Finally, trim the base material with a pair of scissors to give a neat, professional finish to your work. Spray the plant daily and give it an occasional soak in water to

ABOVE **Hartwegia** *(syn.* Nageliella*) purpurea is an interesting species that grows well on wood. The small flowers are produced at the end of long, extremely thin flower spikes. This species blooms for much of the year.*

ORCHIDS FOR GROWING ON BARK

Brassia verrucosa
Dendrobium miyakei
Dendrobium victoria-regina
Encyclia polybulbon
Encyclia vitellina
Laelia anceps
Maxillaria tenuifolia
Oncidium flexuosum
Sarcochilus Fitzhart
Trichopilia tortilis

ensure that the base remains damp. Plants growing in this way will need more regular spraying and watering to keep them moist than ones in pots. Within a few weeks, you will be rewarded with new growth and roots. In some species, such as *Oncidium flexuosum*, a dense mat of roots will be produced that will creep over the bark surface and hang down well below.

Mounting orchids on bark can be taken one step further. If you can find a suitable branch of oak or any type of tree except resinous pine, you can mount several small orchids on the tree to good effect. This will form an attractive feature in a greenhouse and, provided they are sprayed regularly, the plants will thrive. By selecting the right orchid species you can have plants flowering at different times throughout the year. You can decorate the orchid tree further by attaching a few of the smaller-growing tillandsias or ferns.

Orchids growing in this way need the humidity that can only be achieved in a greenhouse. They would not grow well indoors, where it would be extremely difficult to keep the plants sufficiently wet.

Mounting on Orchid Bark

If the orchid is growing out of its pot, and there are aerial roots showing that have not grown into the compost (growing medium), remove the orchid from the pot and mount on to bark.

❶ You will need a slab of tree fern or a piece of cork bark (with a wire hook), some sphagnum moss and coconut fibre, a roll of plastic-coated garden wire, a pair of secateurs (pruners), and a pair of pliers.

❷ Using the pair of secateurs, cut the rhizome at the rim of the pot, leaving a plant with six leaves and a long, thin rhizome. The plant shown here is *Bulbophyllum macranthum*.

❸ Prepare a sandwich of sphagnum moss and coconut fibre to fit the size of the piece of tree fern or cork bark.

❹ Cut a length of the plastic-coated wire and, using the pliers, wire the sphagnum moss and coconut fibre firmly to the tree fern or piece of cork bark.

❺ Position the plant with enough room for new growths, as it will stay in place for some time. Wire the plant firmly, but not too tightly, so that it will be held secure without damaging the rhizome.

❻ These plants will flourish growing suspended in this natural epiphytic manner. They will require daily spraying with water and fertilizer once a week.

PROPAGATION

Orchids can be propagated in a number of ways, depending on their habit of growth. Propagation is a means of keeping the plants healthy, as well as producing new stock. Left to their own devices, they can become quite large specimens, and parts of the plants may become unproductive.

VEGETATIVE PROPAGATION

Orchids can be propagated vegetatively like many other plants, whether from back bulbs, stem cuttings and keikis or adventitious growths. In many cases, the method of propagation depends on whether the orchid is sympodial or monopodial. The monopodial orchids, such as vandas, are those that grow from an upright, extending rhizome, with new leaves coming from the centre. These orchids propagate themselves, or can be propagated from, in a different way to sympodial orchids.

Orchids with pseudobulbs produce a sympodial growth, which means that new growths appear from the base of the previous pseudobulb, adding to their size each year. The new growths form from tiny "eyes", as they are loosely termed, and are the growing tips of the plant. Although a few eyes may form around the base of one pseudobulb, only one, or occasionally two, will be activated and develop into the new growths that eventually mature into pseudobulbs. If the first eye to grow is damaged or otherwise prevented from growing, a second will take over and grow, giving the plant a second chance.

The spare eyes that do not grow at this time remain in a dormant state for as long as the pseudobulb lives, and they can be encouraged to grow by propagation. Each pseudobulb remains on the plant for a few years until it loses its foliage and becomes a "back bulb". When a plant has too many leafless back bulbs, these can be severed at repotting time. Divided singly, these can be potted up on their own in a small pot and placed in a propagator or warm, light spot, where the dormant eye will start into growth within a few weeks.

LEFT *Although new growths usually start from the base of the pseudobulb, occasionally they can grow from the top of a leafless pseudobulb, as on this* Brassia.

PROPAGATING ORCHIDS

Orchids for propagating by back bulbs
Anguloas
Brassias
Bulbophyllums
Cattleyas and allied genera
Coelogynes
Cymbidiums
Dendrochilums
Encyclias
Gongoras
Lycastes
Maxillarias
Stanhopeas

Orchids for propagating by division
Same as for back bulbs

Orchids for propagating by keikis or adventitious growths
Dendrobiums
Epidendrum radicans
Phalaenopsis
Thunias
Vandas and allied genera

Orchids for propagating by stem cuttings
Dendrobiums
Thunias

Orchids for propagating by seed
All orchids

The majority of sympodial orchids with pseudobulbs can be propagated in this way, but there are exceptions, such as orchids from the *Odontoglossum* alliance. It is always worth potting up any spare back bulbs and growing them on to flowering, although this can take a few years. When a back bulb does not grow, it may be too old, and any spare eyes are dead. An old back bulb that gets started into growth sometimes shrivels and dies before the new growth has got very far, and unless it has made its own roots, it is unlikely to survive. Some genera will grow from back bulbs much more readily than others, and it can be a case of trial and error to find out which are most likely to grow for you in this way.

If you find yourself with a handful of various back bulbs left over at repotting time, try placing them all in one seedling tray, then wait to see which start to grow. As new growths appear, take out the relevant back bulbs and pot them up on their own. Those that have not produced new growths within about three months are unlikely to grow and can be discarded.

Odontoglossums

Plants from the *Odontoglossum* alliance are extremely reluctant to grow from the older pseudobulbs. It seems that any spare eyes that are not activated while they are young deteriorate rapidly, losing the ability to grow within a year or two. For this reason, odontoglossums are propagated differently from other sympodial orchids, but the method carries a greater risk to the plant and is not to be undertaken lightly.

ABOVE *Most sympodial orchids can be propagated by removing the old leafless back bulbs from the plant and potting them up. Usually within a few weeks, new growth will have started. The back bulbs shown here are from a* Cymbidium.

This involves cutting off the latest pseudobulb as soon as it has matured, leaving the one behind to grow again and become the leading pseudobulb. If no new growth is forthcoming, the plant has been spoiled. In the meantime, the severed pseudobulb must cope alone, without the support of the old pseudobulbs. This weakened front portion will produce a smaller new growth, which will not be likely to bloom, and it may be several years before either portion of the divided plant will bloom again.

Paphiopedilums and Phragmipediums

Sympodial orchids that do not produce pseudobulbs, mainly the paphiopedilums and phragmipediums, can be propagated from a back portion of growth, which is removed at repotting time in the same way as the old pseudobulbs are removed. This should only be attempted when a plant is large enough and is carrying in excess of four strong growths, otherwise it will reduce the strength of the main plant. Most of the phragmipediums are robust growers that are more easily propagated than many of the hybrid paphiopedilums, which can be slow growing, with the older growths dying before there is an opportunity to build up a very large plant.

Cattleyas

These are sympodial orchids that are also treated slightly differently. The creeping rhizome is much thicker than that of other orchids and is visible on the surface of the compost with the pseudobulbs spaced along it. Most cattleyas have two growing seasons in any year, producing new growth and roots in the autumn as well as in the spring. This makes it possible to start propagation during the autumn by severing the plant, which remains in its pot. You can cut through the rhizome with a sharp pruning knife to separate one or two of the oldest pseudobulbs, then leave them undisturbed until the following spring. By this time, these back bulbs should be showing a new growth, and when the plant is repotted, they can be potted up on their own and grown on in the usual way. Alternatively, this is also a good way of getting a *Cattleya* to make extra growths, if you want to build up a specimen-size plant.

Dendrobiums

These are sympodial orchids, many of which grow tall, thin canes that will readily produce keikis or adventitious new growths along their length. This is particularly true of *Dendrobium nobile* and its hybrids. These growths occur most often as a result of poor cultivation. If the plants are watered too early in the season after the winter's rest, at a time when the flower buds should be developing, these flower buds turn into growths. If you were expecting flowers, this can be an annoying and disappointing habit. However, if you want to produce new plants from one favourite specimen, try cutting off a plump, leafless pseudobulb that has not flowered and dividing this into segments, cutting between the nodes or growing points to produce several pieces, each with one joint at the middle. Dust the cut ends with sulphur or powdered charcoal to

LEFT *The old leafless canes of thunias will produce adventitious growths that can be left until new roots have grown, and then potted up on their own. This should be done in the spring.*

Propagating from Keikis

Orchids such as dendrobiums and thunias produce keikis or adventitious new growths along their length which can be potted up and grown on.

❶ This dendrobium has produced several "keikis" or adventitious growths.

❷ Sever each keiki from the parent with secateurs (pruners) or a sharp knife, making sure it has a good root system.

ABOVE *Dendrobiums are among a few orchids that will readily produce keikis or adventitious growths from nodes along the older canes. These can be removed and potted up as soon as they have made their own roots.*

❸ Pot up the keikis individually using fine bark or sphagnum moss.

❹ Firm each keiki in well, then water. Place in a heated propagator until signs of strong growth appear from the base.

ABOVE *When potting up the rooted preparations of dendrobiums, make sure that they are not buried too deeply in the compost (growing medium), or the base will not produce further new growth.*

prevent rot, and place in a community pot with one end pushed into the compost (growing medium). Most of these will produce a new growth that can be grown on to make a further flowering plant within a few years.

Alternatively, you can take stem cuttings from orchids such as dendrobiums and thunias by laying stem lengths on their sides in a seed tray. A new plant will emerge from the node in a few months. Again, this is a long-term procedure and is only worth doing if you want a number of young plants identical to the main plant.

Epidendrums

A number of the reed-type epidendrums also readily produce adventitious growth from along the older stems and at the

ABOVE *Phalaenopsis such as this* Phalaenopsis *Silky Moon can sometimes produce keikis or adventitious growths which can be used to propagate the plant.*

ends of the extending flower spikes. Leave these until they have grown a good root system, which they do extremely quickly, then carefully remove them from the main stem by cutting them off with a pruning knife. Pot them up and grow them on in the usual way.

Phalaenopsis

These occasionally produce keikis or adventitious growths from the old flowering stems. This is frequently seen with the species *Phalaenopsis lueddemanniana* and related species or hybrids. If you want to encourage new growth in this way, you can treat the flowering stems with keiki paste – a growth hormone enhancement that is available from some specialist nurseries or orchid sundry firms. First remove the small green bract that protects each node along the stem, then apply the paste. If the treatment is successful, a new plantlet will grow, producing its own leaves and roots, which can be removed and potted up when large enough.

Vandas and Related Orchids

These are monopodial orchids, but they are not so easy to propagate from. Generally, a plant that is growing well has no need to produce further growths.

Only when the main stem is damaged and the plant prevented from growing from its centre, perhaps because of rot or mechanical damage, will a new growth be activated near the base.

This ability to propagate can be encouraged in large plants, when necessary, but it is not without some risk, and should only be attempted if it is in the plant's interest to do so. A plant that has become extremely tall, with a length of bare stem at the base and strong aerial roots along its length, can be cut down by severing the rhizome at a point below the leaves and aerial roots. The leafless stump that is left in the pot will, in time, produce a new growth that can be grown on. Where there is a lack of aerial roots on the top portion of the plant, encourage them to grow by wrapping the stem in sphagnum moss or similar moisture-holding material, covering it with polythene (plastic) and tying it into position. Keeping the moss wet will encourage roots to form. Do this before cutting off the top portion of the plant, which will not succeed otherwise.

It can take as much as 12 months before any new roots are seen, and this process is not guaranteed to be successful. You will need to check beneath the sphagnum moss regularly in order to see whether there are any roots growing. As soon as the roots appear, remove the moss covering and spray the roots regularly until they have grown several inches. The plant can then be severed and the top portion potted up and grown on into a new plant.

Taking Stem Cuttings

Some orchids can be propagated by taking stem sections, particularly those that produce long "canes", such as dendrobiums, thunias and epidendrums. The leafless stems are cut from the parent plant at the start of the growing season and divided into shorter lengths, each with at least two growing nodes. The new growth should arise after three to four months, when the new plantlets can be potted up individually in the appropriate choice of compost (growing medium) for the type of orchid. It is important to note here that the sphagnum moss in the trays will grow at the same time.

❶ Cut lengths of stem at least 25cm (10in) long from the plant (in this case *Dendrobium nobile*), cutting just above a node (growing point).

❷ Cut each stem into sections, each with at least two nodes.

❸ Lay the cuttings on trays of moist sphagnum moss.

❹ Place each tray in a clear plastic bag or heated propagator.

❺ New growth should appear within three to four months. The moss also grows.

RAISING ORCHIDS FROM SEED

All living things, both animal and vegetable, are made up of cells that divide as the organism grows. Life starts with a single cell, in the middle of which is a nucleus containing the chromosomes. Each chromosome carries the genes of life. As the cells are the building blocks, so the genes are the blueprint of life. From the moment of conception, when the pollen fertilizes a seed, the characteristics of that potential plant and the colour of its flowers have all been determined by the genes.

There are well-documented accounts of orchids in cultivation that are over 150 years old. These plants are exactly the same as they were when they first flowered. Their colour, shape and size do not alter with age, and all vegetative propagations will remain the same. It is possible to divide or take cuttings many times with the results all being identical to the original stock.

However, propagating orchids from seed enables the grower to produce new orchids that have not been seen before.

In the wild, the pollination of orchids is mostly carried out by insects and occasionally hummingbirds. Orchids often produce large quantities of blooms, all opening at the same time, to ensure successful cross-pollination within the species. Each seed capsule contains hundreds of thousands of minute seeds. It requires only a few of these to germinate for the species to be perpetuated and the cycle of life to continue.

The best results for vigorous seedling growth are obtained from the cross-pollination of two separate clones, although many orchids are self-fertile, whereby the same pollen can be used on the one flower. Commercial nurserymen study the genetic make-up and check the chromosome numbers of two potential parents to ensure that both are compatible. Recessive genes can come to the fore, with the resulting progeny showing characteristics that had lain dormant for generations. The aim of all hybridizers is to produce plants that are new and exciting, and for which there will be a market.

Cross-pollination

When the cross-pollination of two orchids occurs, and the genes of the pollinating parent are mixed with those of the pod plant, a new set of genes is created. The result is unique individuals that have not previously occurred and are unlikely to occur again. Minute, changes will take place each time cross-fertilization occurs, thus making each seedling, or clone, from one capsule a "one off" with its own set of genes.

Most species clones are diploid, indicated by the scientific symbol 2N. Diploids have an even number of chromosomes and ensure fertility throughout the species. Very occasionally, a plant will occur naturally with twice the number of chromosomes. This is a tetraploid, or 4N. Tetraploids are more likely to occur in hybridizing, and when crossed with a diploid the result is a triploid, or 3N. It is also possible to create 5N and 6N hybrids, and so on. To the grower, diploids are usually even-growing, free-flowering plants. Tetraploids produce larger, more robust plants, with superior quality and better-shaped flowers but fewer on a spike. Without the tetraploids, the great advances made in hybridizing would not have been achieved.

Every amateur who tries their hand at hybridizing will be quite successful at crossing two related plants, but the serious breeder will take the time and trouble to study the chromosome counts. These can usually be determined

ABOVE Stanhopea *pollen.*

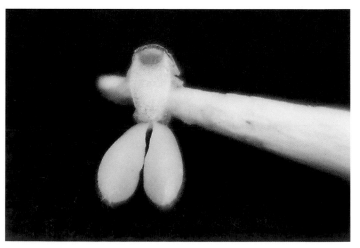

ABOVE Miltoniopsis *pollen.*

by visual examination of the plant, its parents and the size and shape of the blooms. However, the only scientific way is to take root-tip samples. These are sliced into micron-thin slivers and placed on a microscope slide, where a cell in a suitable state of division can be found and the chromosomes counted.

Orchids with uneven numbers of chromosomes will not breed. These can often be converted by treating at a very early stage with Colchicine, an extract from the crocus. This will react by changing the chromosome count in both seed- and tissue-cultured plants. This technique requires some laboratory experience in handling such very small amounts of plant material.

Fertilization

On most flowers the reproductive parts are the stigma and the stamens. The stamens contain the pollen, which is transferred by either insects or wind to the stigma, where the pollen fertilizes the seed embryos situated behind the flower. In orchids, where the pollen is a solid mass, the reproductive parts are the pollinia and the stigma. Some orchids, including *Catasetum* species, produce separate flowers that contain only male or female organs. When catasetums were first introduced, plants with different flowers were thought to be different species. It later became apparent that, within this genus, a plant could produce all-female flowers one year and all-male flowers another, or, very occasionally, to produce both on separate spikes on the same plant at the same time.

This also occurs with *Cycnoches* species, a genus closely related to catasetums. Another feature of this group is that when the pollinator visits the flower, it triggers a mechanism that releases the pollen and fires it, at great speed, towards the head of the insect.

ABOVE *The hybrid* Cymbidium Mini Ice 'Antarctic', *like all orchids, may be propagated from seed.*

Here it sticks firmly by means of a viscose patch, but the slightest knock catapults the pollen from the flowers.

There can be two, four or six pollen masses, depending upon the genus. Each pollen mass contains millions of microscopic pollen grains – a feature unique to orchids. The pollinia are hidden beneath a protective cap, the anther, which ensures that they remain fresh. They are joined by a short thread and a sticky patch, which adheres to the thorax or head of the insect.

Alternatives to Seed Raising

In the commercial world, mericloning, a scientific method of mass-producing one clone to produce identical plants, is now used more than seed raising. This breakthrough was developed by Professor Georges Morel at the University of Paris, who became the first person to produce orchids by meristemming, or cloning, in the early 1960s. He adapted a method devised 15 years earlier in California to rid plants of virus disease, and discovered a new

market in orchids. While, in the past, divisions of the best plants were sometimes available at high prices, now the very best orchids were within the reach of everyone at affordable prices.

Meristemmed plants are produced by removing a small cluster of cells found at the centre, or meristem tip, of a new growth. This is achieved with the aid of a microscope. The removed tissue is placed in a nutritious liquid solution and agitated in suspension to encourage prolification. This results in an ever-enlargening clump of green tissue, which is then cut into smaller pieces until sufficient numbers have been acquired. At this stage, the clumps of green tissue resemble the protocorms that form from the seed, and when these are placed onto an agar base in sterile jars, the meristems grow in the same way as if they were seedling plants.

Pollination

When you are pollinating the orchid flower by hand, use a pointed stick, such as a cocktail stick, in order to lift the pollen from one flower and place it upon the stigmatic surface of the pod parent. The stigmatic surface is found below and beneath where the pollen was situated. Within a few days the fertilized flower will turn red and begin to shrivel. Eventually, the dried-up remains of the flower can be trimmed back in order to prevent infection. In the meantime, the stem immediately behind the flower, which contains the ovaries, begins to swell to form the seed capsule. Be sure to keep a record of the parents used and the date of pollination for future reference. Within nine to twelve months, the seed will ripen. The first signs of maturity are the seed capsule turning yellow and the longitudinal ridges splitting.

Pollinating Orchids

Pollinating orchids is a delicate process, involving the transfer of pollen from the pollinating parent to the pod parent.

❶ A *Miltoniopsis* flower showing the column at the top of which is the anther or pollen cap. Just below this is the stigmatic surface.

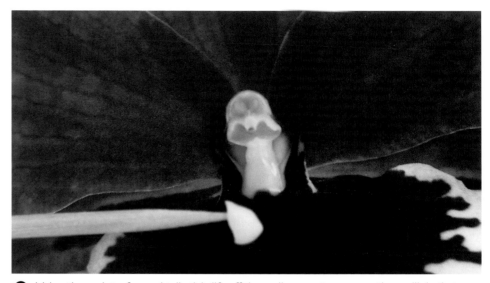

❷ Using the point of a cocktail stick, lift off the pollen cap to expose the pollinia that are attached to the end of the column. Discard the pollen cap.

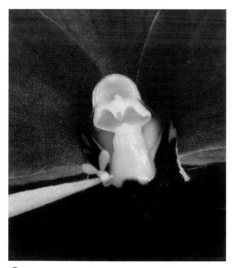

❸ The two pollen masses are joined by a thread to a sticky patch. This is easily removed with the cocktail stick. Place the stick and pollen on one side

❹ Insert the pollen from the pollinating plant on to the stigmatic patch of the pod plant. Once the pollen is in position the flower will collapse quickly, its purpose having been achieved. Within the two pollen masses are thousands of pollen grains which will send roots through the column to the ovaries. Each root must find its own seed to complete fertilization.

POLLEN MASSES

Orchids are classified by the shape of their flowers. Where certain blooms look alike they are classified by the number of their pollens. Orchids have at least two pollen masses and often more in multiples of two. Our picture shows a selection of orchid pollens. Those of a bright, clear yellow are more fertile than the orange brown of the Cymbidium.

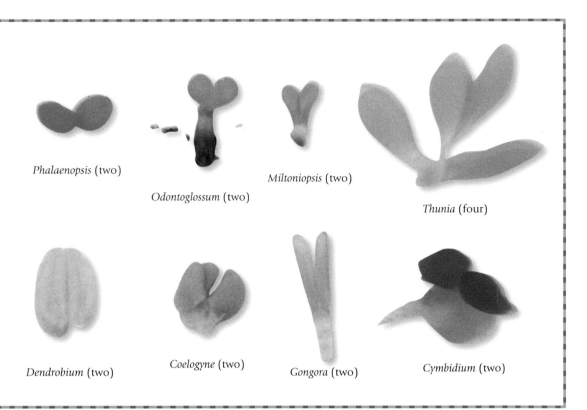

Phalaenopsis (two)

Odontoglossum (two)

Miltoniopsis (two)

Thunia (four)

Dendrobium (two)

Coelogyne (two)

Gongora (two)

Cymbidium (two)

LEFT *A close-up of the column of a* Phalaenopsis *flower. Note the small hook at the base of the pollen cap. Any insect that visits the flower will dislodge this before the pollinia sticks to it.*

Harvesting

Harvest the orchid seed before any is spilt and becomes contaminated. Place the seed capsule in an envelope and cut it from the plant. In this way, none of the seed will be lost. At this stage, you have two options: you can take the seed to a nursery or laboratory that offers a seed-sowing service or raise your own seedlings. If you opt for the latter, you have two further options. One is to use the natural, symbiotic, method, and sprinkle the seed over the prepared surface of a "mother plant", where there is a possibility that a small quantity of seed will germinate and grow.

If you want a more certain future for your seedlings, the artificial, or asymbiotic, method is to sow in sterile jars. These can be obtained from orchid sundry firms, who will supply a seed-sowing kit that contains the ready-made agar-based medium for the containers. You only have to sow the seed on to the agar surface and place the jars in a propagator to await results. Ideally, you need to do this in an air-flow cabinet to prevent the jars being contaminated, or you can work over a bowl of steaming water. You can use milk bottles or jam jars instead of laboratory containers, provided they are sterilized. Dissolve the agar containing the nutrients in distilled water to ensure it is pure. When thoroughly dissolved, pour about 1cm (½in) of the mixture into each jar and screw on the tops. These need to be sterilized using a microwave oven or a pressure cooker. Larger establishments use a sterilizer. Allow to cool and set before sowing.

The Developing Seed Capsule

Once the flower has been pollinated, the plant is carefully tagged and the grooved stem behind the flowers allowed to develop into a seed capsule.

❶ Behind the orchid flower is a grooved stem which swells to become the seed capsule. Its development will commence within days of the flower being pollinated.

❷ This *Cymbidium* shows the longitudinal grooves of the seed capsule. This will develop over many months into a large fruiting body.

❸ After pollination, the flower is tagged with the following information: the date, the number of flowers pollinated and the names of the parents. In this case, the orchid is a self-pollinated *Liparis unata*.

❹ Some seed capsules, here on *Brassia* Rex, hang down while others remain at right angles, or upright from the stem. Every orchid has its own distinctively shaped capsule.

❺ It is advisable to pollinate several flowers on a stem. This increases the flow of sap which in turn ensures the seed capsules are full of fertile seed, although only a very small quantity of the seed will be used. This is *Cymbidium devonianum*.

Harvesting Orchid Seed

When harvesting the seed, remove the seed capsule from the plant by placing it in an envelope and then cutting it from the plant. This will ensure that no seed is spilt.

❶ To harvest the seed, shake it from the seed capsule on to a sheet of clean paper.

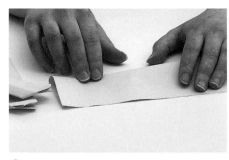

❷ Fold the paper to make a neat packet which can be easily opened when a small amount of seed is needed.

❸ Write all the information on the seed packet as it was recorded on the seed-bearing or mother plant for reference and add the date of harvesting.

❹ Hybridizers keep a detailed studbook. It is necessary for future reference and to avoid making crosses that will prove unproductive. With recorded information, you can follow the seedlings right through to maturity and on to the next generation.

ABOVE *Seed capsules can take from a few weeks, in the case of native European species, to four to twelve months for tropical orchids, before they are ripe. This* Stanhopea *seed capsule has taken nine months to ripen.*

ABOVE *A ripened* Stanhopea *capsule begins to split, spilling thousands of seeds that are so fine that a magnifying glass is needed to examine them. They drift out of the capsule and float away on the wind.*

DIFFERENT ORCHID SEEDS

All orchid seed consists of a single cell that can only be seen with the aid of a microscope. The cell is contained in a casing made up of a network of fibres, varying in density depending on the species. As orchid seed is wind-borne, this husk lightens the load and increases its ability to travel great distances.

Single *Stanhopea* seed as seen under a microscope

Epidendrum seed

Anguloa seed

Cymbidium seed

ABOVE *For the best results when sowing orchid seed, use an air-flow cabinet, working in a sterile zone of filtered air. Use every precaution to prevent contamination taking place, such as donning gloves, mask and a clean overall.*

Sowing

To sow the orchid seed without contamination creeping in is not easy because microscopic fungus spores abound. One spore entering the jar will grow rapidly on the surface of the agar. At this stage, even the seed contains microscopic fungus spores and has to be sterilized. Oversterilizing will kill the seed, so take care. Immerse the seed in a solution of Milton's sterilizing fluid or a very diluted form of hydrochloric acid; this will sterilize the seed without harming the embryo inside. Unscrew each jar and spread the seed carefully on the surface of the jelly using either a pipette or a platinum loop, then close the jar immediately. Even in the most hygienic conditions some contamination will occur at this stage. Fortunately, the orchid is generous with the amount of seed it has provided, so you can afford a 10 per cent failure rate.

Sowing Orchid Seed

Growing orchids from seed is most rewarding, but it will be another five years or so before you see the results of a new flowering orchid, so you will need to be patient.

❶ Pour a small quantity of the seed into the sterilizing solution.

❷ A screw-top jar containing sterilized jelly should be ready to receive the sterilized seed from the test tube.

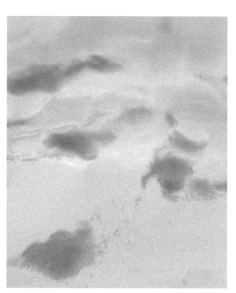

❺ Within a few days the first signs of life appear as the seed, lying on the surface of the agar, turns green.

❻ After a few weeks, the seed masses swell into mounds of bright green protocorms. Each one is an individual plant.

If you are not ready to sow your seed immediately, you can store it in a refrigerator; but since orchid seed is so fine it does not store easily, and the longer you keep it, the less fertile it becomes. However, there is a conservation movement now experimenting with long-term deep-freezing, whereby the seed is dried and kept at extremely low temperatures. Its viability is checked by sowing a small amount of seed every few years. What the end result will be is difficult to predict, but it will be interesting to see if the seed is still fertile after long-term storage.

❸ Using a platinum wire loop, carefully spread the seed across the surface of the jelly. Reseal the jar.

❹ The sown jars are placed on shelves in a seed room where the temperature can be carefully controlled, under special fluorescent tubes.

ABOVE *These large healthy* Zygopetalums, *approximately 25 to 30 in a jar, are ready to be removed and potted up.*

❼ Within several months, each protocorm will have produced a tiny leaf from the top and a root from the base.

❽ The young plants, now with distinguishable leaves, are growing vigorously on a different medium.

ABOVE *Contamination can strike at any time in the form of mould or fungi that will grow faster than the orchids and kill them.*

ABOVE *These are well-established* Laelia *seedlings with roots, leaves and, in some cases, small pseudobulbs.*

Provided the seed you used was fertile, within three weeks the agar surface will turn bright green as the minute seeds swell into protocorms. These are chlorophyll-filled vessels from which leaves and roots are produced within a few more weeks. Any jars that become contaminated with a fungal infection will have to be discarded. The jars should be boiled to destroy infection before opening. These spores will envelop the surface of a jar within a few days, and can be transmitted to the next jar if it is not sufficiently sealed.

Potting Up

The seedlings will be ready to leave the jars when they are about 5cm (2in) tall and have their own roots. This should be done in the spring when the young plants have the summer growing season ahead of them, and there is less danger from damping off. Have ready a shallow bowl of slightly tepid water to which you have added a little fungicide. Unscrew the jar and pour some of the water into the jar and swill it around. This may be sufficient to dislodge the seedlings so that they can be poured out. If the agar is too firm, it may need to be broken up and the seedlings carefully removed with tweezers. Once you have rinsed the seedlings, clean off any agar and lay them out, graded by size, on a piece of absorbent paper towel. Retain only the best-looking plants, discarding the weakest and also any gross plants that have grown significantly larger than the rest. These mutant giants may look exceptionally good, but when grown on to flowering are often found to have inferior flowers.

Your chosen plants are now ready to be potted into small community pots or segregated trays. You can plant six orchid seedlings in one community pot. The pots or trays should have been prepared a week or so beforehand. Place a little drainage material in the base, using your preferred compost (growing medium). An ideal mix is fine bark, with perlite and charcoal added in even proportions, or you can use Rockwool. The latter is less likely to contain any harmful infection that can cause damping off. The community pots can be watered the day before use, which will make the compost easy to handle. Work the seedlings in around the pot rim by making holes with a pointed stick and lowering the plants into the holes, pressing the compost gently around their base. Take care that the seedlings are not buried too deeply, which can cause them to rot, or standing proud and loose, in which case they will not root into the compost. Do not be tempted to place too many seedlings in one larger pot, because if an infection starts it can run through

every plant and all will be lost. Lightly spray the seedlings for a few days before watering the compost. Do this in the morning with a rising temperature. Place the community pots in a propagator, but keep the top open during the day to allow some movement of air. Avoid any dehydration, because, at this stage, the soft foliage can shrivel and die if there is insufficient moisture.

The first few weeks are a critical time for the seedlings, as they recover from the shock of their removal from the sterile conditions and adjust to the harsher outside environment. You will notice a change in the appearance of the plants as they adapt, and, once they are growing strongly, you can start feeding at every watering. Check your seedlings regularly and remove any dead leaves or plants immediately to prevent the spread of rots.

Potting on Orchid Seedlings

Within six to nine months, the seedlings will have reached a stage where they need to be potted on. Do this in the autumn before the winter sets in. By now they should all be large enough to be potted separately in individual pots. Some may already have produced their first pseudobulb and a good root system. The roots made at this time are typical orchid roots, quite different from those made in the agar, which will not have survived the change to conventional compost (growing medium). Repot these plants again the following spring and annually until they reach flowering size in another two to four years.

When the first of your seedlings flower, provided that it is a new cross not previously named, you can register the hybrid with a name of your choice, assuming that it has not been previously used by someone else.

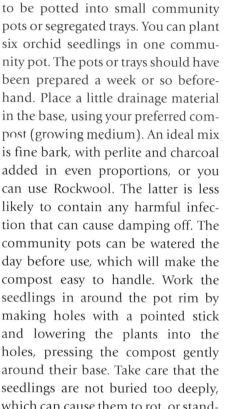

LEFT

Phalaenopsis *Barbara Moler × Spitzberg is a new hybrid in this popular genus. The beautiful, pale lemon flowers can appear at any time.*

Potting Up Orchid Seedlings

Orchid seed that has germinated successfully will result in a great many seedlings. Each jar can contain 50 or more seedlings, so you may finish up with many more plants.

❶ Using a wire hook, remove the seedlings and the agar into the bowl of water. Wear gloves as the water contains a fungicide.

❷ Remove the plants, one at a time, making sure that they are clean and free from jelly.

❸ Grade the seedlings into sizes and discard the smallest and any large misshapen ones. The large ones can be coarse and may produce ugly flowers.

❹ Use a compost (growing medium), perhaps of fine bark and perlite, and pot up each seedling into a segregated tray. Hold a plant by the tip of the leaf and pour the compost in with the other hand. It is not necessary to firm the plant down.

❺ The segregation method ensures that if one plant damps off it is not likely to affect its neighbours.

❻ When the tray is full, label with a stock number or name and the date of potting. Young seedlings placed in a warm greenhouse and kept evenly moist will grow quickly.

❼ Six to nine months later, the tray will be full of vigorous young plants which are now ready for potting on.

❽ The advantage of segregated trays is that when the plant is ready for potting into a larger pot, there is less disturbance of the rootball when it is removed.

❾ Damping off often takes place. The aftercare of orchids, certainly through the first 12 months as well as through winter, can be a trying time for a grower.

ROUTINE CARE

In order to grow orchids successfully, you need to create an environment that imitates their native habitats, which means taking humidity, temperature and light into consideration, as well as their feeding and resting needs. If you are a beginner, it is best to restrict your choice to hybrids that have been bred for ease of care, rather than many species which often have more exacting requirements.

FEEDING

There was a time when the feeding of orchids was frowned upon. It was almost looked upon as "cheating". Orchids were originally thought to be parasites, although it was later understood that they were epiphytes that relied entirely upon fresh air and rainwater to flourish. The first established Victorian growers grew their orchids extremely well, but these plants were imported specimens which continued to grow under their own momentum and needed very little in the way of additional nutrients.

ABOVE *You can foliar feed your orchids by spraying the leaves with a liquid feed added to the water in a watering can.*

During the first half of the 20th century, orchid culture progressed little. Thousands of new hybrids were raised, with seedlings taking up to seven or eight years to flower. The same orchids today can be flowered within three to four years. There can be no doubt that feeding orchids can greatly benefit their performance, but this has to be done with care. Orchids are perennial plants, with a life span of many years. Their rate of growth is slow, and any artificial feeding has to reflect this. The extra nutrients are given not to increase the rate at which orchids grow or to influence their growing cycle, but to maintain a steady momentum and to ensure health and vigour.

The first growers to experiment with feeding orchids were those employed by the private estates, whose owners had the best collections at that time. They used what was at hand, and this happened to be dried animal droppings. This was rubbed through a sieve and mixed with compost (growing medium). This proved very successful with the deciduous calanthes, which have a short, fast growing season. However, the roots were easily burnt by the strong manure and the appearance of virus-like markings on the foliage of cymbidiums and other orchids fuelled the fear that became the basis for the non-feeding rule.

More recently, as the nutritional needs of orchids have become better understood and modern inorganic compost (growing medium) materials have increased, feeding orchids has become scientifically based. Orchids are now systematically fed using any one of a number of specially prepared orchid fertilizers. These are available from most outlets where orchids can be purchased. It is far better to buy a proven product than to make up your own brand of feed, unless you thoroughly understand the requirements of your plants. There remains the danger of overfeeding, with the orchids suffering the consequences. If a specific orchid feed is not available, you can use any one of the popular brands sold for houseplants, using the fertilizer at half the weakest recommended dose. It is important to remember that orchids are weak feeders.

When to Feed

Orchids can be fed at all ages, from young seedlings and propagations to adult plants. Feed only healthy plants, however, because they have the ability to

---

TIPS ON FEEDING
ORCHIDS

Buy a proven product
rather than attempting to mix
your own feed

Only feed orchids that
are actively growing

Apply feed at every second
or third watering

Never overfeed orchids

Feed only healthy plants

Use any one of the popular
brands sold for houseplants,
if necessary, but at half the
recommended weakest dose

LEFT Sophrolaeiocattleya *Brio de Valec* *is a wonderfully coloured, multi-generic* *hybrid that has lost all trace of the* Sophronitis *in its make-up, originally* *introduced to add colour to the hybrids* *and reduce the size of the flowers to* *produce miniature hybrids.*

absorb and convert the chemicals. Do not feed plants that are sick or have lost their roots. They will have no means of taking up the feed, and new roots that appear may be burnt by the residue remaining in the compost (growing medium). For the same reason, do not feed orchids that are resting. Their roots will have become inactive, and the chemicals will remain in the compost where they may cause harm as the plant starts into growth in the spring.

How to Feed

As a general guide, apply feed added to the water at every second or third watering. By using plain water in between the feeds, any leftover chemicals in the compost (growing medium) will be washed through, avoiding the build-up of any residue. Feed very sparingly during the winter and more liberally in summer, when there is better light and higher temperatures to balance the extra nutrients being supplied.

Orchids growing in an inorganic compound such as Rockwool or stone-wool may be given more applications of feed than those growing in a bark or peat mix. An additional foliar feed to provide nutrients through the leaves, can be given occasionally during summer; this also applies to plants that have lost their roots and cannot be fed via the compost (growing medium).

Some manufacturers produce two types of orchid fertilizer. The first is a high-nitrogen feed used to promote growth at the start of the growing season. Later, when the growth has matured, this is replaced by a phosphate-based formula to encourage flowering. Whether this system is preferable to giving a balanced feed throughout the year is debatable, but growers can try out which suits their needs and their orchids best.

Always follow the manufacturers' instructions and read the label carefully. When a liquid concentrate is used, shake the bottle well before using. The solution will have separated, leaving the heavier elements in the fertilizer at the bottom. Preferably, use granular fertilizers, which will not deteriorate over time. Never store fertilizers in the greenhouse or in full sun, but keep them in a cool shed out of the bright light.

You may be tempted to combine different fertilizers to make your own concoction, but this can be dangerous and should only be undertaken by someone who fully understands the chemical formulae of the trace elements. In the same way, do not exceed the recommended dose, or give a double dose because a feeding application has been forgotten. Draw up a regular feeding programme for the year and keep a diary. If watering and feeding are done at the same time, plan this for a certain day of the week so that it becomes part of the routine of your orchid growing.

Applying feed with water is probably the best way to fertilize most orchids. Adding a slow-release fertilizer to the compost (growing medium) when potting does not always work because orchids can be left for two or three years between repotting, by which time any nourishment given at the beginning will have long since deteriorated, with nothing left to benefit the plant.

Early fertilizers consisted of horn-and-hoof or bonemeal powder, which was mixed with the compost (growing medium) at the time of potting or placed in a large tub of water and allowed to ferment. Another product known as cow-tea needs no explanation. In addition to being used on the plants, these mixtures were sometimes poured on to the hot water pipes that ran round the greenhouses, giving off a strong vapour, highly charged with ammonia. Fortunately, today we have progressed to more "scientific" methods of feeding.

WATERING

Watering is the greatest cause of uncertainty among orchid growers, and whether a plant is ready for water or not is always under debate. This is a problem for experienced growers as well as beginners. While they are growing, orchids need to be kept evenly moist, avoiding the two extremes of becoming sodden at the roots or bone dry.

When to Water

There are a number of ways in which you can determine the moisture content of a pot. A good idea is to lift each pot and test the weight, but this is only practical where you have just one or two plants. Nevertheless, it is a good learning experience for the beginner, and as you progress from lifting each pot, you can recognize the dryness of the compost (growing medium) by observing its surface. Dry compost will vary in colour, or you may notice other subtle differences that will only come with experience. If you are still not sure, slip a plant out of its pot, without breaking up the compost ball, and take a quick look underneath to see how wet it is. Take a look also at the plant

itself. This will tell you what has been happening over the past weeks. If the pseudobulbs are plump, all is well. Shrivelled pseudobulbs, or limp foliage, may indicate underwatering or even overwatering. Further study of the roots will ascertain which is the cause, and the problem can be remedied.

Generally, you may expect to water a typical orchid once or twice in any

week during the growing season, and once every two or three weeks while it is resting. Orchids that grow all year round can be watered slightly less in winter than in summer, as the plants take longer to dry out. Much depends, however, upon the size of the plant and the amount of compost (growing medium) around it. A small plant in a large pot will need less water because all that is applied will run into the compost. A large, root-bound plant in a small pot will need far more water to ensure that some of it at least gets into the pot and penetrates to the roots.

Always try to water the orchids at a time when the temperature is rising. This means watering early in the day, and is more important in winter sun when all surplus moisture will have time to dry by nightfall. This avoids the combination of wet and cold that orchids detest. This system is less necessary with indoor growing, and where just a few plants are grown they can be moved individually to the kitchen for watering and allowed to drain before being returned to their growing area, so surplus water is not a problem.

How to Water

Water your orchids using a spouted watering can of a size that reflects the size of your collection. As this grows, you will want to convert to a garden hose in your greenhouse connected to the mains water supply. Use an adjustable nozzle to make the job easier and more enjoyable. When you apply water, give enough to flood the surface, allowing the water to run through, then repeat the process. This will ensure a good soaking. Because of the nature of orchid compost (growing medium), the water will quickly disappear, so you need to use much more than is actually retained.

LEFT *Epiphytes, such as vandas, which like to grow in open wooden baskets without any compost (growing medium), are true air plants. They need regular spraying several times a day in hot weather, especially if the humidity is low.*

Methods of Watering

Water can be given to orchids in a variety of ways, but ensure that it is of the right quality for your orchids.

❶ Water orchids indoors regularly from the rim of the pot, using a spouted watering can. Thoroughly soak the compost (growing medium) right through. The plant shown here is a *Phalaenopsis*.

❷ If a plant, such as this *Doricentrum*, has been allowed to become dry for a considerable time, dip it in a bucket of water and allow it to soak for 10 minutes to wet the compost thoroughly.

Depending upon the water quality where you live, you may be able to use the mains supply straight from the tap. Most orchids prefer a natural pH, and you can find out the acidity of your water from your supplier. If it has a high pH, you can soften the water by storing it in a container and adding a muslin bag full of garden peat. Hung over the edge into the water, it will reduce the acidity. There are other, more expensive methods of converting your water supply, or it may be easier to collect rainwater from outside and use that. If stored water is being used, be sure that it is at room temperature, especially in winter, when icy water will chill the roots. If your water butt (deep sink) is outside, bring in a can-full the day before you need to use it.

Water Quality

Mains tap water is available from several sources. In your area it may have fallen recently as rain and drained into reservoirs. Alternatively, it may be extracted from a river needing treatment

❸ Plants such as this *Coelogyne* that grow on bark in a greenhouse should be dipped in a bucket of water at least once a week and sprayed daily.

before it is suitable for domestic use. It may also be water that has come from deep, underground, natural reservoirs, in subterranean rock formations. This water may be hundreds of years old and contain many minerals. Your water may be fit for human consumption, but epiphytic plants do not like water that contains lime or calcium. Artificial water

softeners are available, which work by adding salts and various ingredients to soften the water. Again, these may be fine for domestic use but not very good for our orchids. In fact, the salts added can be more harmful than the original lime. Water softeners such as reverse osmosis, however, remove impurities to leave a better-quality water suitable for orchids.

RESTING

Most orchids have a growing season followed by a resting period. This rest can last for a few weeks or several months. Those orchids that have the longest resting periods are generally those with pseudobulbs. Paphiopedilums and phalaenopsis do not rest in the same way, but slow their rate of growth during the winter period. The majority of orchids rest during the winter months, which coincides with the dry season in the natural habitats of the species. To ensure the plant's survival, it stops growing and reduces its need for water. Lycastes, pleiones and some dendrobiums are among those that have a deciduous rest, dramatically dropping their foliage at the end of the growing season. Others remain evergreen, losing just a portion of their foliage at about the same time or in the spring when activity restarts.

When Orchids Rest

Cymbidiums are among those that have a very short resting period. As the new pseudobulb matures at the end of summer, the flower spike emerges from the base. It is not unusual for a new growth to appear alongside it, so the plant continues to grow from one season to the next without a break.

Many orchids flower while they are resting. In the wild, this would probably ensure a ready supply of pollinating insects on the wing, and it would prevent blooms from being damaged by torrential rain and winds. Odontoglossums complete their season's pseudobulb and produce their flower spikes at the same time. Only after flowering does the new growth appear, which may be at any time from the early winter onwards. The complex

ABOVE *Calanthes are deciduous orchids which produce their flower spikes at the end of the growing season, as the plant is about to shed its leaves and rest. The flowers will appear while the plant is leafless.*

hybrids in this genus often conform to a nine-month cycle, so that new growth is often started at a different time of the year. This can result in plants growing during the winter and resting and flowering during the summer.

Stanhopeas often prefer to grow during the winter, flowering in mid-summer while at rest. The paphiopedilums and phalaenopsis do not grow and flower at the same time. The phalaenopsis follow a routine of alternately producing one new leaf, then a

flower spike, giving the plant a short rest during flowering.

Most monopodial orchids behave in a similar way. Most of the coelogynes bloom at the start of their growing season, with the flower spikes appearing from the centre of the new growth while it is very young.

There is no definite month when a particular orchid will go to rest or begin to grow again. Watch each plant individually and you will soon get to know from your own observation

After flowering and before the new growth starts, Calanthe *pseudobulbs can be taken out of their pot and left to dry until the new growth is seen.*

whether it is growing or not. Once the season's pseudobulb has matured, having reached its full size, the growing cycle is complete. The plant is now at rest, and only when you can see a new growth extending upwards from the base is the new season commencing.

Caring for Resting Orchids

Orchids that are resting need far less water and very little feeding. Provided that the pseudobulbs remain plump, the plants can be left on the dry side. In some species of *Coelogyne*, it is normal for the pseudobulbs to shrivel slightly; this occurs naturally, but by the time the new growths are starting and normal watering is resumed, they will plump up again.

Orchids that are flowering during their resting period do not necessarily need more water. The flower spike will inevitably take energy from the pseudobulbs for its development, but this has been allowed for by the plant. Once new growth has started, it will be some time before new roots appear. Water sparingly until the growth is a few inches high, then increase the watering and commence feeding. Underwatering during the summer may cause undue shrivelling to occur the following winter, and it may be necessary to water more frequently to prevent excessive shrivelling.

Orchids that rest and lose their leaves at the same time invariably lose their old roots. With the commencement of the new growth, new roots follow and these are the most important part of the plant. Between the end of the resting period and the new growth starting is a good time to repot, catching the plant just before the new roots are made. This is better than potting at the beginning of the resting period, which is the wrong time to disturb the plant.

Thunias are among the very few orchids that produce an autumn display when their leaves change colour before being shed. The leafless canes remain dormant for the winter.

After their winter's rest, thunias commence their new growth in the spring. Repot the plants as soon as this happens and before the new roots start at the base.

TEMPERATURES

It is often mistakenly thought that orchids need a constant temperature in which to grow, yet nowhere in nature does the temperature remain the same both night and day, summer and winter. Wherever orchids originate in the world, there exists a temperature fluctuation, and in cultivation orchids can withstand considerable temperature differences. Indeed, these variations are often the trigger that initiates flowering and regulates growth.

Tropical orchids can be divided into cool-growing, intermediate and warm-growing types, depending upon where the species originated. Each group has its own temperature requirements in which the plants will grow at their best. Within these three temperature bands there is a considerable variation and some overlap of the requirements of each.

Cymbidium **Isobel Saunders**

Cool-growing Orchids

The cool-growing orchids are the largest group, and these include cymbidiums from the Himalayas, odontoglossums from the Andes, and many other genera, most of which are high-altitude plants, coming from elevations as high as 2,500m (8,000ft). They are often subjected to cold nights that drop to freezing, but at high altitudes the air is thinner, and occasional frosts do them no harm.

In cultivation, we grow these orchids in a temperature band that rises from 10°C (50°F) minimum to 30°C (86°F) maximum. The minimum temperature is that experienced on winter nights, and indoors some form of artificial heating will be required to maintain that. A drop of a few degrees is not going to cause any harm, but if the winter night temperature is consistently lower by more than 3°C (5°F), the plants will suffer. Also, in colder temperatures other problems can arise, such as moulds and damp spots on the orchids.

The summer daytime maximum should not exceed 30°C (86°F), which is a comfortable temperature for the orchids. Above this, the plants will inevitably become stressed, and growth will slow down and may even come to a stop. Overheating can be difficult to prevent in a greenhouse and needs to be controlled by sufficient ventilation, shading and damping down. Daytime temperatures should always be significantly higher than those at night, and in winter there should be a rise in temperature of at least 6°C (10°F).

ABOVE *A maximum/minimum thermometer is a vital piece of equipment if you are growing orchids in a greenhouse.*

Where temperatures hardly rise during the daytime, humidity naturally rises, and an imbalance occurs that will result in rots and moulds. Orchids dislike being cold and wet, but they also cannot tolerate the other extreme of being hot and dry.

Intermediate Orchids

The intermediate orchids, which include the showy cattleyas and the handsome, shade-loving paphiopedilums, require a winter night-time temperature that is 3°C (5°F) higher, giving a minimum of 13°C (55°F) at night. Wherever possible, there should be a higher temperature by day, but this should not exceed

ORCHID TEMPERATURE GUIDE

ORCHID TYPE	Minimum temperature	Maximum temperature
Cool-growing such as cymbidiums and odontoglossums	winter night 10°C (50°F) winter day 20°C (68°F)	summer night 13°C (55°F) summer day 30°C (86°F)
Intermediate-growing such as cattleyas and paphiopedilums	winter night 13°C (55°F) winter day 20°C (68°F)	summer night 13°C (55°F) summer day 30°C (86°F)
Warm-growing such as phalaenopsis	winter night 18°C (64°F) winter day 21°C (70°F)	summer night 18°C (64°F) summer day 32°C (90°F)

30°C (86°F). Again, temperatures on either side of these recommendations will cause the plants considerable stress, and over a prolonged period can cause their eventual demise. Summer night-time temperatures should remain at around 13°C (55°F) with no electric heating in the greenhouse. To achieve the higher temperature required on winter nights, you will need to provide heat for longer than is necessary with the cooler-growing types.

Phalaenopsis
San Luca

Warm-growing Orchids

The warm-growing orchids include the popular phalaenopsis, and ideally they should be grown at a minimum winter night temperature of 18°C (64°F), with a summer day maximum of 32°C (90°F). However, in indoor conditions, where the atmosphere is naturally drier than in a greenhouse, they seem to do well at temperatures that are closer to those of the intermediate orchids.

If you are growing your orchids indoors, you can usually find various positions around the home to suit these different temperature-range plants. A useful piece of equipment is a maximum/minimum thermometer, or even several, which can be placed close to the orchids and the temperatures noted. In a greenhouse, it becomes difficult to grow orchids from these three ranges together in one place. What suits one group will not suit another, and you will find that inevitably some orchids will suffer from being too cold or too warm. An ideal

Coelogyne massangeana

situation is to divide a greenhouse into two or three sections, depending upon which orchids you wish to grow. Very small greenhouses are unsuitable because the sections created will be very small and the temperatures extremely difficult to manage. Ideally, two or three small greenhouses where the various temperature-range orchids can each be given their ideal would be best, but this is rather an extravagant option for the home grower.

LIGHT LEVELS

Orchids are shade-loving plants, and while they are growing they need the equivalent of the dappled sunlight they would receive growing in the tree canopy of their natural home. Too much light during the summer will harm the plants by turning the foliage a light green-yellow. In more severe cases, direct sun will burn the leaves, causing black areas where the sun's rays have destroyed the leaf cells. Insufficient light, on the other hand, will create dark green leaves that can become over-extended and limp. The aim should be to give your orchids just enough light to produce a good mid-green, healthy foliage and pseudobulbs that will develop flower spikes at the right time.

Light Levels in Winter

In winter, most orchids, with the exception of the phalaenopsis and paphiopedilums, can take all the light that is available. This will ensure that

sufficient ripening of the pseudobulbs takes place, which is also an important factor in their flowering.

Orchids grown indoors have less light available, and the orchids will only receive this from one direction, so the dangers of giving too much light is not so great a problem. During the winter, it can be a disadvantage if plants are not getting enough light, and it can be difficult to increase this through the window area.

LEFT Growing lights are seldom used by growers in greenhouses but are helpful for plants in dark corners in the home.

Moving the orchids to a lighter area for winter may be the answer, provided that their temperature requirements remain the same. Alternatively, electric lighting, using horticultural fluorescent or high-output tubes above the orchids, may be the answer. However, this system requires a considerable financial outlay and attention to detail to be satisfactory. It works well in colder climates and is used in northern North America with success.

In a greenhouse or heated conservatory, it becomes easier to control light levels, and in the winter the orchids will benefit from full light with no risk of burning from the sun's weak rays. At this time, the glass should be cleaned of any paint shading or green algae to ensure that the orchids receive all the available light. This will also add considerably to the temperature on sunny days, thus saving on the artificial heating.

ABOVE *The variegated foliage of* Vanilla planifolia *var.* variegata *shows in its different shades of green. It needs good light in a greenhouse.*

ABOVE *Orchids growing on a windowsill need to have sufficient light, but must not stand in direct sun during the summer when their leaves will burn.*

RIGHT *Cymbidium Bethlehem 'Ridgeway' is a free-flowering plant which needs plenty of light all year.*

By early spring, as the sun's power gains daily, you need to be careful that the leaves do not get burnt. Shading needs to be put in place early enough so that this does not happen. Shading will also control the temperature, which can rise dramatically, especially in a small greenhouse. Whichever system of shading you use, ideally you should not be able to see the shadow of your hand on the plants when the sun is directly above. If you can see a shadow, the shading is insufficient for the summer.

Light Levels in Summer

Light control in summer is balanced with ventilation, because both factors are used to control the temperature. Those orchids that are placed out of doors at this time will naturally receive as much light as they need, but always in the shade.

Failure to Flower

When an otherwise large and healthy plant fails to bloom in the appropriate season, the causes can only be light and temperature. There is no such thing as a barren orchid that will not flower. Given the right environment, it will produce blooms, because it is the most natural thing for the plant to reproduce itself. One that is growing too well and is extremely healthy can be lazy and sometimes fail to flower. In natural conditions, some plants get too much light and are badly scorched but still produce an abundance of flowers. As gardeners, we are simply trying to get the best of both worlds and to produce a strong, healthy-looking plant with a good display of blooms. By carefully controlling the temperature and light, it is possible

to produce flowers on all your orchids in their regular season. It is harder to achieve this in a mixed collection because individual plants will vary in exactly what they need to induce flowers.

As most amateur collections consist of a selection of "one-off plants", it is helpful to find out the requirements of each orchid. Even in the smallest greenhouse, plants hung higher and closer to the light are more likely to bloom than those lower down on the benches, where it can be just a little too dark and warm. An orchid that fails to bloom in what you consider to be perfect growing conditions need only be moved to the opposite end of the greenhouse to induce it to flower in its season.

ABOVE *The foliage of paphiopedilums can be plain green or patterned. All paphiopedilums require shady conditions.*

MAINTAINING PLANTS AT A CERTAIN SIZE

Whether you are growing your orchid collection in a limited area indoors or in a spacious greenhouse, sooner or later the plants will outgrow their accommodation or become too large to handle easily. This does not usually apply to the monopodial phalaenopsis, however, whose vertical growth is self-regulating. Similarly, although vandas and related orchids can become extremely tall, they rarely create difficulties in terms of headroom. It is mainly the sympodial orchids (those that produce new growths from the base of the previous ones) that cause the most problems. These orchids will spread themselves out over the surface area of the pot and beyond. Some of the coelogynes and encyclias can increase their size in an incredibly short number of years. The small plant acquired in a 10cm (4in) flower pot, which fitted neatly into the one small space left on the ledge, will, after a year or two, require repotting into a larger pot, and before very long it will no longer fit into the allotted space. In time, this neat little plant may grow to giant proportions, and even though it may have been described as a miniature type, when grown to its full size it may be small of stature in height but not in width.

Certain orchids, among them the miniature coelogynes, such as *Coelogyne fimbriata*, and bulbophyllums, including *Bulbophyllum roxburgii*, can be contained in their original pot for several years, even though they will produce numerous new growths. The trick here is to peg down the new growths within the confines of the pot as they grow, carefully pushing them down in between or on top of the existing pseudobulbs. Do this with a small bent piece of plastic-coated wire, rather like a hair pin. This becomes quite easy with those orchids that have an extended rhizome between the pseudobulbs, but take care not to snap the growth by bending it back too far. In time, the plant will grow into a compact mound of pseudobulbs that take up no more room and create a denser display of blooms.

Alternatively, where small-size plants are growing in baskets suspended in the greenhouse, the new growths can be allowed to encircle the pot or basket in which the plant is growing. This is where plastic net-pots, which are often used for aquatic plants, can be ideal. This method will also work well with plants in square wooden baskets. These orchids can be grown on without too much disturbance for many years without taking up any more room than when they first arrived.

Where you suspect that the compost (growing medium) has deteriorated, try gently pushing down new growths that are growing proud of the pot surface.

LEFT *If you do not wish to leave the plants to reach their full size, the alternative is to divide them up into smaller pieces. This* Coelogyne fimbriata *has been divided to produce a plant of a much more manageable size.*

Carefully insert fresh compost, in the form of fine bark chippings, or a mixture of fine bark and peat, in between the pseudobulbs, and tuck it in at the sides to ensure that there is some fresh compost for the new roots to grow into.

Repotting and Dividing

The alternative to keeping your orchids whole, but containing their growth, is to divide them up into smaller pieces. This is regularly done with orchids and is a most successful way of reducing the size of a plant. However, with the smaller-growing species, it is often not until they reach a certain size that their full potential and true beauty can be seen. A single bloom on a small plant very often cannot convey what the same plant would look like when enshrouded in a multitude of exquisite blooms. Specimen plants will also remain in bloom for a much longer period, as not all the individual flowers will open at once.

Sometimes plants have to be divided where they have grown out in various directions, leaving a dead centre in the middle of the pot that cannot be disguised. When this happens, the best remedy is to remove the whole plant from the pot and divide the pieces into single plants, discarding the dead pseudobulbs at the centre. You are then left with several plants, each of which is probably the size of the original purchase. You now have a number of replicas to swap with your friends or to give away as gifts. Many a new orchid enthusiast has been enrolled in just this way!

Where you have the room, and you are happy to watch your plants increase in size and flowering ability over the years, there is no grander sight than a very large orchid frothing over with flowers developed from heaps of pseudobulbs piled high. The delightful and effervescent *Coelogyne cristata* is just such a plant. If you have this species in your collection, given a free hand it can grow to monumental proportions.

Specimen Plants

Wherever possible, specimen plants are always worth retaining intact. It seems a little unfair, when a plant has done its absolute best to grow well to reduce it to a mere seedling that has to start all over again. Often, there can be one place in the home or greenhouse where a single specimen plant can be accommodated in solitary splendour, on a side table in a light corner or a special place in the conservatory or living room. Often it is easier to find space indoors than in the greenhouse, where the temptation is always to cram a few more plants in, which is not always the best idea.

Growing to specimen size is not always possible, however, with large-growing orchids such as cymbidiums. Here, regular repotting and dividing remains the best way to keep them to a reasonable size, when they can be more easily managed and maintained. By removing the oldest, leafless pseudobulbs and retaining the newer, leafed part of the plant, you can ensure that it will always look attractive and continue to bloom regularly.

CALENDAR OF CARE

ABOVE *Scale insects can adhere firmly to the leaf surface, and need to be removed by gentle scrubbing with a toothbrush dipped in denatured alcohol. Rinse in water.*

ABOVE *Nozzles fitted at intervals along the rail will give a misting of very fine water droplets. A burst of water for just a few seconds is sufficient to raise the humidity and cool the greenhouse.*

SPRING

This is the time when the orchids which have been resting all winter start their new season's growth. Many are also flowering.

Commence **watering** regularly and give light **feeding** at every third watering.

In the greenhouse put up the **shading** and increase the **humidity** by **damping down** more often as the temperature rises during the day.

Check for **insect pests**, which will start to become more active now.

Train flower spikes that need extra **support** with a bamboo cane.

Repot as necessary, either as the new growth starts or after flowering.

SUMMER

Keep an eye on the **temperatures** to ensure that your orchids are not getting too hot during the day. If you prefer, take the plants out of the **greenhouse** and place out-of-doors in a **shady** position. Keep well watered and increase the **feed** to once every other watering.

Remove any old flower spikes after the flowers have finished.

Keep a watch for **slugs and snails** and other pests, which will be more active.

Maintain a good **humidity** around the plants left in the greenhouse and **spray** leaves.

If necessary increase the **shade** over the orchids.

ABOVE When looking for mealy bug check the undersides of the leaves where this pest prefers to live. Within a short time, an unchecked colony can lead to an infestation.

ABOVE These Pleione pseudobulbs have remained dormant all winter. The leaves and roots have died away while the pseudobulbs remain as a food store until the spring.

AUTUMN

Return orchids summering out of doors to their **winter** quarters before the first frosts appear.

Check plants over for any **pests** and clean them up before taking them back indoors.

Repot any **young seedlings** or propagations which need it by **dropping on** into a larger pot.

As the sun's power lessens **remove shading** so that the plants can receive full light for the winter.

Pick up all **discarded leaves** as they are shed.

Gradually give less **water** and allow plants to dry out between waterings.

WINTER

Allow orchids that are **resting** to remain dry. Give an occasional watering if the **pseudobulbs** shrivel.

Look for **flower spikes** on many of the orchids and protect them from **slugs and snails**.

Check **temperatures** at night and if necessary provide more **heat** in the coldest periods.

Avoid cold and damp conditions which will encourage **fungal spores**, particularly on the flowers.

Indoors, give your orchids as much **light** as possible, but keep them away from **heat** from radiators or other appliances.

Phalaenopsis and **paphiopedilums** growing indoors need to be kept **watered** and lightly **fed**. These orchids do not have a resting period, but their growth will slow during this time.

COMMON PROBLEMS

Compared with other plants, orchids suffer few problems, although those described here can sometimes occur. From the start, make a habit of practising good hygiene in the greenhouse, for example, by sweeping up dead leaves and other plant material from the floor. This will help in the control of the pests and diseases described here.

PESTS

There are not many pests that will attack orchids, and these are unlikely to gain a hold or reach epidemic proportions where good growing conditions are practised. Most pests are more likely to be encountered in a greenhouse, where the warm, humid conditions are ideal for slugs and snails, for example.

In the home, where there is a much drier environment, it is the smaller, gregarious insects and mites such as red spider mite that might make an appearance. You need to be aware of these pests and to look out for them. More importantly, you need to be able to identify the damage done, which is often the first indication that you have a problem.

Over the years, many dangerous chemicals have been used to eradicate pests, but today less drastic controls are available, which do much less harm to the environment and to ourselves.

Aphids

These include the extremely common and often troublesome greenfly as well as whitefly and blackfly, which are so common in gardens during the summer. Greenfly will be attracted to the softer parts of orchids, such as the very young growths of soft-leaved types like lycastes and pleiones, and the buds of all orchids. They are easily seen, and the observant grower will never allow them to build up into large infestations, which they can do in an extremely short time. When first spotted, this pest can be washed off with tepid water. Fill a bowl with water, add a little insecticidal soap, then immerse the affected part of the plant, swilling it around in the water until all the insects have been dislodged. Alternatively, you can use a cottonbud (swab) to remove them individually, or use an aerosol spray designed for the job. If you are removing aphids from buds, take care not to

LEFT *Aphids can build up into large colonies within a few days. Their sap-sucking activities can distort young growing buds and cause them to abort. Watch out for this pest on young growths and roots as well.*

break any of the buds. Where the pest has remained undetected for some time, it will have caused damage by sucking the sap. Unfortunately, as the buds continue to grow, so does the disfigurement, and when the flowers eventually open, large blotches will show up where the aphids have been. In some cases, the flowers will also appear to be crippled and will not open fully.

Although aphids may be easier to detect and control, they are persistent and can very quickly return, being rampant in the garden during the summer. They need to be watched out for on an almost daily basis: if allowed to breed for just a week there will be a hundred where there was one. Aphids are also responsible for the formation of sticky honeydew, which they excrete. Left on the leaves, this soon becomes infected with a sooty mould. Ants will find aphids and milk them for this honeydew. They will also remove some insects from one place and transport them to another to start a new colony. If you discover ants travelling up and down your flower spikes, find out what they are doing there.

Bees and Mice

These can be classified as pests because they take pollen from the flowers, rendering them useless, for without their pollen intact the flowers will die within one or two days. This is particularly disheartening to the grower when it concerns flowers that are expected to last for several weeks.

The bees will enter a greenhouse from outside, removing pollen as they leave the flowers where they have searched unsuccessfully for nectar. Prevent bees from entering your greenhouse by covering the ventilator

ABOVE *Mealy bug can easily be seen with the naked eye on this* Phalaenopsis *flower spike. It is often found in the axils of leaves or flower spikes, and particularly on new growths.*

ABOVE *A small paintbrush dipped in denatured alcohol is being used to clean mealy bug on this* Phalaenopsis *spike. On new growths, rinse off with water to prevent burning the leaves.*

space with a fine-gauge netting. Remember to do the same to the doorway if this is left open during hot weather.

Mice find orchid pollen particularly attractive as a good source of food. If you suspect you have mice, which will come in from outside as the weather gets cold in winter, lay humane traps and be sure to release them well away from the greenhouse.

ABOVE *Hang up fly catchers in the green-house to catch the small moss flies that can be a nuisance. Their grubs will hatch in the compost (growing medium) and attact the tips of roots. The fly catchers take the form of yellow plastic strips.*

Mealy Bugs

These insects are larger than aphids and therefore more easily seen. They measure about 3mm (⅛in) long. They have soft, pink bodies and cover themselves in a white, cotton-wool-like substance, which gives a clear indication of their presence. They tend to congregate at the base of leaves and in axils on dendrobiums, among others. The damage caused is similar to that done by scale insects, showing up as ugly yellow patches where they settle. Treat this pest in the same way as scale insects. Being slightly more mobile than scale insects, mealy bugs will move on to developing flower spikes, causing harm to buds and flowers alike.

Moss Flies

These breed in the compost (growing medium), which their minute, whitish larvae cause to break down. The grubs will attack seedling roots, but on adult plants are more of a nuisance than a pest. You will see the flies take flight when plants are disturbed. Once a colony has become established, it can breed rapidly into large numbers during the summer. The problem is eliminated by breaking the breeding cycle. To do this, stand the affected plant in a bucket of water so that the water level reaches the rim of the pot in order to drown the grubs. You can leave it there for half an hour without harming the plant.

To control the adult flies, particularly with windowsill orchids, place a few insectivorous plants, such as butterworts (*Pinguicula* spp) and sundews (*Drosera* spp), close to the orchids. These are bog plants and so need to stand in shallow dishes of water at all times. No fertilizer should be used, because this will kill them. Their sticky leaves will catch any moss flies and small midges, making this is an efficient and natural method of control.

Red Spider Mite

This pest will attack most orchids, but in particular the softer-leaved dendrobiums, lycastes and coelogynes, as well as cymbidiums. Individually, they are extremely small, but they can just about be seen with the naked eye, although more easily with a magnifying glass. This will show a yellowish mite, moving across the underside of the leaf surface. Breathing on the leaf will make it speed up, and you may be surprised at how many you can find in a small area. These are sap-sucking mites, which cause a silvery-white film to appear on the leaf where they have killed the leaf cells. In time, an infection creeps into

LEFT Cymbidium *leaves should be green on the undersides. A silvery white speckling as on the leaf on the right shows the damage caused by red spider mite.*

these areas, turning the damaged patches black. Where there is a large infestation, you will see a very fine webbing stretching across the leaf surface. These mites are most active in warm weather and breed fastest in warm, dry conditions. They get on to plants indoors as well as outdoors. In bad cases, they will cause premature foliage loss. You can do much to avoid getting red spider mite on your orchids by regularly spraying the foliage on the undersides as well on top with water. Cymbidiums summering outdoors, for example, can be hosed daily underneath and between the leaves.

Another method of control is to use a systemic insecticide, but take care to read the manufacturers' instructions regarding its safe use. The insecticide will render a plant poisonous and eradicate not only the adult mites but also the new generations that will hatch about ten days later. Alternatively,

use an insecticidal soap, wiping each leaf in turn. This is a contact killer that will destroy adults but may leave eggs unharmed, so repeat after ten days.

False Red Spider Mite

This is a similar pest, which attacks the fleshier leaves of phalaenopsis and paphiopedilums, causing pitting and yellowing of both surfaces. Looked at under the magnifying glass, this pest is similar in appearance to red spider mite. You can get rid of it in the same way as treating the more common red spider mite, but destruction to leaf surfaces cannot be repaired, and a plant has to be grown out of the disfigurement.

Scale Insects

These can take on a variety of forms, but all adults cover themselves with a scale-like shell, which may be soft or hard, white or brown, and usually round or oval-shaped. There is also a woolly scale,

RIGHT *A soft-leaved* Dendrobium *species has become badly affected by red spider mite, which is causing large, white patches and premature leaf loss.*

RIGHT *A bad infestation of scale insects on this* Cattleya *has killed some leaves and badly affected others. It will take much vigilance to eradicate a pest that has got such a hold on a plant.*

this pest is present, it will settle on almost any orchid. The damage is caused when it pierces the leaf surface, which results in unsightly yellow patches. After a while, the scales will move on to another orchid.

If you suspect scale insects on cattleyas or other orchids that protect their pseudobulbs with sheaths, strip these away and you may be surprised at what you find. What appeared to be a few scales around the edge of the sheathing can be the tip of an iceberg, with many more lurking beneath. Remove the pests by washing them off with an insecticidal soap. You may need to use an old toothbrush to dislodge the scale, but do not scrub so hard that you damage the leaf further. An old remedy that was always recommended was to wipe the leaves with denatured alcohol, which kills on contact, but you need to dislodge the shell. Once the visible culprits have been dealt with, treat the plants with systemic insecticide on a regular basis until you can be sure that successive generations have been killed.

Scale insects are more active in the spring and summer, but in a warm greenhouse will continue to breed throughout the winter. They sometimes excrete a honeydew, which in turn will attract ants to "milk" them, in the same way as they do aphids. This honeydew will grow sooty moulds, which can further disfigure the leaf.

Slugs and Snails

These troublesome pests are always with us and can only be kept at bay by constant vigilance. They are likely to be most often encountered in a greenhouse, where conditions are ideal for their survival. The smaller garlic snails can do considerable harm by eating through root tips. The larger varieties, and all sizes of slugs, will eat roots and

which looks similar in appearance to mealy bug but spreads itself more widely over a leaf surface. When eggs hatch, the larval stage is extremely small and relatively fast-moving. When mature, the adults settle down in one position on the leaf under their dome-shaped shell where the eggs are laid, and

at this stage they are quite easy to spot. Some will congregate in large colonies, while others are almost solitary, spacing themselves out well. Various kinds will live on the leaf surface, mostly on the undersides or out of sight beneath the sheaths on cattleyas, which are particularly prone to scale insect attacks. Where

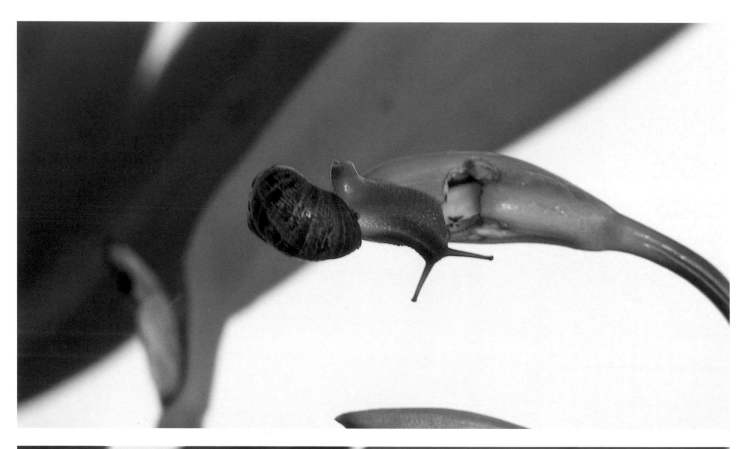

LEFT *Garden snails of all sizes will attack the softest parts of orchids, such as this* Cattleya *bud, particularly the buds and root tips. This pest is more prevalent in a greenhouse, where moisture encourages them to breed.*

RIGHT *A harmless method of catching small slugs and snails is to place slices of apple on the compost (growing medium). The pests congregate underneath the apple and can be picked up in the morning.*

chew into new growths and developing pseudobulbs, often causing a great wound in a single night. Search for these pests after dark with a torch, shining it through the sheaths of *Cymbidium* flower spikes. There are many forms of slug and snail control, but if you want to use non-chemical methods, keep one or two toads in the greenhouse or conservatory as natural predators. Try placing slices of apple around your plants where you suspect these pests are lurking, and the next morning turn each one over. You may be surprised at the numbers of garlic snails that have gathered there to feast on the apple.

Pseudobulbs that have been eaten through will excrete a gluey substance with which to fill the hole. If left untreated, a rot can set into the damaged area, leading to the loss of that season's growth. Dry the hole with a kitchen towel then pack it with horticultural sulphur. This will dry up the wound and prevent infection from setting in. The hole may heal but it will not go away, and will remain an unsightly blemish.

LEFT *Snails and slugs can cause havoc with buds, leaving large holes, which will totally disfigure the flowers when they eventually open, as this* Cattleya *bud shows.*

Weevils and Caterpillars

These leaf-chewing pests will eat large chunks from leaves and flowers in a short time. The weevils are nocturnal, spending their days buried in the compost (growing medium), which makes them particularly difficult to catch. Their grubs also inhabit the compost and harm root tips. Search for these at night while you are looking for slugs. Occasionally, they will be seen by day, as are various kinds of caterpillar. Watering the plant with a solution of insecticidal soap or BT (*Bacillus thuringiensis*) will kill the grubs. Weevils are a common outdoor pest of gardens and will find their way into the greenhouse and home. They may also be brought in on other plants, and should be constantly watched for.

Woodlice, Ants and Earwigs

These pests inhabit cool, damp, shady places, and under the staging in a greenhouse is the ideal home for woodlice. Here they will burrow into the compost (growing medium), breaking it down prematurely and causing it to clog. Ants can set up home in orchid pots, particularly in plants summering out of doors, and again will break down the compost, preventing aeration and suffocating the roots, which then die. Earwigs come into the greenhouse at the end of summer, as the outside temperature drops. They attack new root tips and settle at the base of pseudobulbs and inside cymbidium bracts. They are often found when old bracts are stripped during repotting. To eradicate these pests, water the plants with an insecticidal soap, or use a powder insecticide for that purpose.

DISEASES AND OTHER PROBLEMS

Most diseases are the result of poor cultural conditions and often appear in plants that are under stress from overexposure to light or cold. Cold, damp conditions, such as can occur during the winter if the heating system is inadequate, will cause rots, moulds and blemishes to appear.

Corrugated Leaves

An annoying problem that arises occasionally, particularly on orchids such as odontoglossums and milto-niopsis, is that of corrugated leaves. As the new growth develops, the young leaves become crippled, growing in a corrugated, disfiguring fashion. Although this is often blamed on irregular watering, where the plant has suffered from being too wet followed by too dry, it is also considered to be a genetic fault, arising from interbreeding with certain plants that appear to be prone to this. The problem cannot always be attributed to the grower, who may search in vain for a reason.

Damaged Pseudobulbs

Pseudobulbs can be affected by black watery blotches, which are usually the result of cold and damp conditions over a long period of time. When these are water-filled, you need to cut them open, drain and dry the hole, then fill it with powdered fungicide or horticultural sulphur. Splits that occur suddenly on newly maturing pseudo-bulbs can have other origins. Plants that appear to be growing well and have been fed regularly can sometimes expand their pseudobulbs so fast that

ABOVE *Botrytis (grey mould) is a fungus that appears on old flowers, or on fresh flowers where cold and damp conditions are persistent. Provide a drier atmosphere and, if necessary, increase the warmth.*

they split along their sides. This problem is particularly evident on odontoglossums and some encyclias, as well as lycastes and angulocastes, and can be caused by overfeeding. Provided the crack is kept dry and treated, if necessary, it should not become infected or result in rot.

Rot

Rot in new growths must be treated before it runs back into the main plant, resulting in its loss. Cut away the rotting growth until you get back to a healthy rhizome, then dust the cut area with horticultural sulphur to heal the wound. Black tips appearing on the ends of leaves are a sign that all is not well with your growing conditions. It may be necessary to increase the heat in winter, so check your temperatures. Cut back the black tips to green leaf, and keep the greenhouse slightly drier until you are certain that the problem has been checked. If the affected leaves continue to turn black at the cut tips, the problem has not been solved, and

it is probably an imbalance of the major factors. Check that the humidity, warmth and light are in balance to halt the problem.

Spotting

During the winter, a common fault is premature spotting of flowers. This occurs particularly during spells of damp, sunless weather. Allow the atmosphere to dry out and, if necessary, increase the heat slightly. Alternatively, bring plants that are in flower into the house, where the drier atmosphere will benefit the flowers. This is also a time when bud-drop is most likely to occur. This is due to an imbalance caused by poor conditions. It can happen indoors when the growing area is too hot and dry or the buds have been exposed to too much light.

Sunburn

Sunburn can affect all orchid foliage where direct exposure to the sun has caused a burn mark. This can be seen on the leaf surface directly where the sun has been shining on it. What starts as a whitened area, where leaf cells have been destroyed, turns brown and black as infection sets in. Usually, the area is confined to where the leaf was exposed and will not spread through the leaf. In cases where most of the foliage is affected, it is best left on the plant until the leaves drop naturally in their own time. If only one or two leaves are affected, these can be removed to aid the appearance of the plant without weakening it. Any sudden foliage loss on an evergreen orchid signals a rapid response by the plant to conditions that it has found intolerable. This could be severe cold, for example, and it is the reaction you could expect if the heating system in the greenhouse were to fail on a very cold night. Orchids affected in this way may take years to recover, if they do at all, and sometimes it is not worth trying to bring them back to good health because of the time involved.

Viruses

Poor cultural conditions, particularly during the winter months, are usually responsible for the onset of virus disease. This is the result of stress, when the weakened plant will show black spots, streaks or mottling on the leaves. Virus can also be spread to healthy plants by sap-sucking pests such as red spider mite. Around the middle of the 20th century, virus disease was especially prevalent in cymbidiums. Today, with a better understanding of how it is caused and how to prevent it occurring, it is seldom seen. However, it can appear where poor conditions exist, although an infected plant can continue to grow and flower normally. If you suspect you have a virused

LEFT Bright sunlight, polluted air, cold, wet, or lack of fresh air can cause petal blight. The flowers become blotched and marked with black. When in flower, reduce watering and keep the plants well shaded at an even temperature.

LEFT Mosaic virus leaves dark, sunken patches on the leaves. Affected plants should be destroyed. The problem can be prevented, however, by controlling the damage done by insect pests, which allows viruses to take hold.

orchid, keep it away from other plants to prevent the virus being spread by pests. Grown in isolation where it cannot infect other plants, it can continue to give pleasure for a long time. To prevent cross-infection, always sterilize any tools you use. When repotting or cutting flower spikes, sterilize knives and scissors either by passing them through a flame or dipping them into denatured alcohol.

One of the best ways to keep diseases and bacterial problems at bay is to practise good hygiene in the greenhouse and around the orchids. Collect any dead

leaves that drop off the plants. If they are left to rot underneath the staging in the damp conditions, spores will quickly be dispersed. Wherever possible, ensure that there is some ventilation inside the greenhouse. This is particularly important in the winter, when stagnant conditions can occur, particularly where the greenhouse is double-glazed and there is little air circulation. Always remove flower spikes before the dead flowers drop. These can remain undetected among the orchids, causing rots to start where they have fallen.

LEFT *This strong, healthy* Cymbidium *has plump pseudobulbs, and no surplus of leafless ones. The new growth now showing will mature into a pseudobulb that is larger than the existing ones.*

LEFT *This* Cymbidium *is overburdened with surplus pseudobulbs which should have been removed earlier. The foliage is limp and easily broken. There is healthy new growth that needs to be repotted, with the number of pseudobulbs reduced to two or three.*

TABLE OF COMMON PROBLEMS

Pest	Symptoms	Treatment
Aphids	Found on buds, flowers and new growths, causing deformities and yellowing	Wash off with water or insecticidal soap
Bees and mice	Spoiling flowers by removing pollen	Prevent entry to bees; use humane traps for mice
False red spider mites	Yellow pitting on leaf surface, particularly on phalaenopsis and paphiopedilums	Use systemic insecticide or an insecticidal soap
Mealy bugs	In leaf axils, base of plants on flower spikes; look for woolly exterior covering	Use insecticidal soap
Moss flies	Compost breaking down in pots	Drown grubs in water; use insectivorous plants
Red spider mites	Silvery patches on undersides of leaves, particularly on cymbidiums	Use systemic insecticide or an insecticidal soap
Scale insects	Yellow areas beneath bracts on cattleyas, and in leaf axils	Use insecticidal soap and dislodge the scale
Slugs and snails	Holes in pseudobulbs, flower spikes and on buds	Use slug pellets or lay down apple slices
Weevils and caterpillars	Chewed areas on soft tissue, mainly flowers and buds	Use insecticidal powder or water plants with insecticidal soap
Woodlice, ants and earwigs	Rapidly decomposing compost (growing medium)	Water pots with insecticidal soap or dust with powder

Disease/Problem	Symptoms	Treatment
Fungal disease	Spotty flowers; watery blotches on pseudobulbs	Increase warmth and reduce humidity; treat pseudobulbs with sulphur
Rots	Centre of new growth turning brown, leaves pulling away; base wet and smelling	Cut out rot and dust with sulphur
Split pseudobulbs	Particularly on odontoglossums, which split along their sides	Give less feed; dry up with sulphur
Sunburn	Large blackened areas on leaf surfaces	Increase shade
Viruses	Blackened streaks or yellowish mottling on leaves, often in a defined pattern	Improve culture and hygiene; increase heat in winter; segregate

ORCHID DIRECTORY

We have seen that the orchid family is extremely diverse and so vast that no single work can cover them all. The following section describes and illustrates those orchids that make up the most popular types grown today. Here you will find

recommendations for the beginner, challenges for the serious grower, and other orchids that may be hard to find in cultivation but that have been given a special mention to illustrate the huge differences between the flowers of this amazingly variable family. Every plant, with the exception of the native British orchids, has been grown by the authors, and the descriptions and notes are drawn from personal experience of knowing and growing these undeniably lovely plants.

Explore the world of orchids further and you will encounter many more than are listed here. In time, you will develop your own favourite varieties, and as your knowledge progresses so your orchid collection will become more specialized, housing those that appeal directly to you and that you find easiest to grow. The following selection is just a starting point from which to set out on your voyage of discovering new orchids for yourself.

Phalaenopsis Little Skipper 'Zuma Nova'

POPULAR ORCHIDS

The orchids listed here are suitable for a range of temperatures and situations. The pot sizes given are for adult plants, while the height is for adult plants that are not in flower.

BRASSIA

This small naturally occurring genus of evergreen epiphytic plants originates from Central and South America, including the West Indies. A few of the 25 species are in cultivation and there are a limited number of hybrids. Some startling results have been obtained by intergeneric breeding with odontoglossums and others in this alliance. The results are often large, dramatic flowers with soft colourings, as can be seen in the hybrid

genus *Maclellanara*, which combines *Brassia* with *Odontoglossum* and *Oncidium*.

The species are characterized by the extremely long and narrow petals and sepals, which give rise to the common name of spider orchids. The main colourings are light green and brown. The plants have oval, green pseudobulbs and usually two, though occasionally one, mid-green leaves. The flower spikes appear from the base of the leading pseudobulb in spring and carry up to a dozen flowers on two distinct planes, on arching spikes well above the foliage. The flowering time is early summer, and the flowers, which are wonderfully scented, will last for four to five weeks.

Brassias do well in the company of odontoglossums or in a mixed collection. The plants can be divided when they are

Brassia verrucosa

large enough, and propagation is from back bulbs.

Temperature: Mainly cool-growing.
Cultivation: Grow in 10–15cm (4–6in) pots of bark-based compost (growing medium) or on bark. Water all year, but more moderately in winter. Spray foliage in summer, but keep the buds and flowers dry.
Height: To 30cm (12in).

Brassia Edvah Loo 'Vera Cruz' AM/RHS
The amazingly long – 15cm (6in) or more – sepals and petals on this very fine, awarded hybrid have been produced by crossing the orange-tinted *Brassia longissima* with a further long-petalled species, *B. gireoudiana*. This plant will do best in a warm greenhouse.

Brassia Rex
This older hybrid originated in Hawaii from the green-flowered *Brassia verrucosa* and *B. gireoudiana*. The plant is heat tolerant, making it suitable for cultivation in the warmer parts of the United States and elsewhere.

Brassia verrucosa
The wonderfully long, 15cm (6in) symmetrical flowers of this easily grown species from Honduras and elsewhere ensure its continued popularity as a cool-growing plant for the home or greenhouse. The fragrant flowers appear in early summer.

Brassia Edvah Loo 'Vera Cruz' AM/RHS

Brassia Rex

CATTLEYA ALLIANCE

Cattleyas were the earliest of the showy, tropical epiphytic orchids to be grown and flowered in cultivation. The first was *Cattleya labiata*, introduced from the mountainous forests of Brazil in 1818. Cattleyas form part of a huge alliance comprising many other related orchids, the best known of the natural genera being *Laelia*, *Brassavola*, *Sophronitis* and *Encyclia*. These, and others, have been widely interbred for nearly 200 years to produce the colossal range of variously sized flowers that is available. The species in the alliance originate from Central and South America, and in the genus *Cattleya* there are about 50 species. Most of these are rare in the wild and are found in cultivation in specialist collections, where they have been raised in nurseries from selected clones.

Hybrids can be counted in their thousands, and range from miniature plants containing species of the diminutive *Sophronitis*, mostly with brightly coloured flowers in orange, yellow and red, to the large, frilled excesses of the *Brassavola* crosses. The most well known of these man-made hybrids are *Sophrolaeliocattleya*, *Brassolaeliocattleya* and *Laeliocattleya*. These names can easily be unravelled to identify the specific genera as *Sophronitis*, *Brassavola*, *Laelia* and *Cattleya*, but when more than three genera are involved, the name given to the resulting cross is personalized to one individual, making the name less clear on the label. *Potinara*, for example, is the result of crossing *Brassavola*, *Cattleya*, *Laelia* and *Sophronitis*.

With such a complex alliance, it becomes impossible to describe the typical "cattleya", although all related hybrids are loosely referred to collectively as cattleyas, whatever their make-up.

Among the *Cattleya* species are two distinct groups. These are the unifoliate, which have one leaf, and the bifoliate, which have two. All are evergreen, shedding just an occasional back leaf from time to time. These two groups are well defined in their flowers. The unifoliate species are known for the glistening beauty of their large, frilly-lipped blooms whose dominant colours are white through pink and yellow to exquisite rose-lavender and mauve shades. The bifoliate species have mostly smaller flowers, some with waxy petals and sepals and less frilly lips. Here, other colours, such as green and brown, are found, and the flowers are often heavily spotted or speckled.

Cattleyas produce mostly elongated or club-shaped pseudobulbs, often sheathed while young, with stiffened, dark green leaves. The flower buds are produced from the apex of the pseudobulb, usually encased in a protective sheath, which dries and splits to allow the developing buds to emerge. While most produce their blooms on short spikes, hybrids containing the Mexican species of *Laelia*, such as *L. anceps*, have longer flower spikes.

In most of the fragrant orchid species, the scent becomes lost with hybridizing, but among the *Cattleya* alliance, this fragrance is retained in the vast majority of hybrids, which adds to their allure.

Cattleyas are very much flowers of fashion. During the early and middle part of the last century, the goal was to breed ever larger flowers, which were worn by society ladies. For the grower, the huge heads of blooms required staking to prevent the stems from bending under their own weight. With the popularizing of the smaller flowers achieved by breeding with *Sophronitis*, and the bright colours that appeared, these more easily accommodated hybrids became an instant success with growers. Today, there is still an enormous range of flower types, with something to suit all tastes in this fabulous alliance.

Cattleyas like good light. However, the stiffened foliage is deceptive, and the early spring sunshine can quickly burn their leaves if they are not protected from direct sun. Most cattleyas have a dormant resting period, but this varies from plant to plant. It is not unusual for some to start their new growth in the autumn and continue to grow throughout the winter. The rule is to watch your plant, and when it is not actively in growth, allow it to remain on the dry side until new growth is seen.

Cattleyas make copious roots, which are a joy when they explode from the base of the newly formed pseudobulb. The thick, creeping, woody rhizome connecting the pseudobulbs often results in the development of new growths over the rim of the pot, and, when the new roots follow, this can be a problem for the grower. Although the roots will grow well outside the pot, they can become a problem when the plant is repotted, and will need to be cut back to avoid them becoming rotten. The timing is crucial: repot as soon as the new growth has developed to a stage where the new roots can just be seen, but have not grown sufficiently to be damaged. At this stage, the older roots can be trimmed back with less shock to the plant.

Brassolaeliocattleya **Dorothy Bertsch 'Buttercup'**

Brassolaeliocattleya Malworth × *Laeliocattleya* Honigmond

Temperature: Intermediate-growing.
Cultivation: Grow in pots of 15–20cm (6–8in) or less in coarse bark compost (growing medium) or Rockwool. Water well in summer, and give little water in winter. Mist foliage in summer. Keep shaded in summer, and give full light in winter.
Height: 15cm (6in) or less to 45cm (18in) and above.

Brassolaeliocattleya Mem. Dorothy Bertsch 'Buttercup'

This *Cattleya*-type hybrid has a perfect shape and form. The glistening, apricot-coloured flowers are 15cm (6in) across. Usually one, but occasionally two, flowers are produced in summer.

Brassolaeliocattleya Malworth × *Laeliocattleya* Honigmond

This fragrant, autumn-flowering hybrid is a combination of *Brassavola*, *Laelia* and *Cattleya*. All three genera have contributed something of value to this hybrid. The pink flowers are enhanced by the yellow throat at the centre of the lip.

Cattleya Andean Mist

This pure white *Cattleya* has been line-bred through successive generations of white-flowered species, such as *Cattleya mossiae* var. *alba*, to maintain the clearest colour form. One to three 10cm (4in) fragrant flowers are produced during the summer.

Cattleya Andean Mist

Cattleya skinneri

Laeliocattleya Archange

Cattleya Golden Girl
The bright orange colouring of this autumn-flowering hybrid grex has only been achieved by generations of selective breeding. This has produced a good-size bloom with a strong colour.

Cattleya skinneri
Heralded as the national flower of Costa Rica, this delightful, autumn-flowering species was first collected in Guatemala in 1838. It was discovered by the orchid hunter George Ure-Skinner, after whom it was named. Several colour forms are seen, including white. The plant has been extensively hybridized.

Laeliocattleya Archange
This large-flowered, frilly, pink hybrid shows exquisite depth of colour in the lip. These flowers appear in spring from the previous season's mature pseudobulbs.

Laeliocattleya Beaumesnil 'Parme'
The *Cattleya* parent has influenced the shape of this charming hybrid, which produces a head of two to four large, scented, yellow-centred, mauve flowers during the summer months. The flowers are compact with neat, semi-enclosed lips.

Cattleya Golden Girl

Laeliocattleya Beaumesnil 'Parme'

Laeliocattleya **Carrie Johnson**
This cream and crimson hybrid has peloric markings on the petals that repeat the lip markings. The flower shape resembles the *Laelia anceps* parent, with the blooms on a long stem. The *Laelia* influence allows the plant to be grown cool, indoors or in a greenhouse, where it blooms in late spring.

Laeliocattleya **Chit Chat 'Tangerine'**
Flocks of 5cm (2in) bright orange flowers adorn this pretty, spring-flowering hybrid, which has been raised from the brightly coloured species *Cattleya aurantiaca* from Guatemala and the equally vibrant Brazilian species *Laelia cinnabarina* and *L. harpophylla*. The latter two were crossed in 1902 to give *Laelia* Coronet.

Laeliocattleya **Gypsy Queen**
This American hybrid displays all the qualities looked for in the largest-flowered *Cattleya* alliance blooms. Gorgeously frilled, these huge, pale pink, 10cm (4in) blooms have red lips and yellow centres. They will last for a good three weeks during the summer.

Laeliocattleya **Magic Bell 'New Trick'**
These charming little flowers, 7cm (3in) across, are produced in autumn on a neat, compact plant with slender pseudobulbs and two leaves. With *Cattleya aurantiaca* in its background, giving the open shape and colouring, this hybrid is unusual for its bi-coloured petals and sepals.

Laeliocattleya **Carrie Johnson**

Laeliocattleya **Magic Bell 'New Trick'**

Laeliocattleya **Chit Chat 'Tangerine'**

Laeliocattleya **Gypsy Queen**

Sophrolaeliocattleya Jewel Box 'Dark Waters'

Laeliocattleya Pomme d'Or

Laeliocattleya Pomme d'Or

This hybrid carries smaller flowers with a fleshier texture, which are more abundant on the spike. The rich yellow colouring and red veining in the throat of the lip is a winning combination. This is a spring- and autumn-blooming plant, which lasts for a good three weeks.

Laeliocattleya Starting Point 'Unique'

The exquisite, semi-alba varieties, such as this superb, large-flowered, autumn-flowering hybrid, are hard to resist. The sharply contrasting deep purple lip is framed by the pristine white of the sepals and petals. This is a robust grower that originates from California.

Sophrolaeliocattleya Jewel Box 'Dark Waters'

Clusters of crimson, 7cm (3in) flowers adorn this variety of Jewel Box, which has been inspired by the vivid colour of the *Sophronitis*, while the shape is reminiscent of the *Laelia*. This neat grower easily becomes a specimen plant by continually "breaking double", that is, producing several new growths from one pseudobulb. The flowers appear in spring.

Laeliocattleya Starting Point 'Unique'

COELOGYNE

This is a natural genus of evergreen, epiphytic plants found over a wide area in India, China and throughout most of Malaysia. Those that are found in the Himalayas require cool house treatment and make ideal houseplants. The Malaysian types, which are often larger in growth, are suitable for a slightly higher temperature range. There is a good number of species in cultivation as well as a handful of hybrids, some made many years ago and still highly regarded.

The main colouring in this genus is pristine white with a highly decorated lip; the flowers are often accompanied by a sweet fragrance. Light tawny brown and green are also represented in the colour range. The variably sized plants produce green pseudobulbs, plump and shiny when young, wrinkled when old, which may be less than 2.5cm (1in) high, or over 15cm (6in) tall. Between these two extremes are some truly delightful plants, ideal for windowsill culture or small greenhouses. All support a pair of narrow, oval leaves and most produce their flower spikes from the young growth. The flower spikes can be extremely short and single-flowered, or long and drooping, with a chain of up to two dozen blooms. Coelogynes bloom during late winter and spring, and all are well worth growing.

Coelogynes have well-defined growing and resting periods. Some shrivelling of the pseudobulbs usually occurs during dormancy, which is normal, but they should plump up again when the plant resumes its growth. A number of the species are ideal for growing on into specimen plants – including *Coelogyne cristata*, which can grow to huge proportions – and massive plants are often seen at shows throughout the spring, supporting a frothing mass of effervescent, stunning white flowers.

Coelogyne corymbosa

Temperature: Cool- to intermediate-growing.
Cultivation: Grow in 7–15cm (3–6in) pots depending on the species. Water and feed regularly from spring onwards as the new growth appears. Reduce watering as winter approaches. Keep well-shaded in summer and give full light in winter.
Height: 15–45cm (6–18in).

Coelogyne asperata

This large-growing species from Malaya can reach a height of 60cm (2ft), although the flowers appear on shorter, arching flower spikes. The straw-yellow flowers, which reach 7cm (3in) in diameter, smell strongly of liquorice. This summer-flowering species requires warm house treatment, where it needs plenty of headroom and requires very little rest.

Coelogyne corymbosa

Attractive, pristine white flowers are produced in profusion on this modestly sized species from Darjeeling. The flower spikes arch low beneath the foliage, making it an ideal subject for basket culture. This high-altitude, cool-growing plant blooms in early summer.

Coelogyne asperata

Coelogyne cristata 'Glacier Mint'

Coelogyne cristata var. *alba*

Coelogyne cristata var. *alba*

The lovely, pure white form of the species has no colour adornment at all. The plant grows from a longer rhizome than the type, which results in a rather untidy appearance. It flowers in spring.

Coelogyne cristata 'Glacier Mint'

Undoubtedly one of the most popular of the species suitable for the cool greenhouse or the indoor grower. Left to its own devices, the plants can become huge, resulting in a breathtaking display of brilliant white, 5cm (2in) flowers in early spring. It originates from the Himalayas.

Coelogyne dayana

Coelogyne flaccida

Coelogyne dayana

In summer, the downward-spiralling flower spike carries numerous 4cm (1½in) flowers, which are exquisitely marked in light and dark brown. The plant is tall and slender and needs to be grown in the intermediate greenhouse with good winter light. This species comes from Borneo.

Coelogyne flaccida

Masses of pendent flower spikes adorn this species. The 2.5cm (1in), ivory white blooms are fragrant and produced from the new growths in early summer. The plant is 20cm (8in) tall, and originates from the Khasi Hills in East India. Grow it indoors or in a cool greenhouse.

Coelogyne Green Dragon 'Chelsea' AM/RHS

This is one of the very few really good hybrids within this genus. The dramatic 7cm (3in) flowers have horizontally held green petals that contrast with the black lacing on the lip. The parents are *Coelogyne massangeana* and the apple green *C. pandurata*, which are both warm-growing species from Borneo. The hybrid blooms during the spring and summer.

Coelogyne Intermedia

This plant needs good light all year round and a dry period during the winter while it is resting. It blooms in the spring at the beginning of the growing season. The delicate, white flowers, on a drooping flower spike, last for three to four weeks.

Coelogyne lawrenceana

This species from South-east Asia produces its striking 6cm (2½in), yellow-green flowers on short sprays. The sepals are thin and ribbon-like, but the white lip is large and richly coloured at the centre. It is sequential-flowering, producing its blooms over a long period during summer.

Coelogyne **Green Dragon 'Chelsea' AM/RHS**

Coelogyne Intermedia

Coelogyne lawrenceana

Coelogyne ochracea

Coelogyne **Memoria William Micholitz 'Burnham' AM/RHS**

A combination of the species *Coelogyne lawrenceana* and *C. mooreana* has resulted in this striking hybrid, which produces its flowers in succession from a long spike. The large blooms are pristine white with a deep golden lip, and appear in spring.

Coelogyne mooreana **'Brockhurst' FCC/RHS**

Awarded in 1906, this species is represented by propagations of a single clone from an importation from Vietnam at that time. At 7cm (3in), the flowers are the largest of the white-flowered coelogynes, at their best when blooming in spring. Some hybridizing has been done with this cool-growing species.

Coelogyne ochracea

A compact growing species from Nepal with prettily marked, 2.5cm (1in), white flowers, yellow in the centre, which are produced on upright flower spikes above the pseudobulbs. The flowers are strongly scented and appear from the new growth in spring. Grow cool and rest in winter.

Coelogyne velutina

Long spikes of cream flowers, with brown streaked lips, tumble from the base of this robust Malayan species, which likes a warm greenhouse with good winter light. It produces a plant that is 60cm (2ft) tall and requires plenty of room to grow. It does well in a hanging basket.

Coelogyne Memoria William Micholitz 'Burnham' AM/RHS

Coelogyne mooreana 'Brockhurst' FCC/RHS

Coelogyne velutina

CYMBIDIUM

Species of *Cymbidium* are surprisingly few in number when one considers the tens of thousands of hybrids that have been raised over a period of 100 years. Of the 50 or so species widely distributed throughout Asia, it was hardly more than half a dozen from the Himalayan regions of India and Nepal that became the building blocks for the first hybrids. Those once considered to be the main species in this natural genus are *Cymbidium insigne*, *C. lowianum*, *C. eburneum* and *C. tracyanum*, all cultivated for their showy flowers. Once hybrids began to appear, the species became less attractive to growers, who were looking for improved shape and size. The species, once so plentiful, were often disposed of in favour of the new hybrids, until they were hardly represented in collections. Today there is renewed interest in these and other species, which are considered rare collectors' items, and the finest clones are much sought after.

For the beginner and amateur grower who is not looking to build up a specialist collection of these species, the modern hybrids represent a much better purchase. The hybrids come in a multitude of colours and sizes to suit all situations, and the flowers will last for months rather than weeks. While the first hybrids were all spring-flowering, further breeding lines developed later from alternative species such as *Cymbidium ensifolium*, *C. floribundum*, *C. devonianum* and *C. madidum*, with which the flowering season has been extended to cover most of the year. Some growers concentrate entirely on this one genus, finding that they are continually able to add variation to their collection because they never exceed the choice available.

Cymbidiums are tall-growing plants with several long, strap-like leaves and sheathed pseudobulbs. The plants can grow to 1m (3ft) tall, with flower spikes above the foliage on the standard varieties but shorter on the miniature types. The flower spikes, which are mostly staked upright, can become top heavy so they need to be supported to prevent them snapping under the weight of the buds. A dozen or more blooms are produced, some of which are delicately scented.

Cymbidiums need regular repotting to prevent them becoming overburdened with leafless pseudobulbs. These are the older, back bulbs that have shed their leaves but remain alive for a few more years, supporting the main plant. When there are more out of leaf than in leaf, the older back bulbs will become a drain on the plant and restrict its progress. These should be cut off at repotting time and can be propagated from if wished. Often, the main plant can return to the same size pot when its pseudobulbs are reduced in this way. Large plants can be divided, provided that each piece contains at least one new growth and three supporting pseudobulbs. Repot in the spring as soon as the plant has finished flowering. Cymbidiums grow throughout the year, but more slowly during the winter in balance with the shorter days and colder nights.

Cymbidiums are easily obtainable from various outlets when they are in flower, but beginners to orchid growing often find that they are unable to flower the plants again the following year. The most common cause of this is lack of light, particularly when the plants are being grown indoors. Placing them out of doors for the summer will ensure that the plants receive all the light they require and, as a result, will produce a fine display of blooms in their next season.

Cymbidium **Bethlehem 'Ridgeway'**

Do not allow the plants to stand in the direct midday sun, which will badly scorch their leaves. Give them a shady spot in the garden where they will catch the early morning or late evening sun.

Cymbidiums are grown the world over for the pot-plant trade, as well as for the cut-flower trade. Where they can be grown outdoors all year round, such as in California and parts of Australia, they represent a multi-million pound industry.

The original species from which the hybrids have come are evergreen epiphytic or terrestrial plants. Because of their large size, the hybrids are grown in pots.

Temperature: Cool-growing.

Cultivation: Grow in pots, at least 15cm (6in) in diameter, of coarse bark or Rockwool. Water and feed all year, but in winter allow the plants to dry out partially between waterings. Mist in summer. Keep in good light, but shade from direct sun in summer to prevent leaf scorch.

Height: To 1m (3ft).

Cymbidium Bethlehem 'Ridgeway'

This fine variety of a well-known hybrid is a free-flowering plant which needs plenty of light all year. The white flowers are tinged with pink, with dark pink spotting on the lip. They appear in winter, and will last for eight to ten weeks, produced from flower spikes which emerge from late summer onwards.

Cymbidium Bouley Bay

Bouley Bay, which flowers in winter and spring, is a modern hybrid of *Cymbidium lowianum*, the result of over 100 years of breeding. It retains the green colour.

Cymbidium Bulbarrow 'Will Stuckley' AM/RHS

This spring-flowering, yellow beauty, with its maroon lip, is a hybrid of the epiphyte *Cymbidium devonianum* from Darjeeling, and *C.* Weston Rose, which traces back to *C. insigne*. The size has increased from a 2.5cm (1in) bloom in one generation.

Cymbidium Bouley Bay (left) and *C. lowianum* (right)

Cymbidium devonianum (left) and *C.* Bulbarrow 'Will Stuckley' AM/RHS (right)

Cymbidium Cherry Blossom 'Profusion'

Cymbidium Cotil Point

Cymbidium Embers 'Yowie Bay'

Cymbidium **Cherry Blossom 'Profusion'**
This is a miniature type achieved by
crossing the species *Cymbidium
erythrostylum* and *C. pumilum* (now
reclassified as *C. floribundum*). The plant
will reach flowering size in a 10–13cm
(4–5in) pot with flower spikes 25cm
(10in) long. The flowers, which are pale
pink with a lip heavily spotted with
darker pink, appear in winter.

Cymbidium **Cotil Point**
This fine modern hybrid, which flowers
in spring, has a perfect shape and
colouring. The rich pink has been
brought forward from *Cymbidium insigne*.

Cymbidium **Embers 'Yowie Bay'**
This is a named variety of a popular
hybrid which can be grown indoors in
good light or placed out of doors for the
summer growing season. The blooms,
produced in winter, will last for eight to
ten weeks. Water the plant all year.

Cymbidium erythrostylum

Cymbidium insigne 'Mrs Carl Holmes'

Cymbidium erythrostylum

This delightful species from Vietnam holds its lateral petals thrust forward to hug the lip. Its perfect, pristine-white blooms, which appear in autumn and winter, have produced some excellent hybrids.

Cymbidium insigne 'Mrs Carl Holmes'

Vietnam and China are the home of this tall-growing species. It grows terrestrially and produces flower spikes of up to 1.5m (5ft) long. The flowers are extremely long-lasting and vary from dark pink to white. The flowers appear in spring.

Cymbidium Jocelyn

The flowers of this *Cymbidium* hybrid will last for eight to ten weeks during the winter. The pink petals and sepals are veined, and the cream and yellow lips are blotched and edged with red. The plant should be kept in a cool position, especially at night, while it is in bloom and placed out of doors for the summer growing season.

Cymbidium Jocelyn

Cymbidium **Lady McAlpine**

Cymbidium Lady McAlpine

The white flowers of this spring-flowering orchid have been influenced by the species *Cymbidium eburneum*, which, when crossed with *C. lowianum*, gives the red lip. This is a large-growing, standard-type hybrid that begs a grand setting.

Cymbidium Loch Lomond

This beautiful, modern hybrid, which flowers in winter, can trace its ancestry back to *Cymbidium lowianum*. The large green petals and china-white lip with a red horseshoe are characteristic of this line of breeding.

Cymbidium Maureen Grapes 'Marilyn'

This summer-flowering, highly fragrant variety produces its flower spikes in succession. As one finishes, the next buds are just opening; this greatly extends the flowering season through several months.

Cymbidium **Loch Lomond**

Cymbidium **Maureen Grapes 'Marilyn'**

Cymbidium **Mavourneen 'Jester' AM/RHS**
In this unusual, spring-flowering hybrid, the pink lip patterning is repeated on the petals, giving the appearance of a flower with three lips. This is called peloric marking, and becomes unstable when introduced into hybridizing.

Cymbidium **Mini Ice 'Antarctic'**
Where space is limited, this smaller-growing hybrid is ideal and will provide an abundance of green flowers, with deep red-spotted lips, during early spring. Water all year, and apply feed for most of the year.

Cymbidium **Nevada**
This specimen plant with its multiple flower spikes requires a large setting. The spikes are 1.5m (5ft) tall and the brilliant, golden yellow, non-fading flowers are 13cm (5in) across.

Cymbidium **Mini Ice 'Antarctic'**

Cymbidium **Mavourneen 'Jester' AM/RHS**

Cymbidium **Nevada**

Cymbidium **Pontiac**
An excellent modern, red hybrid with
10–12cm (4–5in) blooms which are
carried on long flower spikes in the
spring. It retains some signs of its
origins from the species *Cymbidium
tracyanum*, which is revealed by the
stripes on the petals and by the beautiful
lip patterning.

Cymbidium **Sarah Jean 'Ice Cascade'**
This is a first generation hybrid from
Cymbidium pumilum. It has small, white
flowers with yellow centres in spring.
The flowers measure 5cm (2in) across
and grow on pendent flower spikes.

Cymbidium **Sarah Jean 'Icicle'**
This spring-flowering hybrid, with its
profusion of delicate, white flowers, will
enhance any situation. Keep the plant
well watered throughout the year, but
avoid overwetting in winter. Place in a
cool room away from any source of heat
or draughts.

Cymbidium **Pontiac**

Cymbidium Sarah Jean 'Ice Cascade'

Cymbidium Sarah Jean 'Icicle'

Cymbidium Scott's Sunrise 'Aurora'
Orange is a colour not generally associated with cymbidiums, but this winter-flowering hybrid, with its red-edged lip, is coming close to a new colour breakthrough.

Cymbidium Summer Pearl 'Senna'
The erect flower spikes of greenish yellow flowers, with lips that are heavily spotted with maroon, appear between spring and autumn.

Cymbidium Summer Pearl 'Sonia'
Between spring and late summer, this lovely orchid produces erect spikes of creamy pink flowers, with lips heavily spotted with maroon.

Cymbidium tracyanum
A late summer-flowering species from Burma and Thailand, this strong-growing plant has large blooms. There are many hidden colours in this flower, but it has mainly contributed its red to hybrids.

Cymbidium Summer Pearl 'Sonia'

Cymbidium Summer Pearl 'Senna'

Cymbidium Scott's Sunrise 'Aurora'

Cymbidium tracyanum

DENDROBIUM

This is an extremely large and varied natural genus containing both deciduous and evergreen types, which are widely distributed throughout India and China, and through the Malaysian peninsula to New Guinea, Australia and New Zealand. Of the 900 or so species, nearly all are epiphytic. Vast numbers of species are in cultivation, in addition to many hybrids. For the hobby grower, the hybrids are mainly confined to the Indian species, and a wonderfully decorative range has been developed using *Dendrobium nobile* as a starting point. With the additional use of related species, hybrids have been produced in a rainbow of colours, with the beautifully rounded blooms amassed on the plant in spring. While hybridizing has been carried out with other distinct groups, only this one has achieved the pinnacle of success associated with the *D. nobile* hybrids.

Dendrobium bigibbum from northern Australia has been responsible for an astonishing variety of hybrids within its group. Numerous varieties are available, with flowers that range from powdery white, through clear yellow, green and pink to the deepest purple and mauve. Unlike the *D. nobile* types, these can be used for the cut-flower trade and are bred extensively and exclusively for this purpose. The cut blooms from plants grown in the tropical conditions of South-east Asia, as well as their native Australia, are flown around the world for sale in florists and other outlets.

Dendrobiums will not all interbreed with each other. Among the several distinct groups that are identified, only those that are closely related will hybridize. The evergreen varieties from Papua New Guinea, such as *Dendrobium canaliculatum*, for example, are incompatible with the Indian species, such as *D. densiflorum*. Between the different divisions within the genus are species that bear little

resemblance to one another. The amazing variety of form, shape and colour is one of the fascinating attractions of this genus. Hybrids apart, the diversity is huge.

Typically, dendrobiums produce short to tall pseudobulbs, which can be extremely long and thin, becoming drooping as they grow, or stout and rigidly upright. They may be leafed along their entire length, the narrowly oval, thinly textured leaves appearing diagonally, as in *Dendrobium pierardii*. Among the evergreen species, one of the most popular is *D. bigibbum*. This species has upright stems leafed to about halfway, and the foliage is more heavily textured. There are extremes, such as

D. cuthbertsonii from New Guinea, which has short, squat pseudobulbs and a single leaf. Among the deciduous types, including *D. nobile*, which becomes evergreen under cultivation, the flowers are produced in ones and twos from nodes that appear opposite the leaf bases. The large, rounded blooms are held on short stems. *D. densiflorum* and others produce a few, roundly oval, heavily textured leaves from the top portion of the squarish pseudobulbs, the blooms hanging on a dense, clustered truss. Most of the Indonesian and Australian species carry their highly specialised blooms on long sprays with up to a dozen flowers.

Dendrobium cuthbertsonii

Most dendrobiums have well-defined growing and resting periods, with new growth starting in spring at the same time as the buds are forming. They produce their growth rapidly during summer, completing it by autumn. Because most are tall-growing plants, there is a tendency to overpot. Some require more specialist culture to ensure a good flowering.

Dendrobium brymerianum

Dendrobium delicatum

Temperature: Cool- to intermediate-growing.
Cultivation: Grow in pots that restrict the roots, in bark compost (growing medium). For anchorage, weigh down the base of the pot with stones or set in a heavier container. Those with long, drooping canes can be grown epiphytically on bark. Allow good light, shading in summer only to prevent leaf scorch. Start watering gradually as soon as new growth appears in spring. Water plants of the *Dendrobium nobile* group very sparingly until the flower buds are defined, or these will develop as adventitious growths rather than as flowers. Water and feed liberally as growth speeds up. Keep all dendrobiums dry in winter.
Height: 15–45cm (6–18in).

Dendrobium brymerianum

An extremely rare, early spring-flowering species not often seen in cultivation, this orchid is a challenge to grow well. Its

deep golden yellow flowers are extraordinary for the deeply fringed, or bearded, lip. The plant is tall and slender and comes from Burma and Thailand, but is no longer imported from the wild.

Dendrobium cuthbertsonii

Among the most concise of the genus, this diminutive, spring-flowering species with short, clustered stems produces comparatively large (2cm/¾in) flowers, variously coloured pink to red, singly from the top of the cane. Rapidly gaining in popularity, the species comes from New Guinea.

Dendrobium delicatum

Long sprays of highly fragrant, densely packed, small, creamy white flowers festoon this tough, hard-caned *Dendrobium* in spring. It is at its best when allowed to grow on into a specimen plant.

Dendrobium fimbriatum var. oculatum

Dendrobium fimbriatum var. *oculatum*

This golden yellow species from India produces its flowers in spring on loose pendent trusses from the top portion of the slender, leafless canes. The deep, almost black "eye" at the centre of the lip makes a striking contrast. This once plentiful species is now considered quite rare.

Dendrobium Gatton Sunray FCC/RHS

This very old hybrid was awarded around the turn of the 20th century. The plant grows extremely tall, to 1.2m (4ft), and the large 10cm (4in) flowers are produced in early summer in loose trusses from the top part of the canes. The striking flowers are a combination of corn yellow with a deep maroon centre to the lip.

Dendrobium infundibulum

A native of India and Thailand, this lovely crystalline, white-flowered species produces its large 8cm (3in) blooms in abundance from the top portion of the black-haired, or hirsute, cane in the spring. It is an easy and rewarding species for the beginner.

Dendrobium Gatton Sunray FCC/RHS

Dendrobium infundibulum

Dendrobium kingianum

Dendrobium kingianum

A hard-caned Australian species that is of compact size, this blooms with a profusion of small 3cm (1¼in) flowers on spikes held above the foliage. The plant will grow indoors or in a cool greenhouse where it likes plenty of good light. Flowering occurs in autumn and also at other times.

Dendrobium miyakei

This rather untidy looking species from the Philippines produces its flowers in pompons along the leafless canes. The flowers are striped mauve and appear throughout the summer at various times. The plant should be grown fairly warm with good light. If the plant is grown in a basket, the canes will droop.

Dendrobium New Comet 'Red Queen'

This is one of the best examples of the breeding qualities of *Dendrobium nobile*, which has helped to produce this hybrid with its deep mauve flowers with maroon lips. The plant flowers along the whole length of the soft canes in early spring.

Dendrobium miyakei

Dendrobium New Comet 'Red Queen'

Dendrobium Seigyoku 'Queen'

Dendrobium New Guinea

New Guinea is the home to some of the most extraordinary species in this genus, and this New Guinea hybrid is one of only a few worthwhile hybrids to have emerged from this group. The nodding, deep yellow flowers are produced in spring and summer on loose trusses from the top of the hard, two-leafed canes. The flowers will last for many months in perfect condition.

Dendrobium Seigyoku 'Queen'

This lovely red-and-white *Dendrobium nobile*-type hybrid, which flowers in spring, was raised in Japan. The flowers appear in profusion on short stems.

Dendrobium victoria-regina

The attractive mauve-tinted flowers are produced in small clusters in spring from the older, leafless canes on this species from the Philippines. The warm-growing plant is deciduous in cultivation and needs a good rest in winter.

Dendrobium New Guinea

Dendrobium victoria-regina

ENCYCLIA

There are about 150 species in this easily recognizable genus, of which a great many have flowers with the lip uppermost. Many are small- or compact-growing plants that will grow into good-sized specimens. All are evergreen, epiphytic plants and most originate from Mexico. While the species are extremely popular and widely grown, there has been very little hybridizing within the genus. Some species have been used with excellent results when crossed with cattleyas or other related genera. When used for hybridizing, the genus is referred to as *Epidendrum*. Hence, a cross between *Encyclia* and *Cattleya* produces *Epicattleya*.

While the dominant colours within the genus are pale, often whitish, these flowers carry a strong fragrance. Especially lovely are *Encyclia radiata* and *E. lancifolia*. These, and others, produce good-looking plants with shiny, elongated pseudobulbs and a pair of mid-green leaves. The flowers come on short to medium, upright flower spikes between the leaves. Distinctly different is *E. vitellina* – the only species with bright vermillion flowers – which has a bluish bloom on its foliage. Further species, such as *E. nemorale*, produce hard, rounded pseudobulbs with long, stiffened leaves; their flowers are held on long spikes and their lips are at the base of the flowers. The plants bloom from spring to midsummer, and last for several weeks.

Encyclias make attractive plants for growing indoors. They are also ideal for the beginner, producing their flowers freely in their season. Most have a decided rest in the winter. A mixed collection should contain at least a few of these endearing orchids.

Temperature: Cool-growing.

Cultivation: Grow in pots or baskets of bark-based compost (growing medium). Water freely, when in active growth, and spray overhead, except when in flower. Keep shaded in summer, although those

Encyclia adenocaula

Encyclia brassavolae

Encyclia cochleata var. 'Yellow Burnham'

with hard, rounded pseudobulbs will tolerate more light. In winter, water just enough to keep the pseudobulbs plump. *Height*: 7–30cm (3–12in).

Encyclia adenocaula

This hard-bulbed type, which comes from Mexico, produces a long flower spike from the top of the rounded pseudobulb in spring and early summer. The mauve flowers have a red-and-white lip. Grow in a cool greenhouse in good light and rest in winter.

Encyclia brassavolae

This handsome species produces tall, slender pseudobulbs. The 5cm (2in), narrow-petalled, green flowers, which are carried on an upright spike, have a white, heart-shaped lip, of which the tip is dipped in rosy mauve. The plant is summer-flowering.

Encyclia lancifolia

Encyclia cochleata var. 'Yellow Burnham'

An extremely popular orchid which does well indoors and which can grow into a large plant over 30cm (12in) high. The flower spikes, with their green flowers with orange-yellow lips, are much taller, and will remain in bloom on mature plants for many months at various times of the year.

Encyclia lancifolia

This neat orchid, 15cm (6in) tall, produces upright flower spikes in summer. The 3cm (1¼in) blooms are starry and ivory-white, with a red-lined lip which is held uppermost. This is a particularly easy and delightful species to grow indoors or in a cool greenhouse.

Encyclia polybulbon
This dwarf plant with clustered pseudobulbs supports two leaves. The single 2cm (¾in) flowers come from between the leaves and cover the plant with their star-like presence. Narrow, light tawny-brown petals and sepals are set off by the large white lip. This cool-growing species flowers in early summer.

Encyclia radiata
An attractive and fragrant species from Guatemala, this makes good-looking plants, 23cm (9in) tall, that bloom freely in the summer. The flower spikes are held upright above the foliage and, like many in this genus, hold their red-lined lip at the top of the flower.

Encyclia vitellina
Of all the species in the *Encyclia* genus, this is unique for its rich orange-red colouring. The plant produces a tall, often branching, flower spike in autumn as the season's pseudobulb is completed. The plant comes from Mexico and Guatemala.

Encyclia polybulbon

Encyclia radiata

Encyclia vitellina

EPIDENDRUM

Epidendrums come in an extremely varied range of sizes, from small tufted plants of less than 15cm (6in) high with clustered, leafy stems (such as *Epidendrum porpax*), to the tall, reedy-stemmed giants of *E. revolutum* and *E. ibaquense*. The latter can attain a height of over 2m (6½ft). In between these extremes are a number of attractive plants with pseudobulbs, including *E. ciliare*, which more closely resemble the encyclias to which they are closely related and with which they were at one time combined.

Widely distributed throughout tropical America, this is a huge genus containing hundreds of species, some of them extremely similar in appearance. Of these, a good number are grown, and there are a few hybrids that are worth looking out for.

Epidendrums are evergreen epiphytic or terrestrial, and sometimes lithophytic, plants with widely varying flowers whose colours range through white, green, brown, pink and red. As a genus it is difficult to get to know, because there are so many distinctly different plants, but this makes their study more interesting. Some of the taller-growing species produce large heads of flowers which, on a large plant, become perpetually flowering, as does *Epidendrum radicans*. Members of this diverse group produce their flowers at different times, but will give a good show during the summer.
Temperature: Cool- to intermediate-growing.
Cultivation: Grow reed-types in 10–15cm (4–6in) pots or prepared beds of coarse bark and sand or peat (or an alternative), and leave undisturbed. Water throughout the year. Grow small, creeping types in small baskets or on bark supports. Water freely when in active growth, and less in winter, when overwatering can cause rotting.
Height: 15–200cm (6–78in).

Epidendrum Burtonii
This is an old-time hybrid from the species *Epidendrum radicans*, which it resembles. Note the extending flower spike where earlier orange blooms have been and the further buds developing at the tip. The flowers can appear at any time.

Epidendrum Burtonii

Epidendrum Plastic Doll
This is one of a very few hybrids developed from the *Epidendrum pseudepidendrum*. The flowers have green petals and sepals set off by a yellow, frilly lip. Several flowers are carried on the flower spike well above the foliage. Grow this plant in the intermediate to warm greenhouse where there is sufficient headroom.

Epidendrum Plastic Doll

Epidendrum pseudepidendum var. *album*

Epidendrum radicans

Epidendrum radicans

Tall, branching stems that produce aerial roots freely along their length typify this species which flowers at any time of the year. Its red flowers have their lip at the top of the flower and are borne on ever-growing flower spikes, which are an extension of the stems; a large plant becomes perpetually blooming.

Epidendrum radicans var. alba

In this white form of the species from Mexico, the flowers lack the bright red pigmentation. The plants are usually smaller growing, but bloom freely all year round.

Epidendrum pseudepidendrum

Epidendrum pseudepidendrum

This orchid has tall, slender, leafy stems, at the top of which several striking flowers are carried loosely in spring and summer. These have deep green petals and sepals, with a distinctive orange lip protruding from the rest of the flower. A native of Costa Rica, this is best grown in intermediate conditions.

Epidendrum pseudepidendrum var. album

This is a paler form of the type which lacks the bright contrast between the pink lip and the yellow petals and sepals. Its paler colouring is nevertheless most attractive, and the flowers are produced in spring and summer on larger clusters at the top of the stem.

Epidendrum radicans var. *alba*

LAELIA

There are about 50 species of *Laelia*, which are found throughout Central and South America, with a high concentration in Mexico. They divide into several distinct groups depending upon their habits, which vary considerably. All the species are lovely and extremely showy, but many had been difficult to find in cultivation until recent breeding programmes increased the availability of some of the finest types, such as the fabulous varieties of *L. purpurata* from Brazil. The genus is closely related to *Cattleya*, and the plants are sometimes difficult to tell apart. From the early days of hybridizing, laelias were crossed with cattleyas to such an extent that there are more laeliocattleyas than interspecific hybrids.

Laelias are evergreen epiphytic plants, their size varying from 15cm (6in) to 1m (3ft) tall. A number of the smaller growing species have petite, brightly coloured flowers held on upright sprays above the foliage. These plants, such as *Laelia cinnabarina*, produce slender pseudobulbs with a single, semi-rigid leaf. The larger types, such as *L. crispa*, resemble cattleyas, while others, which include *L. anceps*, are more distinct with squarish pseudobulbs and a shiny single leaf. Their flowers are carried on tall, slender flower spikes, at the end of which the large, 10cm (4in) blooms are held in a loose cluster. Many of the species bloom in the autumn, while others produce their flowers in the spring at the beginning of the growing season.

Beginners could not do better than to include such beauties as *Laelia anceps* and *L. gouldiana* in their first collections. These plants are good, robust growers that grow with amazing ease and form large, clustered plants within a few years. The small-growing plants such as *L. flava* and *L. cinnabarina* need more specialist care because their pseudobulbs can easily shrivel and the plants quickly dehydrate as a result.

Temperature: Intermediate-growing (cool-growing for Mexican species).

Cultivation: Grow in 10cm (4in) pots of bark compost (growing medium). The smaller species can also be grown on bark. Water well during the summer but allow them almost to dry out in winter when resting. Give some shade in summer and full light in winter.

Height: 15–100cm (6–36in).

Laelia anceps

This delightful, cool-growing species can be grown indoors or in a greenhouse. The flower spikes can grow to a height of 60cm (2ft). The mauve flowers, which are large and variable in appearance, have yellow-centred, deep pink lips and appear in early autumn. The plant comes originally from Mexico.

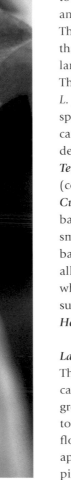

Laelia anceps

Laelia anceps 'Guerrero'

Laelia anceps var. alba

The white form of the species is just as attractive as its coloured form, and has been used to hybridize, retaining the pure colour. The flower spikes are usually shorter than in the type.

Laelia anceps 'Guerrero'

This named variety of the species, which flowers in autumn, is unusual for its exceptionally deep coloured lip. It has been selected for breeding hybrids, some of which retain the rich colouring. There are several further lovely and distinct varietal clones of this species in cultivation.

Laelia milleri × L. briegeri

This primary hybrid was achieved by crossing two of the smaller-flowered species. These compact plants have neat pseudobulbs and golden yellow flowers on an upright flower spike that appears from the top of the pseudobulb in the summer. Grow in an intermediate greenhouse.

Laelia anceps var. *alba*

Laelia milleri × *L. briegeri*

Laelia purpurata var. *alba*

Laelia purpurata

This lovely species from Brazil grows extremely well in the intermediate greenhouse. It produces slender pseudobulbs and carries several 10cm (4in), white flowers with a purple lip on a stem during the spring and summer months.

Laelia purpurata var. alba

There are many examples of albino, or white, forms of species among laelias and cattleyas. This summer-flowering Brazilian species has many named varietal forms, which have been maintained by raising from seed in cultivation.

Laelia purpurata var. carnea

This extremely handsome species resembles the *Cattleya* family in appearance and has been used extensively to produce *Laeliocattleya* hybrids. This summer-flowering variety is unusual because of its salmon-coloured lip.

Laelia purpurata var. *carnea*

Laelia purpurata

LYCASTE ALLIANCE

The lycastes are a relatively small, but influential, natural genus of medium-size plants. They have had a great impact on the related anguloas with which they will readily interbreed to produce some of the most showy artificial hybrids. The majority of the flowers are typically triangular, the shape formed by the widely spread sepals that frame the cupped petals and lip. When crossed with the tulip-shaped anguloas, the superb, large, open-flowered angulocastes are produced, which have done much to promote this alliance. Although the majority of the species within the lycastes and anguloas are of pale colouring, the rosy-red varieties of *Lycaste skinneri* have emphasized rich colours in hybrids such as *L.* Wyld Fire. In the same way, dark red angulocastes have been raised that compare well with the lighter, softer-coloured varieties.

The strongest fragrance in these genera is found among the *Anguloa* species, and this has carried on into the bigeneric hybrids. *A. clowesii* is best known for its sweet perfume.

The lycastes and anguloas share many characteristics. They produce stout, hard, dark green pseudobulbs that are generously foliaged during the summer. The leaves are broad, soft and ribbed, spreading wide as they mature, which makes the plants space-consuming. The foliage is shed during winter or at the onset of new growth in early spring. As the leaves mature, they become spotted and yellowed with age; it is often best to remove them before they drop naturally. The plants have a decided winter's rest. New growth is seen in early spring, and the new shoots are accompanied by numerous, single-flowered spikes, clustering around the base of the pseudobulb. They grow quickly and the flowers appear before being swamped by the spreading foliage. The plants grow rapidly during the summer, producing their large pseudobulbs, 7–15cm (3–6in) high, before winter.

Annual repotting is often preferred for lycastes and anguloas because the plants quickly outgrow their containers. By removing the oldest pseudobulbs each time, plants can be kept to a moderate size. Where specimen plants are wanted, you can leave them to become really large. For these reasons, the hybrids are best contained in a greenhouse where they can be given sufficient headroom.

If you are growing your orchids indoors where space is limited, try one or two of the smaller species among the lycastes such as *Lycaste aromatica*, which is deliciously scented and carries a profusion of golden yellow flowers in the spring, or *L. skinneri*, with its variable white to soft pink varieties. These plants will not grow much bigger than 30cm (12in) high when in leaf.

Most of the 25 or so *Lycaste* species can be found in cultivation, alongside the numerous hybrids. The species may be epiphytic, terrestrial or lithophytic, with most plants preferring shady situations in woodland.

Lycastes are South American orchids whose highest concentrations are in Mexico and Peru. The anguloas are a small natural genus containing about ten species, which exist mainly in Colombia, Ecuador and Peru. Because of their scarcity, only a few species are widely grown. More widely seen in orchid collections are the angulocastes, whose large, fleshy blooms are 10cm (4in) wide.

Temperature: Cool-growing (winter) and intermediate-growing (summer).

Cultivation: Grow in pots of bark-based compost (growing medium) in pots up to 25cm (10in) in diameter. In summer, water and feed freely and maintain good humidity (although excessive spraying can cause leaf marks). Decrease watering as the foliage begins to turn yellow, and water in winter only if the pseudobulbs become dehydrated and shrivel. Give light shade in summer and full light in winter.

Height: 30cm–1m (12–36in).

Anguloa virginalis

Anguloa clowesii

Anguloa clowesii

A most handsome, large-growing, cool-house orchid, this early summer-flowering species has leaves that reach 1m (3ft) tall when mature. The deep yellow flowers, which appear in early summer, are strongly scented, and the rocking lip gives rise to its common name of cradle orchid.

Anguloa virginalis

A single, pale pink, fragrant flower appears in early summer on each spike held below the developing foliage. The sepals and petals remain cupped, not opening fully, as is typical of flowers in this genus.

Angulocaste Jupiter AM/RHS

This older, spring-flowering hybrid retains its youthful looks with densely spotted sepals overlying a light yellow base. This bigeneric hybrid is between *Lycaste* and *Anguloa*.

Lycaste aromatica

This pretty, scented species from South America produces an abundance of golden yellow flowers in spring. The plant is deciduous and rests during the winter. Note the new growth just starting.

Augulocaste **Jupiter AM/RHS**

Lycaste aromatica

Lycaste skinneri

Lycaste Autumn Glow

With strong, brown sepals contrasting with the deep yellow petals and lip, this lovely autumn-flowering, cool-growing hybrid reflects the season well. The plant will rest after flowering.

Lycaste skinneri

A variable species from Guatemala, this is typical of the lycastes with their three-cornered flowers, where the pale pink sepals stand away from the petals that hug the brightly coloured lip. Single flowers, 7cm (3in) wide, are produced in spring on stems that are shorter than the foliage on this deciduous plant.

Lycaste Wyld Surprise

This is one of a range of beautiful hybrids that have been raised using *Lycaste skinneri* as a starting point. Single-flowered stems surround the pseudobulbs at the same time as the new growths are appearing. This lovely, reddish-pink grex is a stunning example of the variation in rich colourings that can be achieved from one cross, where each clone will be unique. The flowers appear in spring.

Lycaste **Autumn Glow**

Lycaste **Wyld Surprise**

MASDEVALLIA

Affectionately known as kite orchids for the long "tails" of some of the flowers in this vast natural genus, the masdevallias are small- to medium-size plants that have single-leafed, short stems on a creeping rhizome. The leaves are oval to long, and mid- to dark green in colour. The slender flower spikes come from the base and may be single-flowered or have several on a stem. The flowers are very variable in shape and colour. While some species, such as *Masdevallia coccinea*, produce some of the most vibrant colours in the orchid flora, others are very drab. Of the 300 or so species, many are in cultivation alongside a small number of hybrids.

The flowers are characterized by the triangular shape of the large, spreading sepals, of which some (such as those of *Masdevallia caudata*) have extended "tails". The petals and lip are much reduced and remain generally hidden at the centre of the bloom. In other species, such as *M. racemosa*, the sepals are fused at the base to create a tube that contains the diminutive other segments. While *M. veitchiana* is outstanding for its vibrant orange and red colouring, others, such as *M. ventricularia*, which has curious brown-spotted, tubular flowers, are nonetheless interesting and worth considering. The largest flower in the genus is that of *M. macrura*, which measures 30cm (12in) or more vertically from top to bottom. This impressive length arises because of the long, tapering sepals.

These evergreen epiphytic, or occasionally lithophytic, orchids inhabit cool, shady and moist areas of forest woodland high in the Andes of South America. In cultivation, they should be disturbed as little as possible, and, when repotting becomes necessary, they can often be "dropped on" into a slightly larger pot without breaking up the root ball. In this way, most masdevallias can be grown on to form good-size clumps without becoming unmanageable. At this stage they are seen at their best and will provide a profusion of flowers during the summer months. A few species, such as *Masdevallia tovarensis*, will produce more of its milk-white flowers from the same stems for more than one year, provided you do not cut them off.

Masdevallias are one natural genus which, in the past, has been combined with a huge number of related genera, including some unusual orchids, among them *Dryadella*, *Dracula*, *Trisetella* and *Pleurothallis*. The latter belongs to another vast group of related plants, which forms one of the largest natural genera with some 900 species. These produce flowers that vary from small to minuscule, where the only way to see them clearly is to view them through a magnifying glass.

Temperature: Cool-growing.
Cultivation: Grow in fine bark in plastic mesh pots of the type used for aquatic plants. Keep in shade year-round. Water carefully throughout the year, never allowing the roots to dry out, but also avoiding overwet conditions, which can lead to rotting.
Height: 15–30cm (6–12in).

Masdevallia coccinea

This elegant, tall-stemmed species carries its single, 5cm (2in), moon-shaped flowers high above the foliage. The bright purple of the spreading sepals is among the richest seen in any orchid flower. The plants bloom mainly throughout the spring and summer.

Masdevallia Falcon Sunrise

Three clones of this new hybrid have combined the qualities of several species to give exciting, orange flowers on medium-length stems. When grown on into specimen plants, these orchids will produce numerous flowers at various times of the year.

Masdevallia coccinea

Masdevallia Falcon Sunrise

Masdevallia Rose Mary

Among the many delightful hybrids that are gaining popularity among the masdevallias is this pretty, short-stemmed, pink-flowered variety. The flowers carry "tails" that adorn the sepals and appear at various times of the year.

Masdevallia Rose Mary

Masdevallia tovarensis

This delightful species comes from Venezuela and is a neat grower with 2.5cm (1in), white flowers which rise above the foliage. The flowers are produced at various times of the year. Each stem produces several flowers and will bloom again the following year, which is an unusual feature among masdevallias.

Masdevallia Whiskers

This tufted plant will produce numerous flowers in succession throughout the summer. The orange flowers stand clear of the foliage and have intensified coloration at the centre of the large, cupped sepals.

Masdevallia tovarensis

Masdevallia Whiskers

Maxillaria rufescens

MAXILLARIA

Inhabiting vast regions of Central and South America are the 300 or so evergreen, epiphytic or lithophytic species of *Maxillaria*. These are small- to medium-size plants that vary greatly in structure. The majority produce pseudobulbs, which may be small and round, with a single, grass-like leaf (such as *Maxillaria tenuifolia*), or large and spectacular (such as *M. sanderiana*). The latter, with its fleshy white, red-spotted flowers and triangular shape, resembles *Lycaste*, a genus into which most maxillarias were originally placed. Many of the species, and a very few hybrids, are grown. Of these, a number are often incorrectly named due to the similarity of some plants, which often cannot be told apart until they bloom.

Any number of the smaller-growing species are ideal beginners' orchids. They have a great willingness to grow and flower under extreme conditions and are more tolerant of a hot, dry environment than many other orchids. Those with the showiest flowers should be searched out; among these can be counted *Maxillaria picta*, which has deliciously fragrant blooms produced in abundance in autumn. Maxillarias bloom from the base, with a single flower on short to medium stems. The colours are variable, with yellow, buff-brown and red being the most frequent.

Most maxillarias prefer to be grown on, rather than continually divided into smaller pieces, when the limited number of flowers does not do justice to the plant when seen in its prime.

Temperature: Mainly cool-growing.
Cultivation: Grow in pots, larger varieties in coarse bark, smaller ones in fine bark. Those with a creeping rhizome can be grown in baskets or on bark. Keep in good light. Feed and water freely during summer, but give less in winter, without allowing the plants to dry out completely.
Height: 15–30cm (6–12in).

Maxillaria acutipetala

Maxillaria acutipetala

In summer, this pretty, distinctive species has pure yellow flowers with darker, reddish lips. The flowers are 2cm (¾in) across on stems less than 15cm (6in) high. This species is less often seen in collections and is rather rare.

Maxillaria coccinea

Unusually bright red colouring enhances these small, 2cm (¾in) wide, single flowers on thin, clustered stems well below the foliage. This is an easily grown, summer-flowering plant for the cool greenhouse or a shady position indoors.

Maxillaria luteo-alba

These 4cm (1½in) wide, cream flowers, with orange-brown sepals and yellow petals, are produced in early summer around the base of the leading pseudobulbs on 13cm (5in) stems, well below the foliage. This free-flowering, cool-growing species comes from Costa Rica and elsewhere.

Maxillaria ochroleuca

A spidery mass of fragrant flowers surrounds the base of this modestly sized, cool-growing plant from Honduras. The creamy white, spring flowers have either yellow or orange-red lips.

Maxillaria coccinea

Maxillaria luteo-alba

Maxillaria ochroleuca

Maxillaria praestans

Presenting a uniform face, these alert brownish flowers with their almost black lips will last for several weeks during the summer months. The larger the plant, the more flowers it can be expected to produce.

Maxillaria tenuifolia

This gem produces long, straggly plants with pseudobulbs spaced along an upward-creeping rhizome. The single flowers, which appear in summer, are on short stems, with never more than one or two from one pseudobulb. The flowers are yellow, densely or lightly peppered with red, and fragrant.

Maxillaria praestans

Maxillaria tenuifolia

MILTONIOPSIS

These orchids are without par in the orchid flora. They are the much-loved pansy orchids, so called because of their likeness to that flower. Their growth is compact compared with the large size of the showy, flat flowers, and this, combined with the fact that they are easy to grow and flower reliably, makes them the number one orchid for indoor culture. Their rise in popularity over recent years has been responsible for vast numbers of gorgeous hybrids being made available to the home grower.

These plants come in a wide range of colours, from dazzling white, through delicate pastel pinks and yellows, to the deepest of reds. The flowers are always adorned with a "mask" – a butterfly-shaped design at the centre of the bloom, on the base of the lip. The design takes many forms; it can be small and neat, or expand across the lip to form the "waterfall" patterns of great beauty and contrast. Two flower spikes are regularly produced from one pseudobulb, with from three to six 7cm (3in) wide blooms on each. Often blooming twice a year, in early summer and autumn, and accompanied by a delicate fragrance, it is easy to see why these orchids are so popular.

In a natural genus with thousands of hybrids, there are surprisingly few species. Of the five, all endemic to Colombia, four have contributed to the vast breeding programme that has enhanced the colour range tenfold. The evergreen, epiphytic species are all rare in cultivation and belong in specialized collections where they can be treasured for future generations.

Miltoniopsis are closely related to odontoglossums, with which they will readily interbreed, along with other members of this great alliance. When combined with odontoglossums, the resulting flowers have enlarged lips and strong colours. Miltoniopsis were originally placed in the genus *Miltonia*, which is now confined to about ten species found in Brazil, so when crossed with *Odontoglossum* they make *Odontonia*. Other intergeneric combinations that include *Miltoniopsis* (still called *Miltonia* for registration purposes) are *Miltassia* (*Miltonia* × *Brassia*), *Miltonidum* (*Miltonia* × *Oncidium*) and many others.

Hybrid miltoniopsis produce light green pseudobulbs that carry two apical and two basal, light green, narrowly oval leaves. The plants grow throughout most of the year, starting new growths as soon as the previous pseudobulb has been completed, and often before the plant has finished flowering. The flower spikes come quickly as the pseudobulb matures, and produce their blooms in an arching habit just clear of the foliage. The plants are seldom higher than 30cm (12in), which makes them ideal for the home grower.

Like all orchids, miltoniopsis thrive when surrounded by the foliage of other plants, and growing them in company means that the humidity can be maintained around them.

Miltoniopsis **Herr Alexandre**

Miltoniopsis **Jersey**

Temperature: Cool-growing.
Cultivation: Grow in pots of fine bark compost (growing medium) or in Rockwool. Keep them out of direct sunlight at all times. Water throughout the year and feed from spring to autumn.
Height: To 30cm (12in).

Miltoniopsis **Herr Alexandre**

This boldly marked, enchanting, white hybrid has all the hallmarks of a winning combination. The large flowers, 10cm (4in) wide, stand well clear of the foliage, appearing in early summer and autumn. Two flower spikes may be produced by the leading pseudobulb.

Miltoniopsis **Jersey**

A lovely red and white modern hybrid for summer flowering, this clone will produce up to six large blooms, 8cm (3in) wide, known affectionately as pansy orchids.

Miltoniopsis **Marie Riopelle 'Portland Rose'**

This wonderfully decorative hybrid has the exquisite lip marking, which combines with the deep, rosy pink of the rest of the flower to create a ravishing effect. Plants like this can be grown indoors or in a cool greenhouse where it is shady and moist. It flowers in late spring and early summer.

Miltoniopsis **Marie Riopelle 'Portland Rose'**

Miltoniopsis **Rozel**

Miltoniopsis **Red Knight 'Grail' AM/RHS**
Producing a single, large flower in late spring and early summer, this hybrid has the appearance of deep red velvet. Young plants often produce one flower, but there can be up to six on an older plant.

Miltoniopsis **Rozel**
Many hybrids such as this have been bred to show the "waterfall" or "water droplet" patterning on the lip, which is a feature of these varieties. Note the occasional "droplet" on the petals. The combination of dark pink sepals and the beautifully patterned lips with their pink edge in this hybrid is captivating. The flowers appear in late spring and early summer.

Miltoniopsis **Saint Helier 'Pink Delight'**
A superb shape and rich pink colouring combine to make this lovely hybrid an absolute beauty. The deep crimson, butterfly-shaped mask at the centre of the blooms sets the scene for the paler heavy veining on the lip. Flowering occurs twice a year, in late spring and early summer.

Miltoniopsis **Red Knight 'Grail' AM/RHS**

Miltoniopsis **Saint Helier 'Pink Delight'**

Miltoniopsis vexillaria

Miltoniopsis vexillaria 'Arctic Moon'

Miltoniopsis vexillaria

This soft pink form of the species, which comes from Colombia, is now a rare collectors' item. It is behind the majority of today's fine hybrids, which retain its lovely shape and gently arching habit. It flowers in late spring and early summer.

Miltoniopsis vexillaria 'Arctic Moon'

A pale form of the species, this lacks the delicate pink colouring of the sepals, petals and lip, but has an enhanced colour at the centre of the flower. It flowers in late spring and early summer.

Miltoniopsis Zorro 'Yellow Delight'

Selected breeding has produced this yellow hybrid, which flowers in late spring and early summer, although the colour does not exist in the species. It has been brought out from *Miltoniopsis roezlii*, the influence of which is also seen in the red marking.

Miltoniopsis Zorro 'Yellow Delight'

ODONTOGLOSSUM ALLIANCE

Odontoglossums are at the pinnacle of this complex alliance, which is made up of a number of closely related natural genera, all of which will interbreed to produce the fantastic range of flower types.

The species number about 60 evergreen epiphytic plants, which originate from high in the Andes of South America. Adored from the beginning of their introduction, the pristine white flowers of the splendid *Odontoglossum crispum* earned them the name "Queen of Orchids". They were so highly prized that demand led to their near extinction in the wild. Many superb varieties were grown that exist today only in the illustrations and descriptions of old publications. The comparatively few species grown today are confined to specialist collections, while in their place have come hundreds of hybrids that, for the hobby grower, constitute a much better buy. The hybrids have a spectrum of colours and a vigorous habit that are not found in the species, and are much more suited to mass-production for the hobbiest.

Typically, odontoglossums and related genera produce green pseudobulbs with an apical pair of mid-green, narrowly oval leaves, and two shorter leaves at the base. The plants may be 30–45cm (12–18in) high, and the flower spikes can be twice this. The flowers of the pure *Odontoglossum* hybrids are well rounded, with sepals and petals of equal size, and a neat, often frilly-edged lip. All colours are possible, with intricate patternings not found to the same extent in any other orchid. The flowers, which may number up to a dozen and are 6cm (2½in) wide, may be boldly marked or self-coloured. They will last for many weeks at almost any time of the year.

More numerous than the pure odontoglossums are the intergeneric hybrids. These include *Odontioda*, which is *Odontoglossum* crossed with the

smaller, lesser-grown genus *Cochlioda*. This latter genus found fame for its bright red colouring, which it imparted to the *Odontioda* hybrids and which distinguishes them from odontoglossums. When combined with *Oncidium*, which is a genus dominated by smaller-flowered, longer-spiked, generally yellow flowers, the resulting *Odontocidium* produces some very pleasing results. There are many more combinations, all containing the genes of odontoglossums and exhibiting various characteristics belonging to the

other partners. Some lines of breeding have concentrated on producing plants for the cooler climate, and include *Vuylstekeara* (*Cochlioda* × *Miltonia* × *Odontoglossum*) and *Wilsonara* (*Cochlioda* × *Odontoglossum* × *Oncidium*). By introducing the warmer-growing oncidiums to the equation, multigeneric hybrids have been raised that are heat-tolerant and can be grown in the tropics. These include *Beallara* (*Brassia* × *Cochlioda* × *Miltonia* × *Odontoglossum*) and *Aliceara* (*Brassia* × *Miltonia* × *Oncidium*).

Miltonidum **Pupukea Sunset**

Odontioda Avranches

Odontioda La Couperon

Odontoglossums can suffer easily from heat stress, and if you cannot keep the plants cool enough in summer, try putting them out of doors in a well-shaded place where they can be kept moist and humid. If placed in too much light, the leaves will turn a reddish hue. If not overdone, this is an acceptable colour that will return to green when the sun loses its power. However, if the exposure is excessive, the whole leaf surface will become dark red and premature leaf loss may result. Odontoglossums that lose too many leaves at one time will go into decline, and the plants will need to be repotted at the earliest opportunity, and the leafless pseudobulbs removed to restore the balance of the plant.

All the intergeneric odontoglossums are extremely lovely plants to grow, but care must be taken to ensure that the pseudobulbs stay plump throughout the year. On occasion, a mature plant will produce a tall, well-flowered spike that is more than it can support. As the buds develop to opening stage, the plant will suddenly shrivel badly, which is an indication that the flowers are sapping

its strength and it cannot support them and live. Remove the flower spike immediately. You can still enjoy the flowers by placing them in water. Repot the plant if necessary and encourage it to produce a new growth as quickly as possible, after which a slow recovery can begin.

Odontoglossums originally extended from the Andes in South America north to Mexico. Recent reclassification has created new genera, until the only true *Odontoglossum* species left occur in the Andes. Horticulturally, many of the older generic names are retained, hence both names, which remain in common usage, are given here. The exception is the genus *Rossioglossum*, where the species are so distinct that they are listed separately under Specialist Orchids.

Temperature: Cool-growing; keep below 24°C (75°F) in summer.

Cultivation: Grow in fine bark in 5–7cm (2–3in) pots that restrict the roots. Keep well shaded in summer, but give more light in winter. Water and apply feed all year, but give less in winter.

Height: 30–45cm (12–18in).

Miltonidum Pupukea Sunset

An unlikely cross between the tall-growing *Miltonia warscewiczii* and the diminutive *Oncidium cheirophorum* has resulted in this extremely attractive primary with flower spikes that reach 23cm (9in) in length. The flowers, with their cream, pink and green colouring appear in spring.

Odontioda Avranches

The artificial genus *Odontioda* (*Odontoglossum* × *Cochlioda*) was first produced to give the red colouring of the *Cochlioda* genus to the usually pale-coloured odontoglossums. In this largely spring-flowering hybrid, all *Cochlioda* influence has disappeared to return to the white colouring of the *Odontoglossum*.

Odontioda La Couperon

The vivid pink colouring and fine, deep pink patterning of the flowers on the long, arching flower spike reveal the influence of *Cochlioda* on this striking hybrid, which has given the flower its bright, vibrant appearance. The flowers appear at various times, but usually in the spring.

Odontioda Mont Felard × St Aubin's Bay

Odontioda Les Plantons

The colouring and patterning seen in this largely spring-flowering hybrid is typical of the diversity that is being bred into this man-made genus. The spots and blotches appear in a kaleidoscope of changing colours unequalled by any other orchid.

Odontioda Mont Felard × St Aubin's Bay

This is a neat-growing orchid, which, in varying seasons, produces spikes of white flowers spotted with rich pink; the lips are stained the same colour towards the edge and have yellow centres. The petal edges are ruffled and frilled.

Odontioda Pontinfer

With its beautifully proportioned flower in stunning red on white, this large, often branching flower spike shows the influence of the species *Odontoglossum pescatorei* in its background. The flowers appear at various times.

Odontioda Les Plantons

Odontioda Pontinfer

Odontocidium **Isler's Gold Dragon**
Bright colour combinations and a tall flower spike make this plant an indoor favourite. Grow in a cool situation where there is good light all year. The flowers, which appear at various times, will last for several weeks.

Odontocidium **La Moye**
This complex hybrid is robust and free-flowering. Keep the plant in a cool room in good light. Water and apply feed all year. The white flowers, with their pink and yellow patterning, will last for several weeks and appear at various times.

Odontocidium **Russikon's Goldbaum**
This bigeneric hybrid has inherited the large yellow lip and brown marking on the petals from the species *Oncidium tigrinum*. This has also contributed to the upright, branching habit of the spike. The flowers appear at various times, usually in spring.

Odontocidium **Russikon's Goldbaum**

Odontocidium **Isler's Gold Dragon**

Odontocidium **La Moye**

Odontoglossum cariniferum

Odontoglossum cariniferum
(syn. *Oncidium cariniferum*)
This lovely species celebrates its abundant spring flowering with a tall, branching spike which is heavy with blooms. Individually, these are rich chocolate brown, and the petals curve inwards to welcome the bloom's pollinator.

Odontoglossum cordatum
(syn. *Lemboglossum cordatum*)
This compact species carries its elegantly pointed, brown-blotched flowers in spring on a neat spike, about 15cm (6in) tall. Originating from Honduras, it is easy to grow and flower, and will do well indoors or in a cool, shady greenhouse.

Odontoglossum crocidipterum
Many *Odontoglossum* species are very rare today, as is this delicately patterned variety. The light yellow and brown markings are typical of a number in the genus that are mostly high-altitude plants from the Andes. This species flowers in spring.

Odontoglossum cordatum

Odontoglossum crocidipterum

Odontoglossum hallii

Odontoglossum laeve

Odontoglossum Jorisianum

Odontoglossum hallii

With its strangely twisting, fragrant flowers and needle-like point to the lips, this summer-flowering species from Ecuador has contributed its basic yellow colouring to many early hybrids. It is quite rare in cultivation today.

Odontoglossum Jorisianum

This classic hybrid was first raised around the beginning of the 20th century, when hybridizing was not far advanced. It is the result of crossing two excellent species, *Odontoglossum purpureum* and *O. triumphans*, both of which are rare today. The red-marked, yellow flowers bloom in spring.

Odontoglossum laeve
(syn. *Miltonioides laevis*)

Strongly perfumed, this species carries its yellow and brown flowers with lips that are pink at the centre and held on a 45cm (18in) spike, well clear of the foliage. Flowering is in late summer and is long lasting. The plant is a robust grower, and comes from Honduras and Mexico.

Odontoglossum oerstedii
(syn. *Ticoglossum oerstedii*)
An unusual and rarely seen species, this orchid has small pseudobulbs and leaves about 15cm (6in) tall. The pretty, waxy, white flowers with a golden yellow blotch on the lips appear on short spikes just above the foliage. Flowering in spring, this Costa Rican species can be grown warmer than most in the genus.

Vuylstekeara **Cambria 'Lensings Favorit'**
From the multitude of mass-produced Cambria 'Plush' came this "sport", showing sufficient variation of colouring to warrant its own specific varietal name. A lovely distinct form, with pink-blotched, red sepals and petals and a pink lip with a red central marking, it is suitable for indoors or a cool to intermediate greenhouse. The flowers bloom at various times of year.

Vuylstekeara **Cambria 'Plush' FCC/RHS**
One of the most popular orchids of all time, this multi-generic hybrid, with red and white colouring, has been produced in its thousands for the world pot-plant market. The large flowers, 7cm (3in) wide, are richly coloured and produced at various times throughout the year.

Odontoglossum oerstedii

Vuylstekeara **Cambria 'Lensings Favorit'**

Vuylstekeara Cambria 'Plush' FCC/RHS

ONCIDIUM ALLIANCE

Among the 400 or so *Oncidium* species are many extremely varied plants, which range from diminutive equitants – small, fan-like, foliaged plants with brightly coloured flowers – to large-bulbed, long-spiked beauties such as *Oncidium macranthum*, now also known as *Cyrtochilum macranthum*. In between, are numerous, delightful plants of modest size with brightly coloured blooms which are predominantly yellow. Many of the species are in cultivation, and these are easy to grow and flower, finding favour among beginners for their reliability. To this pretty and interesting selection can be added a huge array of hybrids, mostly intergenerics resulting from crossings with odontoglossums and other related genera. The result is that many exciting and desirable plants are regularly seen that will grace any small orchid collection to perfection.

Oncidiums are evergreen plants, typically with neat, green pseudobulbs and a pair of narrowly oval leaves. The flower spikes come from the base of the leading pseudobulb as it matures, and this can be at almost any time of the year, although flowering peaks during the autumn months. The species originate from throughout tropical America and are found in varying epiphytic habitats. A number of species are know affectionately as "mule ear" types, a reference to their thick, solitary leaves that are supported by an often diminutive pseudobulb. These plants, which include *Oncidium luridum*, exist in hot, dry environments that are different to the Brazilian home of *O. flexuosum*, which resembles the typical *Odontoglossum*. The latter produces its pseudobulbs well spaced along an upward-growing rhizome. Grown on a piece of cork bark and given its freedom, this species produces a mass of white aerial roots, forming a curtain of a yard or so long.

In cultivation, some oncidiums are more favoured than others. The most popular kinds are cool-growing and do well when grown with odontoglossums, where they will co-exist under the same conditions. The mule ear types and others that come from the more tropical parts of America need to be kept warmer, and intermediate to warm conditions suit them best. They are high-light plants, requiring more light then their cooler-growing relations. In the northern hemisphere, some of them, such as *Oncidium splendidum*, can be challenging to flower because of the lack of year-round sunshine.

If you have limited growing space, look out for a few of the smaller-growing species or hybrids. These include *Oncidium cheirophorum*, which has short flower spikes of densely clustered, curiously shaped, bright yellow flowers.

Oncidium
Boissiense

Similar in size is the highly fragrant *O. ornithorhynchum*, with its pretty pink blooms produced in profusion; this is a must. *O. flexuosum*, mentioned earlier, produces long flower spikes which terminate in a shower of numerous, bright yellow blooms which last for three or four weeks during the autumn.
Temperature: Cool-growing; some intermediate- to warm-growing.
Cultivation: Grow in 5–10cm (2–4in) pots of bark-based compost (growing medium). *O. flexuosum* can also be grown on bark. Shade cool-growing types in summer, but keep mule-ear types well-lit at all times. Water and feed hybrids throughout the year; keep species dry during winter, when growth stops.
Height: 15–30cm (6–12in).

Oncidium Boissiense
This striking hybrid bears large, bright yellow flowers with the huge lip being derived from the species *Oncidium varicosum*, among others. This strong, robust, autumn-flowering plant can be grown indoors or in a cool to intermediate greenhouse.

Oncidium obryzatum
The tall, wispy flower spikes of this yellow-flowered species provide a dense swarm of tiny blooms that hover above the 20cm (8in) plant in winter. This species should be grown in an intermediate greenhouse.

Oncidium Sharry Baby 'Sweet Fragrance'
This lovely, chocolate-scented hybrid produces a profusion of cherry-red blooms with white-tipped lips. It blooms at various times and is cool-growing. The flowers show a strong influence from the species *Oncidium ornithorhynchum*, which appears in its background.

Oncidium sphacelatum
This is one of the taller-growing *Oncidium* species. The branching flower spikes can reach 1m (3ft) tall, with numerous flowers on side branches. This native of Mexico needs good light in order to bloom well in the spring.

Oncidium Sharry Baby 'Sweet Fragrance'

Oncidium obryzatum

Oncidium sphacelatum

PAPHIOPEDILUM

Aeons ago, the paphiopedilums, and other related slipper orchids, split from the mainstream to evolve along their own path. This led to the characteristic pouch that defines this and related genera. The pouch, or slipper, is a modification of the third petal, which appears in other orchids as the lip. In developing the pouch, the typical *Paphiopedilum* modified its other parts accordingly. The two lateral sepals, for instance, have largely become fused and are mostly hidden from view behind the pouch. The pouch is designed to trap a pollinating insect by first enticing it to the edge, where it then loses its grip on the slippery surface and tumbles in. Once inside the pouch, a ladder of small hairs enables the insect to force its way out between either side of the pouch and the column. As it does so, the insect takes the pollen with it.

The paphiopedilums include about 65 species found throughout the Far East, from India, China and South-east Asia to the Philippines, Indonesia and New Guinea. They are evergreen plants without pseudobulbs, mostly terrestrial, producing tufted growths, from the centre of which extends the flower spike. The spikes may have a solitary flower, or carry from two to a dozen blooms. Some of the most striking of all orchid blooms are those produced by the Borneo species, *Paphiopedilum rothschildianum*, where the lateral petals have become extremely long and narrow, held horizontally and dramatically striped. When seen on a tall flower spike, the result is nothing short of heart-stopping.

New introductions from China, brought into cultivation during the last two decades of the 20th century, have revolutionized new breeding lines. Species such as the golden yellow *Paphiopedilum armeniacum* and the delightful, pink *P. micranthum*, among others, have resulted in some superb hybrids with unique colour combinations.

Paphiopedilums are noted for their longevity. Among the first of the orchids to be hybridized in the 19th century, there are plants in collections today that are over 150 years old. These grand plants have become classics in their own right and are treasured possessions in the collections of those fortunate enough to have acquired them.

So great is the appeal of the paphiopedilums that whole collections are devoted to this one genus. For the beginner or collector, there are several kinds to look out for. The complex hybrids produce plants with stout green foliage and a single, large, rounded bloom in a variety of colours, from yellow and green through to red, brown and bronze. The flowers may be self-coloured, or heavily spotted and shaded with other colours. All produce highly glossed blooms, mostly during the winter months when they will last for many weeks.

The mottled-leaved types produce plants of a smaller stature, and can be extremely free-flowering on a large, multi-growthed plant. The flower spikes are taller, up to 30cm (12in) tall, with a single, open-shaped bloom. These less heavy blooms can be green or red, with the darkest colours being deep purple bordering on the elusive black. These

Paphiopedilum **Claire de Lune**

handsome blooms are usually striped or spotted, often with dramatically flamed dorsal petals. Their flowering season extends into the summer, overlapping a further group that produces multi-flowering spikes. These are hybrids bred from species such as the extremely long-petalled *Paphiopedilum sanderianum* and *P. rothschildianum*, with its rigidly held petals. These, and *P. parishii*, with its long twisting petals, have produced some lovely hybrids that add a dramatic dimension to the genus.

Paphiopedilums produce sparse roots compared with other orchids; these are brown and hairy. Repotting is best done on an annual basis but with minor disturbance to the root system. They should be kept in as small a pot as possible, often being placed back into the same size pot after repotting and having the compost (growing medium) replaced with a fresh supply.

When in bloom, paphiopedilums will need some support. Use a thin split bamboo cane to hold the spike upright, and wait until the bloom is open and has become "set". At this stage, tie the cane at the base of the flower to bring it up to eye level, where it can be fully appreciated.

Temperature: Intermediate-growing.
Cultivation: Grow in bark-based compost (growing medium) or Rockwool, in pots that restrict the roots. Place them away from direct sun and keep them evenly moist all year. Feed regularly. Mist only lightly (if at all) to avoid water running into the centre of the growths, where it can lead to rotting.
Height: 15–30cm (6–12in).

Paphiopedilum Claire de Lune

This is an older hybrid that has stood the test of time and is as popular today as it was over 100 years ago. The plants have beautifully mottled leaves and the elegant green-and-white flowers are carried on slender stems in winter and spring.

Paphiopedilum delenatii

Paphiopedilum Corbiere 'La Tuilerie'

Paphiopedilum haynaldianum

Paphiopedilum Corbiere 'La Tuilerie'
The elegant lines of this older-type, spring-flowering hybrid with its rich red colouring and deeply veined dorsal petal make an attractive combination. The stems are 23cm (9in) tall on a green-leaved plant.

Paphiopedilum delenatii
Originating from Vietnam, this enticing, pale pink species, with its slightly deeper pink lip, makes an attractive plant with mottled foliage. The flowers of this species, which bloom in the spring, have passed their delicate pink colouring on to many newer hybrids.

Paphiopedilum haynaldianum
One of the finest of the multi-flowered species, this large-flowered plant, which has flowers 13cm (5in) across, originates from India and carries its delectable flowers in green, brown and pink on a 60cm (2ft) flower spike in winter.

Paphiopedilum insigne
This was once a very popular species, grown by the million to provide cut flowers. Today, it makes a lovely houseplant, with its green and brown colouring. It grows well in a cool room out of the sun where it will bloom freely during the winter.

Paphiopedilum insigne

Paphiopedilum Leeanum

Paphiopedilum Lady Isabel

Paphiopedilum Jersey Freckles
This combination of chocolate brown, lime, cream and pale pink is very striking in this large-flowered hybrid. It grows in a fairly warm situation so long as the leaves are not exposed to direct sun. The flowers appear in winter.

Paphiopedilum Lady Isabel
This hybrid is an offspring of *Paphiopedilum rothschildianum*. The multi-flowered spike on a tall stem has cream flowers, streaked with brown and with a pale red lip, which appear in winter and spring. The long, green leaves can become quite large.

Paphiopedilum Leeanum
This fine old hybrid was raised in Victorian times. The flowers have green lateral sepals, a pink-speckled, white dorsal sepal and a brown pouch. They appear during winter and last up to three months on the plant.

Paphiopedilum Jersey Freckles

Paphiopedilum Les Landes

Among the green-leaved hybrids, such as this large, red-brown variety, are a number with highly glossed flowers in all shades from dark red and bronze through green and yellow. The flowers, usually appearing singly on the stem in spring, can be as much as 10cm (4in) across.

Paphiopedilum micranthum

This species from China has neat, mottled leaves and huge-pouched, pale pink flowers with deep pink and yellow stripes on the petals. The flowers appear singly on medium-length stems in spring. The blooms have the bulbous pouch more usually associated with the cypripediums.

Paphiopedilum Quetivel Mill × Rod McLellan

This is a tall-stemmed, green-leaved hybrid which is suitable for indoors or a shady intermediate greenhouse. These hybrids mainly bloom in winter, when the red-freckled, yellow flowers will last for many weeks. The dorsal sepal is edged with white.

Paphiopedilum Les Landes

Paphiopedilum micranthum

Paphiopedilum Schillerianum

This old primary hybrid, which flowers in winter, could be over 200 years old, but may well be from a later remake of the same cross. The dominant parent here is the slender-petalled *P. rothschildianum*. The creamy green flowers are striped and spotted with deep purple, and the bulbous pouch is similarly coloured in purple.

Paphiopedilum Yellow Tiger

This lovely, multi-flowered cross between the similar, long-petalled species *Paphiopedilum stonei* and *P. granduliferum* was raised in California in 1984. The creamy white, winter flowers are striped with chocolate brown, while the pouch is raspberry coloured. The pale green petals complete the subtle effect.

Paphiopedilum Quetivel Mill × Rod McLellan

Paphiopedilum Yellow Tiger

Paphiopedilum Schillerianum

PHALAENOPSIS ALLIANCE

These orchids enjoy an extremely high profile among growers and beginners alike. The genus has probably done more in recent years to popularize orchids than any other. This has arisen from the mass-hybridizing that has taken place in parts of the world where these orchids can be raised with comparative ease and shipped to the wholesale market. Hybridizing continued at an amazing rate during the latter part of the 20th century, when more phalaenopsis were being produced for the mass-market than any other orchid, even beating cymbidiums in the popularity stakes. This has meant that phalaenopsis are sold in various outlets from florists to DIY stores, where they offer extremely good value for money.

Phalaenopsis are everybody's orchid – they can be grown with great ease indoors, where they require the minimum of care to produce numerous flowers over an extended period. They are ideally suited to the home environment, and their popularity was established when it was realised what excellent houseplants they make. Being warm, shade-loving plants, the interior of most houses is an ideal environment for them, often better than an overheated, over-bright greenhouse.

Phalaenopsis will also interbreed with other related genera such as *Ascocenda* and *Doritaenopsis*, and through *Rhynchostylis* to *Vanda*, resulting in some extremely complex and incredible, artificial genera.

The natural genus of *Phalaenopsis* is made up of almost 50 species, originating from the Old World through India, South-east Asia, Indonesia and parts of Australia. Most are evergreen epiphytic plants. The greatest concentration, and the species that have had the greatest influence on hybridizing, come from the Philippine Islands. These include *Phalaenopsis amabilis*, *P. stuartiana*, *P. sanderiana* and *P. schilleriana*, which are long-stemmed varieties with pink or white flowers. The plants are mostly extremely attractive, their broad, fleshy leaves often marbled with light and dark green mottling. They are monopodial in their growth, each new leaf extending from a centre, with the flower spikes coming from the base of the lower leaves. Phalaenopsis do not grow overly large, because leaves are shed from the base at about the same rate as new ones are developed. Their roots are exceptionally good-looking, often appearing above the pot and remaining airborne. These are flattened and silvery white, with clearly visible, green-growing tips. They have a tendency to adhere to any surface with which they come into contact. In a greenhouse, they often attach themselves to the bench upon which they are growing. Roots that have meandered over the rim of the pot are impossible to get back without snapping. Allow them to wander at will, and, when repotting, leave any live aerial roots outside the pot. Any that have died and are shrivelled can be cut off.

In addition to the long-stemmed, large-flowered kinds, there are numerous other hybrids raised from smaller, yellow- or brown-coloured species, which have given rise to a further dimension within the alliance. Many delightful miniature varieties are now available, with a colour range that extends from white, through yellow, to pink and red. These include pure phalaenopsis and intergeneric hybrids. The choice has become immense.

Phalaenopsis can bloom at almost any time, and it is not unusual for one plant to bloom two or three times in one year and to remain in bloom for many months. It is important, however, that the plant continues to make new leaves at the same time as flowering. If too many leaves are shed, you should cut off any flowering spikes and allow the plant to grow on until it has three or four leaves before allowing it to produce flowers. With half a dozen plants in an indoor environment, you can achieve almost perpetual, year-round flowering.

Temperature: Warm-growing (winter minimum 18°C/65°F with a rise during the day of 12°C/20°F).

Cultivation: Grow in 10cm (4in) pots of coarse bark or Rockwool. Water and feed throughout the year, but avoid

Doritaenopsis **Kiska**

Phalaenopsis **Barbara Moler × Spitzberg**

Phalaenopsis Brother Lancer

Phalaenopsis Claire de Valec

Phalaenopsis Catalina

Phalaenopsis Culiacan

waterlogging. High humidity is not necessary; placing plants on a humidity tray provides the appropriate level. Wipe the foliage with a damp cloth to clear of dust, but do not allow water to run down into the centre of the plant, where it can lead to rotting.
Height: 15cm (6in).

Doritaenopsis Kiska
This bigeneric hybrid, which combines the genera *Phalaenopsis* with *Doritis*, is usually darker in colour. This pale variety shows a new colour breakthrough with the striking orange lip. The flowers bloom in all seasons.

Phalaenopsis Barbara Moler × Spitzberg
This is a new hybrid from this extremely popular genus which adapts so well to indoor culture. The plant likes to be kept warm and moist all year, but out of direct sun. The pale lemon flowers have an orange lip and can appear at any time.

Phalaenopsis Brother Lancer
This is a smaller-flowered hybrid that carries its pretty blooms on a shorter, more compact spike, making it ideal for growing indoors where space is limited. The flowers, which can appear at any time of year, are pale lemon, striped and speckled with pink, and have a deep orange lip.

Phalaenopsis Catalina
Many *Phalaenopsis* hybrids are pure white with lovely marking on the lip. This varies between similar hybrids; in this case, the lip is orange. The flowers bloom in all seasons.

Phalaenopsis Claire de Valec
This robust grower produces long sprays of pale pink flowers in all seasons. It has proved to be consistent as a show plant and is a parent of further fine crosses.

Phalaenopsis Culiacan
This lovely hybrid has white flowers with a golden yellow lip. A well-grown plant will bloom two or three times a year.

Phalaenopsis **Fajan's Fireworks**

Phalaenopsis **Flare Spots**

Phalaenopsis Follett

Phalaenopsis Golden Hat

Phalaenopsis Happy Girl

Phalaenopsis **Fajan's Fireworks**
Intricate pink veining overlies the white background on this lovely hybrid, which are affectionately known as candy stripes. The sprays of flowers, 7cm (3in) wide, can last for many weeks at various times of the year.

Phalaenopsis **Flare Spots**
This hybrid has a compact flower spike, with the blooms set close together on the 30cm (12in) tall stem. The blooms are just under 8cm (3in) across. The white flowers, which appear in all seasons, have purple speckling and a crimson lip.

Phalaenopsis **Follett**
This tall-stemmed, large-flowered, pink-striped hybrid, which flowers in all seasons, is typical of those being produced in vast quantities for the houseplant trade. These orchids are unbeatable for indoors.

Phalaenopsis **Golden Hat**
Slight red peppering at the centre of these light yellow flowers makes an interesting combination of colour. In this modern hybrid, numerous flowers are produced on a branching flower spike in all seasons.

Phalaenopsis **Happy Girl**
This white hybrid, with lovely rounded petals and a cherry-red lip, provides an ideal combination of colours. The flowers, on an arching flower spike, fall into a cascade and appear in all seasons.

Phalaenopsis Hawaiian Darling

Phalaenopsis Lady Sakhara

Phalaenopsis Little Skipper

Phalaenopsis Hawaiian Darling

This almost-white flower has fine red peppering at the centre of the bloom, and the lip is leopard-marked with red spotting. This is an ideal hybrid for growing indoors. The flower spikes can reach 45cm (18in) in height. The flowers appear in all seasons.

Phalaenopsis Lady Sakhara

Throughout the year, this striking epiphytic orchid produces racemes of pink flowers that are veined darker; the lips are glowing cerise pink and have yellow centres.

Phalaenopsis Little Skipper

Miniature hybrids are really taking off now, as this popular variety shows. In all seasons, the branching sprays produce numerous, pale pink, small flowers, each no more than 2.5cm (1in) across, to create a charming picture.

Phalaenopsis Little Skipper 'Zuma Nova'

Raised in the United States to give large sprays of small, pink flowers in all seasons, this variety offers a distinct contrast to the larger-flowered types. The plants are more compact and take up less room.

Phalaenopsis Little Skipper 'Zuma Nova'

Phalaenopsis Mad Milva

Phalaenopsis Purple Valley

Phalaenopsis Mystik Golden Leopard

Phalaenopsis Rendezvous

Phalaenopsis Mad Milva
This plant will do well as the centrepiece of an orchid display, provided it is kept out of direct sunlight. The flowers are delightful, with cerise pink petals and sepals, and a darker pink lip. The flowers appear in all seasons and will last for several weeks.

Phalaenopsis Mystik Golden Leopard
This lovely yellow hybrid was produced from species such as *Phalaenopsis amboinensis* to give a compact flowering spike on a smaller plant. The orange-red lip provides a striking colour contrast against the yellow flower. Flowering can occur at any time of the year.

Phalaenopsis Purple Valley
The deep cherry-red blooms of this hybrid are a huge step forward in the production of exciting new phalaenopsis varieties. The plant blooms on a tall flower spike in all seasons, which will remain for months on end.

Phalaenopsis Rendezvous
This superb, deep pink hybrid has darker veining covering the sepals and petals while the lip is a vibrantly rich red. This plant will bloom two or three times during the year.

Phalaenopsis Yellow Treasure

Phalaenopsis schilleriana

This is one of the species from the Philippines from which most of the modern hybrids have been raised. The pale pink flowers, which appear in all seasons, are daintier and lack the rounded shape of the hybrids. The foliage is attractively mottled.

Phalaenopsis Silky Moon

This white orchid with an orange-red lip has tall flower spikes, which make an impressive display in any room in all seasons. When not in flower, keep in a warm situation away from direct sunlight.

Phalaenopsis Yellow Treasure

The light yellow-green colour of this neat hybrid is coming close to the more unusual green that has evaded hybridists to date. The flowers appear at any time of year. This is a flower with a future.

Phalaenopsis schilleriana

Phalaenopsis Silky Moon

PHRAGMIPEDIUM

Phragmipediums, like paphiopedilums, are also known as slipper orchids. However, there is no slipper orchid alliance as appears within the other major orchid groups, because phragmipediums will not interbreed with similar-looking, related genera. This is surprising when we consider the similarity between the flowers, especially among the multi-flowered paphiopedilums. The plants resemble the paphiopedilums, with their large, tufted growths.

Phragmipediums are mainly terrestrial or lithophytic plants, originating from South America, where they number possibly less than 20 species. The genus remained in the background of orchid cultivation until the last quarter of the 20th century, when a sensational new discovery revolutionized this previously drab-coloured genus. This new introduction was the famed *Phragmipedium besseae*, a plant with a flower of such brilliant red that it caused a sensation wherever it was seen. Its natural home was on the sheer rock faces of the inaccessible mountainous regions of Peru and Ecuador, and it was this precarious and impossible-to-reach habitat that kept the species under nature's wraps for so long. Invisible from the ground, it was only discovered when spotted from a helicopter flying over the area on a plant-hunting expedition. By the end of the 20th century, most of its former sites had been systematically stripped of these precious plants, which were quickly spread around the world. Today, this one plant has projected the genus to a high profile not previously enjoyed. Numerous red hybrids have resulted that are now at the forefront of all *Phragmipedium* breeding. We have yet to see the full potential this species is capable of reaching.

The majority of hybrids raised using the red-flowered *Phragmipedium besseae* have predictably produced blooms in the red to orange range. These are large-pouched, short-petalled, nicely balanced flowers, and are in sharp contrast to the species *Phragmipedium caudatum* and its old hybrid *P.* Grande, which possess extremely long, ribbon-like, twisting petals that reach down for 30cm (12in) or more. When held horizontally by the petal tips, the flower stretches over 60cm (2ft), making this the largest orchid flower in the world.

Phragmipediums become considerably large in their growth, and some of the modern hybrids raised from the species *Phragmipedium longifolium* produce extremely long, almost perpetually blooming flower spikes that go on for many months, even years, producing more blooms from an ever-extending tip. These large plants need plenty of headroom wherever they are grown. Their root system is similar to paphiopedilums, but more robust. The plants are at their best when allowed to reach their full potential and flowering

Phragmipedium Dom Wimber

ability, rather then being divided into small pieces. Give them the room they require and they will reward you with plenty of flowers.

Temperature: Intermediate-growing.
Cultivation: Grow in 15–20cm (6–8in) pots of coarse bark chips or Rockwool. Water freely throughout the year to keep the roots evenly moist. Feed at every other watering. Provide shade in summer, and give more light in winter.
Height: 30–60cm (1–2ft).

Phragmipedium besseae

This is the only known red-flowered *Phragmipedium* species, and one that was discovered as late as 1981 in Peru. This species, which flowers in summer, has revolutionized the genus by adding its red colouring to a new generation of hybrids.

Phragmipedium Don Wimber

This is an example of the lovely results that are being obtained by breeding with the species *Phragmipedium besseae*. The other parent is the hybrid *P.* Eric Young. The orange flowers are tinged with yellow, and appear in winter and spring on spikes up to 1m (3ft) high.

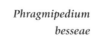

*Phragmipedium
besseae*

Phragmipedium Grande

Phragmipedium Eric Young

Phragmipedium pearcei

Phragmipedium Eric Young

This superb, winter- and spring-flowering modern hybrid was produced from the species *Phragmipedium besseae* to give the red colouring. The other parent of this primary hybrid is the long-petalled species *Phragmipedium longifolium*.

Phragmipedium Grande

This old hybrid produces large, green, long-petalled flowers in winter and spring, which droop from the multi-flowered spike. Although a great favourite, it lacks the colour of the modern hybrids.

Phragmipedium pearcei

This dwarf species from Central America has tufted growths and flower spikes 15cm (6in) high. The 10cm (4in) long, pale green flowers appear in spring and summer and have typically ribbon-like petals. Several flowers can appear on a stem.

PLEIONE

Pleiones are charming, miniature orchids with about 16 species in the genus. These are mainly terrestrial, sometimes lithophytic or epiphytic, deciduous plants, which produce rounded or coned pseudobulbs with a single, narrowly oval, ribbed leaf. The flowers are borne singly, but with occasionally two, on a slender stem that arises from the new growth when it is very young. The flowers are large for the size of the plant, and vary little in their appearance. Typically, the flowers have narrow sepals and petals of equal length, with a large, frilled, trumpet-shaped lip. The colours extend from pristine white to glistening pink and delicate mauve shades. Yellow is a rarer colour, but comes through in a number of the hybrids derived from the yellow-flowered species *Pleione forrestii*. While this species is rare in cultivation, others are common and easily grown alongside the larger, more richly coloured hybrids, which can have flowers 7cm (3in) across. Their flowering period is in the spring, although there are a few autumn-blooming species, such as *Pleione humilus*. The flowers will last for about ten days, after which new roots appear and the growth continues to complete the pseudobulb throughout the summer. As autumn approaches, the leaves will turn yellow before being discarded by the plant.

The pseudobulbs are only of two years' duration, so each spring pot up last season's pseudobulbs and remove the previous ones, which will be shrivelled and dead.

Pleiones like to be grown very cool, and a frost-free position will suit them during the winter. In summer, while they are growing, keep them on a cool windowsill or outdoors, if a suitable place can be found for them, once the flowers have finished. They can be planted out in rockeries in sheltered places, but the biggest danger here is of their being eaten by mice or slugs. Whatever other orchids you grow, find a small place for a few dainty pleiones.

Pleione formosana **var.** *alba*

Temperature: Very cool-growing.
Cultivation: Grow in groups in shallow pans or half pots of terrestrial orchid compost (growing medium), or a fine mixture of peat (or peat substitute) and perlite to which a little charcoal has been added. Give some shade in summer and full light in winter. Water only when in growth, from spring to autumn and feed at every other watering. Overwinter in a cool, dry place.
Height: To 15cm (6in).

Pleione formosana var. alba

This is the white form of the variable species that has done much for hybridizing within this genus. These deciduous orchids need a very cool winter's rest. The flowers appear in early spring.

Pleione speciosa

This very pretty species from China blooms in early spring from the centre of the new growth. The mauve flowers, with yellow at the centre of the lip, are 5cm (2in) across and appear on a stem less than 15cm (6in) tall. Many hybrids have been produced from this species.

Pleione speciosa

STANHOPEA

These are among the strangest of orchids, with their unusual habit of producing downward flower spikes that carry large, unwieldy flowers with fantastic fragrances and amazing shapes. To some, their appeal is irresistible, and they are worthy of interest.

About 25 species exist, originating from Central and South America where they grow as epiphytes on stout tree branches. The plants are evergreen, producing stout pseudobulbs with a single, large, semi-rigid leaf. They are grown in open hanging baskets to allow their flower spikes to penetrate the base and emerge through the bottom during the summer-flowering season. Under good culture they make extensive aerial roots, which form a dense and protective mass around the base of the plant. A good number of the species are in cultivation, in addition to a few hybrids, which are generally little improvement upon the fantastic species. Although the flowers are extremely short-lived, lasting for just a few days, plants that are grown to specimen size will produce several flower spikes, which open in succession to extend the flowering season.

Stanhopea Boileau

These orchids have a definite resting period during which they need to be allowed to dry out. This period may be while they are flowering in the summer, with new growths appearing during the autumn and continuing throughout the winter.
Temperature: Cool- to intermediate-growing.
Cultivation: Grow in open hanging baskets in bark-based compost (growing medium) in good light throughout the year. Water while in active growth and feed during the same period. Mist during summer, except when in flower.
Height: 30cm (12in).

Stanhopea Boileau
This is one of the very few hybrids in the genus. The blooms are short-lived, lasting just three to four days, but several flowerings can be expected in summer.

Stanhopea graveolans
Grow stanhopeas where you can provide them with plenty of headroom and space to accommodate their hanging flowers. This strongly fragrant species from Mexico and Guatemala, blooms several times throughout the summer.

Stanhopea wardii
Stanhopeas are grown in open slatted baskets and their extraordinary flowers are produced on vertical flower spikes that hang below the plant. This highly fragrant species needs a cool greenhouse where it will flower throughout the summer. The yellow flowers have orange markings.

Stanhopea graveolens

Stanhopea wardii

VANDA ALLIANCE

Vandas are a natural genus of over 30 species, originating from a wide area of the Old World, from India, South-east Asia and Indonesia to the Philippines, New Guinea and Australia. They head a huge alliance of intergeneric hybrid forms, which include other natural genera such as *Ascocentrum, Rhynchostylis, Renanthera, Arachnis*, and many others, including *Phalaenopsis* and *Doritis*. The majority of these plants are warm-growing, light-loving types that grow best in the tropics, where a massive breeding programme has continued apace. The results can be seen in florists' shops where the cut flowers are in great demand.

Vandas are monopodial evergreen plants that grow from a central tip on an ever-extending rhizome. As new, semi-rigid leaves are produced from the apex, the lower ones are eventually lost. After a few years, the plants become "leggy" with a length of bare stem above the pot. Stout aerial roots, formed along the base stem, are a feature of these plants. At the right stage, the plant can be reduced in length by cutting through the bare rhizome below the aerial roots. The top portion is potted up, leaving the aerial roots outside the pot. In time, new roots will be made inside the pot and the plant will continue its upward progression. The flower spikes emerge from the axils of the lower leaves at various times throughout the year.

Some varieties are more easily flowered than others. Try a few of the fantastic blue or mauve hybrids, containing the species *Vanda coerulea* and *V.* (syn. *Eulanthe*) *sanderiana*. The crossing of these two plants produced the lovely, deep blue *V.* Rothschildiana, and this one hybrid has done more to promote the genus in the northern hemisphere than any other orchid. *V.* Rothschildiana will grow with exceptional ease and bloom two to three times a year. The plants can grow considerably tall, up to 1m (3ft), making an impressive specimen when in bloom. The large, rounded blooms are over 7cm (3in) across and will last for several weeks at a time. In addition, there are other variously coloured vandas and intergeneric hybrids available. Look out for the brilliantly coloured, often smaller-flowered ascocendas (*Vanda* × *Ascocentrum*). These are often more popular than the pure vandas because of their neat habit and upright flower spikes, which are crowded with beautiful, symmetrical flowers in fiery reds, gorgeous oranges and deep yellows. While some are self-coloured, others display extreme tessellating or mottling on the petals and sepals.

Temperature: Warm-growing.

Cultivation: Grow in open slatted baskets in a compost (growing medium) of coarse bark chips to which a few pieces of horticultural charcoal or pumice have been added. Maintain good light all year. Water freely and feed weekly in summer to encourage aerial roots. Mist the foliage on a regular basis.

Height: 30–100cm (12-36in).

Ascocenda **Crownfox Mystique**

Ascocenda **Crownfox Gem**

Ascocenda David Peterson × *Rhynchostylis coelestis*

Trudelia cristata

Ascocenda **Crownfox Gem**
The rich russet-brown of this summer-flowering orchid is an unusual colour combination. The colour is the result of several lines of breeding using the colourful *Ascocentrum* species with *Vanda* hybrids.

Ascocenda **Crownfox Mystique**
The wonderfully rich colouring of this bigeneric cross has come from the *Ascocentrum* parent, which has also reduced the size of the summer flowers.

Ascocenda David Peterson × *Rhynchostylis coelestis*
This is a tri-generic genus in the huge *Vanda* alliance, which has produced vanda-like flowers, well rounded and tessellated, on an upright flower spike. The *Rhynchostylis* parent has reduced the overall size of the flowers, which otherwise closely resemble the pure *Vanda*. The striking, purple-blue flowers appear in abundant clusters in the summer.

Trudelia cristata
Closely allied to *Vanda*, where it was originally placed, this green-flowered species with a vivid, red-striped lip makes a slender plant that can grow to 30cm (12in) tall. This popular species, which flowers in the spring, comes from India.

Vanda coerulescens

Vanda **Fuchs Magic**

Vanda **Gordon Dillon 'Lea' AM/AOS**

Vanda coerulescens

One of the smaller-growing species, this plant has terete leaves in pairs with the loosely flowered spike coming from the leaf axils. The pale mauve flowers with a violet lip are 3cm (1¼in) across. This highly variable species can bloom at various times.

Vanda Fuchs Magic

Among the numerous hybrids in this genus is a multitude of colourful varieties where the rich mauves and purples excel. This stunning variety, which flowers in summer, shows delicate tessellating over the sepals and petals.

Vanda Gordon Dillon 'Lea' AM/AOS

Awarded by the American Orchid Society for its unusual colour combination and flower quality, this striking hybrid speaks for itself. The flower spike is compact, and the heavy, textured blooms are evenly marked. The flowers appear in the summer.

Vanda Julia Sorenson

Vanda plants such as this hybrid can grow considerably large with many pairs of leaves. The large, 10cm (4in) flowers, which appear in summer, are produced on spikes that come from the axils of the leaves.

Vanda Manuvadee 'Sky'

Blue is a colour seldom met in orchids other than vandas. The deep purple-blue of this outstanding hybrid has come from several blue-flowered species, including *Vanda coerulea*. The flowers bloom in summer.

Vanda **Julia Sorenson**

Vanda **Manuvadee 'Sky'**

ZYGOPETALUM

Strong colourings, fragrance and upright flower spikes typify this South and Central American genus. The plants are mainly epiphytic with stout pseudobulbs and leaves which can grow to 30cm (12in) or more in height. They produce a thick rooting system, not unlike that of cymbidiums. For this reason they need to be repotted on a regular basis, as if left too long in one pot they push themselves out by their roots. The flower spikes appear from the base of the new growth while it is still at a young stage in the spring. The flowers are characterized by their bold colourings, the petals and sepals (of equal length) being mostly green-brown or green speckled brown, and the bold lip usually white, veined, dotted or dashed with mauve or indigo blue. Of the 20 or so species that occur in the wild, only a few are generally found in cultivation, the most popular being *Zygopetalum mackaii*.

Until recently very little hybridizing had been carried out with this genus, but the last few years have witnessed an upsurge in the breeding of intergeneric hybrids from Australia. Zygopetalums have been crossed with *Colax* to produce *Zygocolax*, *Neogardneria* which gives *Zygoneria*, and with *Aganisia*, *Batemannia*, *Otostylis* and *Zygosepalum* which created the multigeneric hybrid *Hamelwellsara*. These new hybrids are increasing the range of highly fragrant, free flowering, modest-size orchids for the cool and intermediate greenhouses. The plants most frequently seen for sale are cool growing.

While these orchids are considered more of a challenge they are nevertheless well worth growing once you have gained some experience with easier types.

Temperature: Cool- to intermediate-growing.

Cultivation: Grow in pots or open slatted baskets of bark-based compost (growing medium). They require shady conditions for most of the year, and need to be watered more in the summer and less in the winter. Feed can be applied while they are growing. The foliage of zygopetalums is easily marked if water rests on the surface for too long. For this reason they are better not sprayed on a regular basis with water, but watered only through the roots. *Height*: 30–45cm (12–18in).

Zygopetalum Artur Elle 'Stonehurst'

The bold colours of the flowers, which are lime-green with deep purple spotting and have a purple lip, make this an unusual orchid for indoor cultivation. The plant blooms from the new growths in the early spring. Grow in a fairly cool room with good light, but out of direct sun.

Zygopetalum **Artur Elle 'Stonehurst'**

SPECIALIST ORCHIDS

The orchids described on the following pages can be grown alongside most of those already mentioned in order to add variety to any collection. All are intriguing plants, which you will grow to appreciate as they become more familiar.

ACINETA

Of the 15 species of *Acineta*, which all come from South America, only a few are in general cultivation. These evergreen epiphytic orchids produce stout, cone-shaped pseudobulbs with usually two, occasionally more, semi-rigid, broad leaves. The plants resemble the stanhopeas, being of a similar size at around 30cm (12in) tall. The flower spikes come from the base of the latest pseudobulb and develop over the rim of the container, eventually becoming pendent. The flowers, clustered on the spike, have a heavy, waxy texture and are strongly coloured. The plants bloom mostly during the summer.
Temperature: Intermediate-growing, with a minimum winter night temperature of 13°C (55°F).
Cultivation: Grow in hanging, open, slatted baskets in a coarse bark compost (growing medium), in good light all year round. Commence watering immediately new growth is seen, usually in the spring. During the growing season, water and apply feed at every other watering. Spray the foliage and maintain a good humidity. Allow the plants to rest when dormant during the winter.
Height: 30cm (12in).

Acineta superba
These robust orchids from South America need to grow in baskets to enable their downward-growing flower spikes to hang freely. The fragrant flowers, which appear in spring and summer, are cupped, with the smaller petals standing close to the lip.

Acineta superba

AERANGIS

There are about 50 species in this natural genus of monopodial orchids, which hail from Africa and Madagascar. The plants produce a fan-like assemblage of semi-rigid leaves that grow from a central rhizome. Most of the species resemble the phalaenopsis in habit, but their leaves are thicker. The flower spikes may bear from just one to numerous flowers on pendent spikes, over 30cm (12in) long. The flowers are mostly white, with a long spur at the back of the flower. This spur is an extension of the back of the lip, and is used by the flower to ensure pollination by a moth with a tongue of the same length. The white flowers are attractive to night-flying moths.

Limited hybridizing has been done with this genus, and intergeneric hybrids have been made crossing *Aerangis* with *Angraecum* (*Angrangis*) and others. When you look at the clear, natural beauty of these often pristine white blooms, it is difficult to see how hybridizing can improve upon them. The species are exquisite, and if you grow any of the orchids from this group, you will want to obtain as many as possible.

A greenhouse suits them best, where they can be suspended from the roof in open baskets to allow their flowers to be shown to their best advantage.
Temperature: Warm-growing.
Cultivation: Grow in a fine bark compost (growing medium) in slatted baskets in good light. Small species can also be mounted on bark. Keep them moist all year round and mist them regularly to maintain humidity. Feed lightly at every second watering. Leave plants undisturbed, but add a small amount of compost (growing medium) to the base of the plant from time to time. If on bark, add a wad of fibre or moss around the base.
Height: From 15cm (6in).

Aerangis luteo alba var. *rhodostricta*
This is an attractive dwarf species from parts of Africa, where it grows on twigs in dry, exposed areas. The plant is only a few inches high, and the white flowers, which appear in winter, have an unusually bright red column and are large in comparison.

Aerangis luteo-alba var. *rhodostricta*

ANGRAECUM

Related to the smaller-growing *Aerangis* are the lovely angraecums. These superb epiphytic, lithophytic or terrestrial orchids come from all over southern Africa and Madagascar. The monopodial plants vary in size, and, of the 200 or so species, many can be found in cultivation. Among the smallest is *Angraecum distichum*, a dwarf plant with plaited (braided), herringbone-like foliage, whose oval leaves overlap along a curving rhizome, which rarely exceeds 15cm (6in) in length. The minute flowers (5mm/¼in wide) are produced singly all over the plant, to resemble stars in a night sky. The giants of the genus include the magnificent *A. sesquipedale*. In between these extremes are further desirable and collectable species as well as a few hybrids.

These evergreen plants make attractive specimens, even when they are not in flower. Their blooms are produced mainly during the winter and spring, when they will last for several weeks.
Temperature: Intermediate-growing, with a minimum winter temperature of 13°C (55°F) at night.
Cultivation: Grow smaller angraecums in half pots or mounted on pieces of cork bark. The larger plants need to be grown in pots with an open, coarse compost (growing medium). As the temperature rises in summer, increase the humidity to maintain the balance. These are low-light plants, which need good shade in summer and filtered light in winter. Water all year round and apply feed, but give less to those in pots in winter because they will take longer to dry out.
Height: 15cm (6in) to over 30cm (12in).

Angraecum sesquipedale
The comet orchid from Madagascar is so called because of its extraordinarily long spur. The waxy, ivory-white flower is 15cm (6in) across, and the plant will grow to over 30cm (12in). Several flowers can be carried on one spike and appear in winter.

Angraecum sesquipedale

Bifrenaria harrisoniae

BIFRENARIA

About 30 species make up this natural genus of mainly epiphytic plants, which originate from Brazil, Peru and as far north as Panama. Several species are in cultivation, the most popular being *Bifrenaria harrisoniae*, with its strikingly beautiful colouring. This species can be grown with comparative ease and blooms regularly in late summer, thus making it an ideal orchid to grow, even for the relatively inexperienced orchid-grower.

Typically, the plants produce cone-shaped, yellowish to green pseudobulbs with a single, wide, ribbed leaf. The flowers are produced on short flower spikes that huddle below the foliage, bearing two or more flowers.

These orchids do well in a mixed collection, being easily accommodated among other plants. When they are large enough, the plants can be divided into smaller pieces, provided there is a new growth on each division. Alternatively, new plants can be grown from the backbulbs that are removed from the main plant at repotting time.
Temperature: Cool-growing.
Cultivation: Grow in 10cm (4in) pots in a fine bark compost (growing medium) in good light. Water and apply feed regularly during the summer growing season. The foliage can be lightly sprayed in summer while the plants are out of flower. Allow the plants to dry out while resting in winter. Water should be given during this time only if the plants shrivel.
Height: To 30cm (12in).

Bifrenaria harrisoniae
A most pleasing species for the cool greenhouse or indoors, the large flowers, 8cm (3in) wide, which bloom in early summer, are waxy, creamy white and have a deep mauve, hairy lip. One to two flowers are produced on a short spike below the leaves.

BULBOPHYLLUM

The bulbophyllums comprise a huge genus of upwards of 1,000 species, among which can be found some of the most extraordinary and outlandish flowers. The plants are extremely variable, ranging in size from tiny plants with little rounded, pea-size pseudobulbs (such as *Bulbophyllum roxburghii*) to the giants such as *B. fletcherianum*, whose ungainly flowers resemble the gaping mouths of baby birds. This plant has leaves that hang down over 30cm (12in), resembling the old-fashioned razor strops. In between are literally hundreds of species and a very few hybrids, all with amazing flowers. Some are decidedly ugly and have a strong odour reminiscent of carrion. Others are exceedingly pretty, while others produce flattened stems with beetle-like flowers, which typify one small group among this extremely diverse genus. All the plants are evergreen and epiphytic, some of the

Bulbophyllum barbigerum

smaller species being known as "twig epiphytes" because they cling to the very extremities of the smallest branches.

Bulbophyllums are widely distributed throughout South-east Asia as well as Africa, Australia and tropical America. They must be regarded as one of the most successful genera among the orchids. If you cannot recognize one orchid from a display at an orchid event, the chances are that it is a *Bulbophyllum*!

Try some of the smaller plants indoors, where they will do well in pots, baskets or on bark. The smaller species will grow with great vigour, multiplying their pseudobulbs each year until a large specimen plant is built up. When placed in a hanging basket, the plants can grow into huge leafy balls completely surrounding their container. The numerous flowering spikes that are produced will cover the plant to create a most eye-catching sight.

These are really fun orchids to grow, but watch out for the bad-smelling ones. Go instead for those gems with a rocking lip, such as *Bulbophyllum lobbii*, or those with the amazingly long sepals, such as *B. medusae*, or the alluring, tantalizingly mobile flowers of *B. barbigerum*. You will not be disappointed.
Temperature: Cool-growing (some are best in intermediate conditions).
Cultivation: Grow on bark or in pots or baskets of bark compost (growing medium). Water well in summer, but give less in winter. Do not allow those with small pseudobulbs to shrivel. Feed every second watering. Once established, give plenty of light, but avoid direct sunlight. In winter they need as much light as possible.
Height: 7–30cm (3–12in).

Bulbophyllum barbigerum
These tantalizing 1cm (½in) dark red flowers have a movable lip that is adorned with bristling hairs. The slightest movement causes them to wave in a way that is likely to attract a pollinator. The plant will remain in bloom for months.

Bulbophyllum dayanum

Bulbophyllum dayanum

This small plant, less than 15cm (6in) in height, produces its modest flowers in clusters around the base in summer. Each 5mm (¼in) bloom has short hairs to the edges of its sepals and petals and the lip is blood red. Its appearance is intended to mimic an open wound on an animal's hide.

Bulbophyllum purpureorachis

Among the bulbophyllums can be found some of the strangest flowers in the orchid family. This curious species from Africa carries its small, beetle-like flowers along two sides of a tall, flattened stem.

Bulbophyllum purpureoachis

CALANTHE

This is a genus of about 150 terrestrial species spread through parts of Asia. Of these, only a handful of species and hybrids are in general cultivation.

The genus can be divided into two distinct groups. The first, which is more widely grown, contains deciduous plants that have large, silvery pseudobulbs and wide, spreading, ribbed leaves. They are short-lived and die in their second year. The flowers – mainly pink and white – are spread along a tall, arching flower spike, which emerges from the base of the leafless pseudobulb during the autumn and winter, while the plant is at rest. Modern hybridizing within this group has resulted in some highly desirable deep red clones. The flower stems are soft and hairy, and the blooms have a delicate appeal.

The second group are the evergreen types. These come mainly from across China and Japan and are highly regarded by the Japanese, who grow them to perfection, creating new hybrids along the way. This group produces small, diminutive pseudobulbs with wide, spreading foliage. The flower

Calanthe **Baron Schroder**

Calanthe **Corbiere**

and discontinue for the winter while the flower spike is extending and the flowering period lasts. After flowering, remove the plants to a position in full light, but take care to retrieve them as soon as you see the new growth the next year.
Height: To 1m (3ft) when in leaf.

Calanthe **Baron Schroder**

One of the older hybrids among the genus raised in 1894, this plant produces its pink and white flowers over many months in winter and spring. The silvery pseudobulbs can be up to 15cm (6in) high. In summer, the plants are in leaf and need plenty of headroom in a warm greenhouse.

Calanthe **Corbiere**

This milk-white hybrid is from the group of deciduous calanthes produced from *Calanthe* Harrisii. These plants bloom during the winter and spring while the plant is dormant.

Calanthe **Gorey × Grouville**

Numerous flowers are produced over an extended period during the winter. Over 2.5cm (1in) wide, they are carried on a very tall flower spike that can grow to over 1m (3ft) as it develops.

Calanthe **Gorey × Grouville**

spikes come from the base, and carry numerous colourful flowers with yellow, pink, white and green being popular.

Calanthes have a short, fast-growing season. Because of the speed at which they grow, these are really exciting orchids to cultivate, but they do need plenty of headroom while in leaf. Repot each spring when the growth starts. If the oldest pseudobulb is dead and shrivelled, remove it; if it is still firm and plump, it may be potted separately to give you two new plants next season.

Temperature: Intermediate-growing, with a minimum temperature of 16°C (60°F) at night.
Cultivation: Grow in pots of a terrestrial orchid mix containing some peat and perlite. Begin watering and feeding as soon as new growth is seen in the spring. While in growth, the plants should be kept well shaded. Too much humidity, as well as spraying of the leaves, can cause the foliage to spot. This is not a great problem because it is shed in autumn, after turning yellow. At this time, reduce the watering

CIRRHOPETALUM

While some authorities consider all cirrhopetalums as part of the huge, closely related genus *Bulbophyllum*, others keep them distinct. There are obvious similarities between the plants, which often cannot be distinguished out of bloom, but the flowers can be horticulturally recognized by the extremely long and tapering sepals produced by the majority of the species. They are mentioned here as a separate genus firstly because the older name is retained for horticultural usage and secondly to enable the reader to distinguish readily between them. For hybrid registration purposes, both *Bulbophyllum* and *Cirrhopetalum* have been recognized, with four bigeneric hybrids being registered as *Cirrhophyllum* in 1965.

Culturally, cirrhopetalums require the same conditions and treatment as bulbophyllums. The species exhibit their twirling flowers in close umbels at the end of slender flower spikes. The overall effect of the closely aligned flowers, with stumpy petals touching and the elegantly tapering sepals forming a distinct waterfall, is quite captivating. The colours can be strong, with red being the main colour. The small, often glossy or wet-looking, projecting lip attracts flies on the lookout for raw meat. *Cirrhopetalum rothschildianum* carries a fringe of small hairs on the tips of the petals and dorsal sepal like an exclamation mark, creating an alien air.

Temperature: Cool-growing (some are best in intermediate conditions).

Cultivation: Grow on bark or in pots or baskets of bark compost (growing medium). Water well in summer, but give less in winter. Do not allow those with small pseudobulbs to shrivel. Feed every second watering. Once established, give plenty of light, but avoid direct sunlight. In winter they need as much light as possible.

Height: 15cm (6in).

Cirrhopetalum Elizabeth Ann 'Bucklebury' AM/RHS

This is one of only a few exciting hybrids to be produced from this genus. The flowers, which appear at various times, extend their long, tapering sepals for several centimetres (inches), and the dorsals are adorned with small tufts of hairs.

Cirrhopetalum guttulatum

In winter and spring, little flowers less than 1cm (½in) wide adorn this pretty, easily grown and flowered species, which does well indoors or in a cool greenhouse. The flower spikes are under 15cm (6in) tall.

Cirrhopetalum umbellatum

A robust species with plants over 15cm (6in) tall, this has drooping flower spikes that terminate in umbels of large flowers where the sepals are extended to form the edge of the ring. The petals and lip are very small. The flowers bloom in spring.

Cirrhopetalum guttulatum

Cirrhopetalum umbellatum

Cirrhopetalum Elizabeth Ann 'Bucklebury' AM/RHS

CYRTOCHILUM

This genus contains about 150 evergreen epiphytic species, which originate from South and Central America, often at high elevations in the Andes. The plants were at one time included in the genus *Oncidium*, but are now considered distinct, although the latter name persists in orchid-growing circles. Very few of the species, and virtually no hybrids, are cultivated. Mostly the species are rare and much treasured. The main appreciable difference between *Cyrtochilum* and *Oncidium* is the size of the lip, which, so often exaggerated in the oncidiums, is much reduced in favour of broad, spreading sepals in the cyrtochilums.

The plants, which can be over 30cm (12in) tall, produce robust pseudobulbs with narrowly oval leaves. Typically, the flower spikes are extremely long, often reaching 4–5m (12–16½ft) in length. The flowers are spread out, appearing in little clusters along most of their length. These long flower spikes can be trained into a hoop, which makes accommodating them easier and enables the flowers to be seen more clearly.

Cyrtochilums do well alongside other members of the *Odontoglossum* alliance. Some of the species produce their new pseudobulbs along an upward-creeping rhizome, with a long gap in between. One good way of growing these is to insert a mossy pole into a heavy flowerpot and allow the plant to extend upwards. Aerial roots soon become a feature of these plants.
Temperature: Cool-growing.
Cultivation: Grow in 10cm (4in) pots in a coarse bark compost (growing medium) or insert a moss-covered pole in the pot for the orchid to climb up. Provide shade during the summer and give more light in winter. Water throughout the year, but give less in winter. Apply feed in summer at every other watering.
Height: 60cm (2ft).

Cyrtochilum annulares
Clusters of chocolate-brown, yellow-edged flowers are produced in summer at intervals along an extremely long stem, which is best trained into a hoop.

Cyrtochilum annulares

DENDROCHILUM

Dendrochilums are evergreen epiphytic orchids, which come from the continent of Asia, but are also found in the Philippines and New Guinea. Of the 120 or so species, very few are generally grown, and there appear to be no hybrids. This rarity in cultivation reflects the plants' scarcity in the wild, and it is possible that they have never been that abundant.

The plants are neat, with evergreen pseudobulbs and a single, narrow, oval leaf, seldom reaching more than 25cm (10in) tall. The slender flower spikes come from the base of the new growth, and most are autumn-flowering. When grown on into large specimen plants, their sight and fragrance is not something to be forgotten, for these are among the prettiest of little orchid flowers.

Do not be tempted to divide these orchids until absolutely necessary: the larger the plant, the better they look.

The common name for these delightful, modestly sized orchids is silver chain orchids, or in some instances golden chain orchids. This refers to the slender flower spike, which is densely packed with small, white or yellow flowers, arranged in two distinct rows along most of its length.

Temperature: Cool-growing.

Cultivation: Grow in pots or hanging baskets of fine bark compost (growing medium). Provide shady conditions when in growth, but full light during the winter. Water all year, but give much less during the winter while the plants are resting. Feed only in summer, at every other watering.

Height: 23cm (9in).

Dendrochilum cobbianum

Dendrochilum glumaceum

Dendrochilum cobbianum

This sweetly scented, cool-growing species from the Philippines, which grows to about 30cm (12in) tall, carries hundreds of small, white flowers on drooping spikes. It blooms in early summer and is suitable for indoor or greenhouse culture.

Dendrochilum glumaceum

An easily grown species, this blooms freely during the early summer with cascading sprays of small, whitish flowers with orange lips, densely packed in a herringbone pattern along the flower spike. The flowers carry a very strong, attractive scent.

EULOPHIA

Over 200 species of *Eulophia* are distributed throughout the African continent. These are terrestrial orchids, which produce large pseudobulbs from a strong rhizome, with wide, spreading leaves. The flower spikes come from the base of the newly completed pseudobulb. The genus is extremely varied, and plants of differing sizes are found, although not many are in general cultivation. In their natural state, these orchids may exist in wet marshland or on dry and arid hillsides. Their different cultural requirements may be one reason for their lack of popularity in cultivation. Nevertheless, these are excellent plants to grow and not all are space-consuming giants.

An interesting feature of some of the species is the unusual flower shape: the petals turn on a flat plane, possibly offering a wider landing platform for insects.

These are specialist plants, whose requirements need to be addressed for successful cultivation.

Temperature: Cool- or intermediate-growing, depending upon the species.
Cultivation: Pot in an open coarse mix of chunky bark and peat, to which has been added a portion of perlite. Water and feed while in active growth. Water or rest in winter according to its natural habitat (only water if the plant is in active growth).
Height: 30cm (12in).

Eulophia euglossa
An unusual terrestrial species from Africa, this produces slender, leafy pseudobulbs and showy flowers on an upright spike in summer. The pointed blooms are apple green with a white lip.

Eulophia euglossa

GONGORA

This is a small, natural genus of about 25 species, a number of which are cultivated, mostly by specialist growers mesmerized by the small, curiously formed flowers. A plant in bloom most often conjures up images of birds in flight, or, occasionally, insects flying in formation. There are no hybrids, probably because the species offer all that anyone could require from this type of orchid.

Closely related to the stanhopeas, the gongoras are mainly smaller plants with ribbed, cone-shaped, green pseudobulbs, supporting a pair of narrowly oval to wide leaves. The flower spikes come from the base of the newly completed pseudobulbs in the early summer, and some are extremely fragrant. The spikes hang around the edge of the plant's container, often in profusion. These evergreen epiphytic species hail mostly from Brazil, with others coming from Peru and further north to Mexico.

Further fanciful attempts to describe the flowers have given rise to the name of Punch and Judy orchid: turn one flower on its side and see the two quarrelling figures appear to be battling it out with each other!

Although not plentiful in cultivation, these orchids are well worth growing, but need to be bought from specialist nurseries.
Temperature: Cool- to intermediate-growing.
Cultivation: Grow in pots or in hanging baskets in fine bark compost (growing medium). Give shade in summer, and full light in winter. Water and apply feed throughout the summer. Water sparingly during the winter to keep the pseudobulbs plump.
Height: 23cm (9in).

Gongora maculata
Among the strangest of flowers produced by any orchid, this species from tropical America projects a cascade of flowers, 4cm (1½in) long, like birds in flight, from the base of the pseudobulb in summer. It is lightly scented.

Gongora maculata

Jumellia sagittata

JUMELLIA

Coming mainly from Madagascar, these monopodial, clump-forming, evergreen epiphytic plants resemble angraecums in their growth, which is robust, with long, fleshy leaves. Of the 40 or so species, only a very few are grown, none of which is plentiful in cultivation, and the genus has not produced any hybrids except for a very few intergenerics with related genera such as *Angraecum* and *Aeranthes* (syn. *Angranthellea*).

The flowers, which are disappointingly small for the size of the plant, are produced on slender flower spikes and are typically solely white, with sepals, petals and a lip of equal proportions. This structure as well as the presence of a long spur indicates pollination by night-flying moths, which means that the flower has no need of other coloration or indeed fragrance.
Temperature: Warm-growing.
Cultivation: Grow in 15cm (6in) pots or baskets containing a coarse, chunky compost (growing medium) to accommodate the long roots, which often

meander at will. Provide shade and high humidity, as for *Phalaenopsis*. Water and feed throughout the year, giving less in winter.
Height: 45cm (18in).

Jumellia sagittata

A robust-growing species from Madagascar, this produces *Vanda*-like growth. The flowers, 4cm (1½in) wide, are carried singly on spindly spikes that are shorter than the height of the plant. A profusion of blooms crowds around the base in winter.

LOCKHARTIA

Lockhartias are not common in cultivation, and of the 30 or so evergreen epiphytic species endemic to Mexico and nearby, only a very few are grown. The plants are nevertheless interesting, having distinct foliage that forms two ranks along the entire length of the erect stems. The flowers, which are small and yellow, not unlike *Oncidium*, appear in groups from between the leaves at intervals along the stem.

These orchids have a fine rooting system that will quickly adhere to any bark surface, provided there is sufficient moisture. They do not have a noticeable dormant period but will slow their growth during the winter months.
Temperature: Intermediate-growing.
Cultivation: Grow in small pots of fine bark compost (growing medium) or mounted on bark. Spray regularly during summer to keep the foliage from dehydrating. Water all year, and apply feed lightly during the summer.
Height: To 30cm (12in).

Lockhartia oerstedii
This species produces leafy stems, up to 30cm (12in) tall. The small, overlapping leaves create an unusual plaited appearance. The small, bright yellow flowers are produced over a period of several weeks in summer.

Lockhartia oerstedii

Ludisia discolor

LUDISIA

Members of this genus of attractive terrestrials, which originate from China, are known as jewel orchids. This is one of a very few orchid genera that are cultivated for their foliage rather than for their flowers. The leaves of this pretty orchid are exquisite: dark velvety green is overlaid with silver and gold veining in intricate lines all over the leaf surface. At night, shine a torch on to the leaves and see them glisten; the same effect is achieved by allowing the sun to shine momentarily upon them. But these are essentially shade-loving plants, used to growing as terrestrials or lithophytes along the banks of rivers and streams where the light is poor and the sun seldom filters down. In their native home across India and China, they grow upon mossy rocks close to water, but they often do well indoors, where the drier atmosphere suits them.

The plants produce rosettes of leaves at intervals along a creeping rhizome. Shortly after the appearance of the new growth, roots appear around the base and these will penetrate the compost (growing medium). The flowers appear from the centre of the maturing growth on an upright flower spike. The curious, pretty blooms are white with yellow on the lip. A large plant that has been allowed to grow on, producing multiple growths, will create a lasting impression, with numerous flower spikes open all at once.
Temperature: Warm-growing.
Cultivation: Grow in pans with an open, gritty compost (growing medium) suitable for terrestrial orchids. Keep well shaded all year. Keep evenly moist. If the plants become overwet at any time, rotting is quick to follow. Water carefully in summer and sparingly during the winter. Feed the plants lightly at every third watering.
Height: 15cm (6in).

Ludisia discolor
This species is grown for its beautiful, velvety, dark green and veined foliage. It is a terrestrial plant that blooms from the centre of the growth, producing flower spikes, about 30cm (12in) tall, of delightfully curious white flowers. The flowers bloom in summer.

MEXICOA

This genus contains just one species, which has been moved from *Oncidium* and given monotypic status. *Mexicoa ghiesbrechtiana* is small in stature, with oval pseudobulbs and a pair of narrowly oval leaves. As its name suggests, it originates from Mexico and grows epiphytically. This is an ideal subject for inclusion in a collection of miniature orchids, since this little plant rarely exceeds 15cm (6in) in height, even when in flower. It associates well with other members of the *Odontoglossum* alliance. The attractive blooms, on short flower spikes, are yellow and the petals and sepals are shaded with brown. The lip is large, reminiscent of *Oncidium*, and dominates the flower. The flowers appear mainly during summer and will last for a few weeks.

Temperature: Cool-growing.

Cultivation: Grow in pots of fine bark compost (growing medium) or mounted on bark. Grow in good shade in summer, but give more light in winter. Water all year, but give less in winter. Feed lightly at every third watering in summer. Lightly mist the foliage in summer.

Height: To 15cm (6in).

Mexicoa ghiesbrechtiana

A delightful miniature species from Mexico, this requires a cool situation. The plants are no more than 15cm (6in) tall and the pretty flowers, which come on arching spikes, are yellow and brown. The lip is large and flared. The plant blooms mainly during the summer.

Mexicoa ghiesbrechtiana

MILTONIA

There are about ten species of *Miltonia* and very few pure hybrids. The genus was divided from *Miltoniopsis*, the true pansy orchids, the notable difference being the lack of the large, flat lip, and the distribution of the plants. Miltonias are confined to Brazil, whereas miltoniopsis are spread mainly throughout Colombia. Some confusion can arise when the incorrect name is used for miltoniopsis, where, for hybrid registration purposes, *Miltonia* is retained.

Miltonias are evergreen epiphytes with neat, green pseudobulbs, often produced along a creeping rhizome. The flowers come from the base of the new growth and are spread along an arching or upright flower spike. The flowers are variable, and the most spectacular have been used for hybridizing with other related members of the *Odontoglossum* alliance.

Temperature: Warm-growing.
Cultivation: Grow those that produce their pseudobulbs at intervals along a rhizome in half-pots or baskets of a shape that easily accommodates their elongated outline, using a bark-based compost (growing medium). Give good shade in summer, but more light in winter. Feed at every other watering in summer, and maintain a good humidity.
Height: 23cm (9in).

Miltonia confusa (syn. *Miltonioides confusa*)
This lovely fragrant species from Costa Rica produces its eye-catching, red and green flowers mainly during the winter and spring. The flowers are long-lasting.

Miltonia flavescens
Suitable for warm growing, this species has slender pseudobulbs and numerous pale-coloured flowers on a spike. It will last for several weeks during the summer.

Miltonia confusa

Miltonia warscewiczii
(syn. *Miltonioides warscewiczii*)
This warm-growing species is unusual for the "window" of almost translucent tissue that can be seen in the middle of the lip. The flowers, which appear in early summer, are cherry red. Some handsome hybrids have been raised from this species.

Miltonia warscewiczii var. *alba*
(syn. *Miltonioides warscewiczii* var. *alba*)
The albino form of the species, which comes from South America, has near-white flowers in early summer, and is quite rare. It carries fewer flowers on the spike than the type. This plant does best when grown in a warm greenhouse.

Miltonia warscewiczii

Miltonia flavescens

Miltonia warscewiczii var. alba

NEOFINETA

Neofineta has been settled upon a single species, which has undergone numerous name changes since its discovery in 1784. It is a small-growing, monopodial, evergreen species from Japan, which has a large following of devoted growers who cultivate the plant for its often-seen, variegated foliage, considered in Japan to be highly decorative. The plant seldom reaches more than 10cm (4in) in height, producing semi-rigid, fleshy leaves from the apex. The flowers, usually two or three on a short stem, are white with a long, curving spur.

Temperature: Cool-growing.
Cultivation: Grow in a small container of fine bark compost (growing medium) or mounted on bark. Maintain good light and high humidity by spraying the foliage regularly. Keep moist all year, and apply feed during the summer.
Height: To 10cm (4in).

Neofineta falcata
This is an attractive, modestly sized, monopodial plant with flower spikes of pure white blooms, each with a long spur. Grow in good light in a cool greenhouse. Flowers appear at various times.

Neofineta falcata

PLEUROTHALLIS

This is one natural genus among several that comprise a huge alliance of miniature orchids, known as the Pleurothallidinae alliance. These often tiny, always delightful, orchids have a large following of devoted growers, and specialist societies are confined entirely to the promotion of this group. Among these can be found some of the smallest orchids in the world, which need the assistance of an eye glass in order to study their tiny but intricate flowers.

There are considered to be about 900 species distributed throughout Central and South America. Some have been transferred to separate genera, but often appear under the older name in cultivation. Many of these are grown, but little hybridizng has been attempted.

Various sections within the genus are characterized by the habit of the plant. Notable are those with short, slender stems that support a single wide leaf. The flowers appear at the apex and "sit" on the leaf surface, resembling a little beetle, as with *Pleurothallis matuadina*. Others deliver an explosion of minute flowers from the leaf axil, as with *P. octomerioides*. Yet others produce leafy stems, their cotton-thin flower spikes coming from near the base and carrying several tiny flowers on stems only just taller than the foliage. Some of the smallest, such as *P. grobyi*, compare with the giants of the genus, including the dark, brooding flowers of *P. roezlii*.

Pleurothallis are extremely easy plants to grow, and large specimens can be attained with a few years of growing. They flower freely, and those that produce sequential flowerings will continue to flower for months.

Temperature: Cool-growing.

Cultivation: Grow in pots of fine bark compost (growing medium). Keep shaded in summer, and admit full light in winter. Water all year, but give less in winter. Feed lightly at every third watering.

Height: 5–23cm (2–9in).

Pleurothallis peduncularis

From a huge genus of often minuscule orchids comes this little plant, whose tiny blooms explode from the base of the leaf in early autumn. These are off-white, with a tiny, jewel-like lip at the centre.

ROSSIOGLOSSUM

At one time grouped with the odontoglossums, this magnificent genus has been afforded separate status. The evergreen epiphytic plants come from Central America, where six species have been identified. All are highly desirable plants, not at all common in cultivation. Although defined as members of the *Odontoglossum* alliance, rossioglossums will not cross breed with any other genus; in fact, they are extremely difficult to hybridize within their own select genus. As a result, there are very few hybrids available.

The plants have dark green pseudobulbs and a pair of dark green, oval leaves that are peppered with brown when the new growth is young. This unusual feature is often mistaken for insect infestation. The flower spikes come from the base of the new growth in the autumn and produce several flowers on a stem. These are mostly large, strongly coloured flowers, typically yellow and red-brown. The plants commence their new growths late in the year, and it is often early summer before these show.

Rossioglossum Rawdon Jester

Pleurothallis peduncularis

Temperature: Cool-growing.
Cultivation: Grow in 10cm (4in) pots of bark-based compost (growing medium). Shade in summer, but allow full light in winter. Water while the plants are in growth, decreasing gradually as the pseudobulbs mature. When no growth is visible, allow the plants to remain dry but without undue shrivelling of the pseudobulb. Feed at every other watering in summer.
Height: 23cm (9in).

Rossioglossum Rawdon Jester

This is the only successful hybrid in a genus that is extremely reluctant to produce seed or hybridize. The striking, huge flowers, 12cm (5in) wide, are boldly coloured in chestnut brown and yellow. The flowers appear in autumn and winter. This hybrid will grow indoors or in a cool greenhouse.

SARCOCHILUS

This is a small, monopodial genus of modestly sized plants that come from Australia. Of the 15 or so species, only a very few are seen in cultivation. These, and one hybrid, grow with comparative ease, and excellent specimens are seen which are an indication of the plants' reliability. These mostly epiphytic plants produce pairs of semi-rigid leaves on stems that do not become too tall. New growth is produced from the base. In this way, a tufted plant is created that will bloom profusely during the winter months. The flowers, held on upright flower spikes, are white with red circular spotting at the centre.

Temperature: Intermediate-growing.
Cultivation: Grow in 5–10cm (2–4in) pots of fine bark compost (growing medium). Shade in summer, but provide more light in winter. Water all year; feed in summer at every other watering.
Height: 15cm (6in).

Sarcochilus Fitzhart

This is an attractive primary hybrid between two species, *Sarcochilus fitzgeraldii* and *S. hartmannii*, from Australia. The plant produces tufted growths, and blooms freely in spring on flower spikes held well above the foliage. The petite, rounded flowers are white with a central red marking.

Sarcochilus Fitzhart

Thunia Gattonense

THUNIA

A few species make up this small genus of beautiful orchids from India. These, and one very old hybrid that has stood the test of time, make superb-looking plants in summer with tall, fleshy stems softly leafed along their length. When mature, they will reach 60cm (2ft) or more. The papery flowers appear in a frothy cascade at the apex of the stem and last for about three weeks in summer. These are usually white, with yellow or pinky red on the lip.

Thunias are very exciting plants to grow. From the moment the new growth is seen in early spring, they race forward at a great pace, completing their season's growth in record time, so that by early summer, growth is complete and the flower spikes are showing.

The canes are short-lived, and shrivel and die after one year. In autumn, the plants shed their foliage, which turns from green to golden yellow before being discarded. When this happens, take the bare canes out of the pot and place them in a seed tray in full light. Leave them completely dry for the winter. In spring, remove the old dead canes, and pot up the plump ones when you see the new growths.

Temperature: Cool- to intermediate-growing (the warmer you grow them, the earlier in the year thunias will bloom).
Cultivation: Grow in 10cm (4in) pots of bark-based compost (growing medium), or try growing in Rockwool. Water well once the roots have started, and feed, but keep the foliage dry to avoid spotting. Keep dry in winter. Keep in shade all summer, but give full light in winter.
Height: To 60cm (2ft) or more.

Thunia Gattonense

A old classic hybrid raised 100 years ago, this is a delightful plant to grow, with beautiful foliage and large, frothing heads of flowers, 10cm (4in) across, in summer.

TRICHOPILIA

Of the 30 or so species in this evergreen epiphytic genus, which occurs in Central and South America, only a few are occasionally seen in cultivation. There are no hybrids within this genus, which is a pity because those species that are grown have much to commend them, and hybridizing could possibly combine their separate qualities.

The plants are modestly sized, fitting nicely into a mixed collection indoors or in a cool greenhouse. Most do not exceed 15cm (6in) in height, with flower spikes below the foliage, often drooping. The petals and sepals of *Trichopilia tortilis* are long and narrow, twisting along their length, which gives rise to the common name, corkscrew orchid. This, and others in cultivation, are extremely pretty and easy to grow and flower. The plants bloom in late summer or autumn and last for a few weeks. They are seen at their best when grown on into specimen plants but, if preferred, they may be divided when large enough to maintain them at a desired size.

Temperature: Cool-growing.
Cultivation: While most do well in pots of fine bark compost (growing medium), they can also be grown mounted on bark or other suitable bases. Water all year, but give less in winter while the plants are resting. Keep shaded in summer, and give more light in winter. Feed lightly in summer.
Height: To 15cm (6in).

Trichopilia tortilis

This corkscrew orchid has distinctive, twisting sepals and petals, which are long and narrow. The large, flared lip is white with some pink at the centre. The flowers are carried singly on drooping spikes during the summer.

Trichopilia tortilis

TEMPERATE TERRESTRIAL ORCHIDS

The following terrestrial orchids can be artificially raised from seed, and are sometimes available from hardy plant nurseries, while in growth and flower. Many more can be found in the wild, where they are all protected plants.

ANACAMPTIS

Although just two species make up this genus of European terrestrial orchids, only one is generally seen. This is the pyramidal orchid (*Anacamptis pyramidalis*), which occurs in abundance in parts of Britain, usually on dry hillsides and areas close to the sea. The name is derived from the shape of the inflorescence, which is densely packed with pretty, pale pink flowers. A white form is occasionally seen.

The plant, which also occurs in parts of Africa, blooms in early summer, after which it dies down, leaving a head of seed capsules.

Temperature: 1–5°C (34–41°F).
Cultivation: Grow in pots of coarse grit and leaf mould or a similar compost (growing medium) in a frost-free greenhouse or cold frame. Water while in active growth. Keep dry in winter. Alternatively, plant out in beds in well-drained situations. Allow to spread and leave undisturbed so they will colonize.
Height: 10cm (4in).

DACTYLORHIZA

Closely related to the genus *Orchis*, there are about 40 species spread throughout Europe, Asia and elsewhere. In Britain, this is a widespread and commonly seen genus, with plants covering large areas in marshy or boggy places. One of the largest species occurring in Africa is *Dactylorhiza foliosa*, and this can be seen in long-established colonies in botanical gardens. When planted out and left undisturbed, this species, and others, can be cultivated.

Dactylorhiza foliosa

The plants produce leafy stems that terminate in the flower spike. Dactylorhizas will often hybridize within a colony, making it difficult to determine the true species, which can be highly variable, giving rise to several distinct colour forms from white, through pale pink to deep mauve.
Temperature: 1–5°C (34–41°F).
Cultivation: Grow in pots of coarse grit and leaf mould or a similar compost (growing medium) in a frost-free greenhouse or cold frame. Water while in active growth. Keep dry in winter. Alternatively, plant out in beds in well-drained situations. Allow to spread and leave undisturbed so they will colonize.
Height: 10cm (4in) or larger.

Anacamptis pyramidalis

Ophrys apifera

Orchis mascula

OPHRYS

Of all the terrestrial orchids native to Europe, the ophrys are perhaps the most intriguing for the shape of their flowers and their mimicry of the insects that pollinate them. Fly orchid (*Ophrys insectifera*), spider orchid (*O. sphegodes*) and bee orchid (*O. apifera*) give some idea of the adaptation of the lips of the flowers to resemble the male pollinator, which is duped into attempted copulation with the flower, thus resulting in pollination. Of the 30 or so species that have been identified, there exist numerous sub-species, varieties and colour variations, which can make positive identification difficult.

While the majority of the species are found in the Mediterranean region, some can be seen in Britain, especially in coastal areas and grassland. In recent years, they have been successfully cultivated in pots.
Temperature: 1–5°C (34–41°F).
Cultivation: Grow in pots of coarse grit and leaf mould or a similar compost (growing medium) in a frost-free greenhouse or cold frame. Water while in active growth. Keep dry in winter. Alternatively, plant out in beds in well-drained situations. Allow to spread and leave undisturbed so they will colonize.
Height: 5cm (2in).

ORCHIS

This attractive genus of terrestrial European orchids contains about 30 species spread throughout Europe and extending their range into North Africa and western Asia. In Britain, the early purple orchid (*Orchis mascula*) is the first of the native orchids to bloom, in late spring. Among this genus are some apt descriptions of their common names, which include the military orchid (*O. militaris*), named for the soldier-like appearance of the lip topped by a "helmet" of sepals and petals, and the monkey orchid (*O. simia*), whose extraordinary lip perfectly mimics the shape of a monkey. These species are extremely rare in Britain, but may be seen in profusion in other parts of Europe. Protected from disturbance in the wild, they are not cultivated in gardens.

These orchids rely heavily upon the mycorrhizal association with their own specific fungus, and their colonies can vary in number from year to year. The foliage appears in spring and forms a rosette of leaves from the centre of which extends the flower spike. Most *Orchis* favour dry meadows or heathland sites.
Temperature: 1–5°C (34–41°F).
Cultivation: Grow in pots of coarse grit and leaf mould or a similar compost (growing medium) in a frost-free greenhouse or cold frame. Water while in active growth. Keep dry in winter. Alternatively, plant out in beds in well-drained situations. Allow to spread and leave undisturbed so they will colonize.
Height: 16cm (6in) or larger.

PLATANTHERA

It is thought that there are about 100 species of this widely distributed orchid, which appears naturally across Europe, North America and elsewhere. The plants have widespread leaves and produce their flowers on a tall, upright flower spike. These are mostly white with a long spur, and are pollinated by night-flying hawk moths. With the decline of their natural habitats of old pasture or land that has not been used extensively for agriculture, these orchids, once numerous, have dwindled in number. The greater butterfly orchid (*Platanthera chlorantha*) produces greenish white flowers, 30cm (12in) tall, on spikes which arise from two rounded, green leaves in early summer.
Temperature: 1–5°C (34–41°F).
Cultivation: Grow in pots of coarse grit and leaf mould or a similar compost (growing medium) in a frost-free greenhouse or cold frame. Water while in active growth. Keep dry in winter. Alternatively, plant out in beds in well-drained situations. Allow to spread and leave undisturbed so they will colonize.
Height: 15cm (6in) or larger.

Platanthera chlorantha

GLOSSARY

Adventitious growth
Roots or growths that are produced from the stem or other unusual places.

Agar solution
Formulated culture base containing nutrients for the germination of seeds in vitro.

Alliance
A term applied to closely related orchid genera.

Anther
The part of the stamen that contains the pollen sac.

Apical
Flowering stem that arises from the top of the stem or pseudobulb.

Back bulb
The oldest, leafless pseudobulbs on a plant.

Bark compost
An organic, chopped-up material obtained from matured pineforest trees after felling.

Basal
Flowering stem that comes from the base of the stem of pseudobulb.

Bifoliate
A term used to describe those plants from the *Cattleya* alliance that have two leaves.

Bigeneric
An artificially made hybrid containing two related genera.

Zygopetalum Artur Elle 'Stonehurst' AM/RHS

Bulbil
Matured adventitious growths, which appear on pleiones in particular, and are too small to produce any flowers.

Cane
An elongated pseudobulb, as on thunias.

Clone
An individual plant, from which all propagations will be identical.

Colchicine
A method of chemically treating chromosomes in order to enhance growth and flowers. Colchicine is extracted from the crocus.

Column
The single, finger-like structure at the centre of an orchid flower that contains the male and female reproductive parts.

Diploid
Refers to the number of chromosomes, in this case 40 (2N), which indicates that the plant is fertile.

Dorsal sepal
The sepal opposite the lip, usually at the top of the flower.

Dropping on
Removing a plant from one pot to a larger one, but without disturbing the rootball.

Epiphyte
A plant that grows upon a host tree as an "air plant".

Equitant
A plant whose leaves form an overlapping fan shape, like an iris.

Horticultural foam
A rubber-based spongy material manufactured for horticultural purposes.

Humidity tray
A water-holding tray that provides humidity in a dry atmosphere.

Hybrid grex
Indicates any number of plants in a cross with the same parents.

Intergeneric
The same as bigeneric, but with more than two genera involved.

Keikis
A small offshoot from a plant which can be produced naturally or by artificial means.

Labellum
Another term for the lip or the third petal.

Lithophyte
A plant that grows on mossy rocks or rock faces.

Mericloning
A method of multiplying a plant, or clone, to produce identical plants.

Meristemmed plants
Those plants that have been produced by mass-propagation or mericloning.

Monopodial
A plant that grows continually from its apex or terminal bud.

Miltonia confusa

Monotypic
A genus in which only a single species is known to exist.

Multigeneric
An artificially produced hybrid genus containing several separate genera.

Mycelium
The microscopic fungus that must be present in order for orchid seed to germinate.

Mycorrhizal
The symbiotic relationship that exists between the orchid roots and its micro-fungus.

Node
The part of the stem that is jointed and produces leaves or buds.

Peloric
An abnormal formation in which the petals resemble the lip in some way.

Perlag
An aggregate that is made from pumice stone and used in orchid compost.

Perlite
A finer material which is the same as perlag.

Petal
The inner whorl of an orchid flower is made up of three petals, two lateral petals, and the lip.

Pollinating parent
The parent in a cross from which the pollen has been taken.

Pollinia
The solid pollen masses found beneath the anther or pollen cap.

Pod parent
The parent in a cross that has been fertilized, and will carry the seed capsule or pod until the seed inside is ready for harvesting and sowing.

Protocorm
The chlorophyll-containing embryo that forms from the seed of an orchid before leaves or roots are able to develop.

Pseudobulb
A swollen stem used for water storage above ground.

Rockwool
An artifical material which is made from spun volcanic rock and used as an inorganic potting material. Most shop-bought orchids are growing in Rockwool.

Saphophyte
A plant that lives on dead trees.

Cymbidium Bethlehem 'Ridgeway'

Seed capsule

The vessel that develops from the stem behind the flower to carry seed until it matures.

Sepal

The outer whorl of modified leaves that surrounds the petals.

Sequential flowering

A term used to describe those plants that do not produce all their flowers at once.

Stamen

The male part of the flower, which carries the pollen.

Stigma

The part of the plant that receives the the pollen and induces fertilization. It is found beneath the column in the flower.

Symbiosis

The natural means by which orchids relate to their mycorrhiza.

Sympodial

A term used to describe growth in which the new shoots develop from the base of previous growths or from pseudobulbs.

Taxonomist

A botanical scientist who is responsible for the naming and classification of plants.

Tepal

Reference to both the petals and sepals as joint segments of a flower.

Terete

Leaves that have become thin and rounded, like a pencil, usually in order to save moisture.

Phalaenopsis Mount Kaala *(left); Phalaenopsis* Hakalau Queen *(centre); Phalaenopsis* Silky Moon *(right)*

Terrestrial

An orchid that grows in soil or leaf litter, usually producing tubers or matted roots.

Tessellation

A term used to describe a mottling effect on flowers or leaves.

Trigeneric

An artificially made hybrid that combines three separate genera.

Umbel

Flowers that are formed in a flat-topped inflorescence arising from a single point.

Unifoliate

A term that is used to describe those members of the *Cattleya* alliance that bear a single leaf on each pseudobulb.

Velamen

The white, absorbent outer layer that covers the roots.

Viscid

The sticky disc attached to the pollen sacs or pollinia which adheres to the body or head of the visiting insect pollinator, so aiding the process of pollination.

SUPPLIERS

EUROPE

Useful Organisations
British Orchid Growers' Association
38 Florence Road, College Town
Sandhurst, Berkshire GU47 0QD
Tel: 01276 32947
Contact Mrs. Janet Plested

Orchid Society of Great Britain
10 Willoughby Close
Helpringham
Sleasford, Lincolnshire NG34 0RX
Tel: 01529 421521
Contact Mrs. Mary Smallman

Nurseries
Burnham Nurseries Ltd.
Forches Cross
Newton Abbot
Devon TQ12 6PZ
Tel: 01626 352233
Fax: 01626 362167
Email: burnhamorchids@eclipse.co.uk

David Stead Orchids
Greenscapes Horticultural Centre
Brandon Crescent
Shadwell
Leeds LS17 6JH
Tel/Fax: 0113 2893933

Deva Orchids
Littlebrook Farm
Stryt Isa
Pen-y-ffordd
Chester CII4 OJY
Tel: 01978 762454

Equatorial Plant Company
7 Gray Lane
Barnard Castle
Country Durham DL12 8PD
Tel/Fax: 01833 690519
Email: equatorialplants@onyx.net.co.uk

Ivans Orchids
Great Barn Dell
St. Albans Road
Sandridge, St. Albans
Hertfordshire AL4 9LB
Tel: 01727 863178
Fax: 01727 858545

Kenntner Orchideenzucht
D- 89555 Steinheim-Sontheim/St.
Birkelweg 12
Germany
Tel: 073 29/55 88
Fax: 073 29/1576

Mansell & Hatcher Ltd.
Cragg Wood Nurseries
Woodlands Drive
Rawdon
Leeds
Yorkshire LS19 6LQ
Tel: 01132 502016

McBean's Orchids
Cooksbridge
Lewes
East Sussex BN8 4PR
Tel: 01273 400228
Fax: 01273 401181

Lycaste deppei

Orchid Answers Ltd.
113 Second Avenue
Almodington
Birdham
Chichester
West Sussex PO20 7LF
Tel: 01243 511322
Fax: 01243 511474

Vacherot and Lecoufle
La Tuilerie
29 Rue de Valenton
94470 Boissy-Saint-Leger
France
Tel: (1) 45 69 10 42
Fax: (1) 45 98 30 14

Greenhouse and Equipment Suppliers
C H Whitehouse Ltd
Dept J
Buckhurst Works
Bells Yew Green
Frant, Tunbridge Wells
Kent TN3 9BN
Tel: 01892 750247

Simply Control
139 Commercial Centre (BOG99)
Picket Place
Andover
Hampshire SP11 6RU
Tel: 01264 334805 (24 hours)
Fax: 01264 335755

UNITED STATES

Useful Organisations
The American Orchid Society
6000 South Olive Avenue
West Palm Beach
FL 33405
Tel: (561) 585-8666
Tel: (561) 585-0654
Email: TheAOS@compuserve.com
www.orchidweb.org

Dendrobium spectabile

Nurseries
Cal-Orchid, Inc.
1251 Orchid Drive
Santa Barbara, CA 93111
Tel: (805) 967-1312
Fax: (805) 967-6882

Carter and Holmes Orchids
629 Mendenhall Road
PO Box 668
Newberry, SC 29108
Tel: (803) 276-0579
Fax: (803) 276-0588
Email:
orchids@carterandholmes.com

Orchids by Hausermann Inc.
2N134 Addison Road
Villa Park
Illinois 60181-1191
Tel: (630) 543-6855
Fa: (630) 543-9842
Email: hausermann@compuserve.com
www.orchidsbyhausermann.com

AUSTRALIA

Nurseries
Adelaide Orchids
16 Pine Road
Woodcroft
South Australia 5162
Tel: 61 8 83812011
Fax: 61 8 83221546
Email: stephen@adelaideorchids.com
Internet home page:
http://www.adelaideorchids.com

Warrnambol Orchids
32 Riverside Terrace
Warrnambol 3280
Victoria
Tel: 613 556 2373
Fax: 613 556 12433
Email: altmann@standard.net.au
http://www.standard.net.au/-altman

INDEX

Miltonia spectabilis var. *moreliana*

Zygopetalum maxillare

Dendrochilum glumaceum

ACKNOWLEDGEMENTS

All special photography in this book was provided by Derek Cranch, except for the following:
KEY:- t = top   b = bottom   c = centre
r = right   l = left

Peter Anderson: 9t; 20bl; 30; 141 (all); 167tl and tr; 191; 200t; 215tc

Jonathan Buckley: 79tl and tr; 83tl; 126tr

Helen Fickling: 1; 2; 4; 6; 7; 52t; 54 (all); 56; 57; 58t; 59 (all); 60t; 62 (all); 63; 64tr; 64bl; 65t; 65bl; 66; 86t; 87; 93; 94; 98 (all); 99 (all); 100; 108; 111; 118; 129t; 144 (all); 145 (all); 158bl; 160; 162b; 163b; 165t; 166br;

201bl and br; 209b; 210tl; 210b; 212r; 213br; 215br; 216t; 216c; 217br; 248; 249; 250; 251; 256

The publishers would like to thank the following individuals and picture agencies for allowing their photographs to be reproduced:

Ancient Art & Architecture Collection: 32l

A–Z Botanical Collection: 6tl; 28r; 31

Ed Gabriel: 12 (all)

The Garden Picture Library: 52b (Vaughan Fleming)

Sarah Rittershausen: 16; 17 (all); 18 (all); 19 (all); 21 (all); 67; 70 (all); 71 (all)

Tim Shepherd: 14bl and br; 15 (all); 20br

Simply Control: 76; 78 (all); 79b; 81tl; 81br; 82bl

CH Whitehouse & Co.: 74

Peter Williams: 22 (all); 23 (all); 24 (all); 25 (all)

The vast majority of the orchids in this book were photographed at Burnham Nurseries Ltd., Forches Cross, Newton Abbot, TQ12 6PZ, in England, or on location in Thailand and Brazil.